Lucy Prebble
Plays 1

CW00548982

The Sugar Syndrome; Enron; The Effect; A Very Expensive Poison

The Sugar Syndrome: 'Prebble's play is excellently wrought, and courageous in its engagement with taboo.' *The Times*

Enron: 'An exhilarating mix of political satire, modern morality and multimedia spectacle.' *Guardian*

The Effect: 'The material is complex but always accessible, the drama serious and informative yet deeply human, with the odd jolt of piercing humour. *The Effect* confirms her as one of the most intelligent voices in British theatre.' *Evening Standard*

A Very Expensive Poison: 'A brilliantly bold and ferociously intelligent drama about our slippery times.' *Financial Times*

Lucy Prebble is a writer for film, television, games and theatre.

Lucy is Co-Executive Producer and writer on the BAFTA, Golden Globe and Emmy Award-winning HBO drama *Succession*, for which she has also won a Writers Guild Award and a Producers Award.

For television, she has written and co-created *I Hate Suzie* with her close friend Billie Piper for Sky Atlantic, to be aired in 2020. She is the creator of the TV series *Secret Diary of a Call Girl* (ITV/ Showtime), and has recently made a pilot for HBO starring Sarah Silverman. Lucy also writes for Frankie Boyle's *New World Order* (BBC) and appears on the TV show as a guest as well as appearing regularly on *Have I Got News for You*.

For theatre, Lucy recently wrote the political and emotional meta-thriller *A Very Expensive Poison* which was a huge five-star hit for the Old Vic in 2019, winning Best New Play at the Critics' Circle Awards, Best New Production of a Play at the Broadway World

Awards and winning Lucy the Susan Smith Blackburn prize. It has alos been nominated for the Olivier Award for Best New Play. Her play *The Effect*, a study of love and neuroscience, was performed at the National Theatre and also won the Critics' Circle Aware for Best New Play. Before that she wrote *Enron*, a hugely successful piece about the infamous corporate fraud, which transferred to the West End and Broadway after sell-out runs at both the Royal Court and Chichester Festival Theatre. Her first play, *The Sugar Syndrome*, won her the George Devine Award and was performed at the Royal Court Theatre.

Lucy is the recipient of the 2019 Wellcome Screenwriting Fellowship, allowing her to explore where the world of film meets science and research.

Lucy also writes video games and is fascinated by new technology and storytelling. She contributes to major publications as a journalist and wrote weekly tech column for the *Observer* newspaper. In video games, she was Head Scene Writer for Bungie's massively successful first person shooter *Destiny*.

Lucy Prebble
Plays 1

The Sugar Syndrome

Enron

The Effect

A Very Expensive Poison

With an introduction by the author

methuen | drama

LONDON • NEW YORK • OXFORD • NEW DELHI • SYDNEY

METHUEN DRAMA
Bloomsbury Publishing Plc
50 Bedford Square, London, WC1B 3DP, UK
1385 Broadway, New York, NY 10018, USA

BLOOMSBURY, METHUEN DRAMA and the Methuen Drama logo are
trademarks of Bloomsbury Publishing Plc

This collection first published in Great Britain 2020
Reprinted 2020

Cover design: Ben Anslow
Cover image: Lovers kissing, coloured X-ray (© GUSTOIMAGES / SCIENCE
PHOTO LIBRARY

A catalogue record for this book is available from the British Library.

A catalog record for this book is available from the Library of Congress.

ISBN: PB: 978-1-3501-7509-9
ePDF: 978-1-3501-7510-5
eBook: 978-1-3501-7511-2

Series: Contemporary Dramatists

Typeset by Newgen KnowledgeWorks Pvt. Ltd., Chennai, India
Printed and bound in Great Britain

To find out more about our authors and books visit www.bloomsbury.com
and sign up for our newsletters.

Contents

Contents

Introduction

In 2002 I went for an interview at the National Theatre for a job as an assistant to an assistant in the Director's Office. It had been advertised in the Guardian Media section and I was sure I wouldn't get it. But, down to the last two, I decided to lie about my typing speed and got the job. After this, when artistic director Nick Hytner would dictate a letter, I would sit behind my desk, terrified, and wildly tap away, mostly nonsense coming up on the screen, because I just couldn't keep up. Eventually, brilliantly, I came up with a scheme where I would record him as he dictated, as I pantomimed writing it up, and then later I would type the letter up from the recording. But one day, in real time, he wandered around behind me, to check on what he had dictated so far, only to see a wall of gobbledygook on the screen. I panicked. I died inside. I thought about passing out, faking my own death, pretending to smell smoke and run from the room. Ever classy, Nick just walked back around to the front of my desk and continued dictating.

I tell you this because I, like all writers, sometimes feel like a fraud.

I didn't come from a theatrical background. My parents bettered themselves into Commuterville, then wisely left me and my siblings to take care of ourselves. My passion was for books and video games. I read constantly, voraciously, anything too grown-up for me. I'm a believer in having wildly inappropriate books lying around. Printed words became, to me, the place where adults spoke honestly.

Whenever I write, I still feel like that bullshitting secretary. I always expect the sheer nonsense I am banging out on the screen to be greeted with a bemused, blank stare from a more powerful employer. It is from these nerves that I suspect my passion for research was born. I have always felt that, armed with enough information and insight, writing will get easier. It never does.

The plays contained here are the product of dozens of drafts, of long and complex research journeys that have taken them from that first desperate draft to how they're presented to you now. It is only with the help of those kind enough to be interviewed by me, and of course the casts and crews of each play, that the best moments have been forged. It was the most fun when we were building these plays together.

I have never been a writer who would prefer to write than live. That's why I'm not so prolific. It is the living behind these plays that gave me the most pleasure: the friends made and hearts broken and rehearsal rooms filled. I remember the kindness and support of the Young Writers Group I attended at the Royal Court, run by Simon Stephens, that led to writing *The Sugar Syndrome*. I recently travelled to the Orange Tree Theatre to see a revival of that first play. I was delighted to find myself genuinely disturbed by it. I'd assumed it would be dark in a sort of performative, adolescent way, but it left me with nightmares. It was odd to face my younger self after so many years. But I was aware that I was watching the burgeoning careers and friendships of a new, young cast and crew all over again. Lives intertwining. Plays always feel like beginnings, even old ones.

I assume you're reading a collection of plays because you plan to perform them or would like to write plays yourself. In either case, you must. Theatre is the warmest and most democratic of artforms. It requires only other people to do it and there are lots of them, everywhere. I humbly suggest that whether you want to perform or to write, you make the effort to live as well as work. It's very hard to do both, but I honestly think both must be done.

In the spirit of life over work, I won't bother pontificating on the themes of these plays. What I would like to do is mention the people whose lives met mine over this period. Anthony Neilson remains the most important person and artist to advise and inspire me. He always told me the truth and believed in me as a playwright from the moment we met. I will always love him. My professional journey was helped immensely by my time with Headlong Theatre, run by Rupert Goold, who deserves the thanks and blame in equal measure. The enthusiasm and kindness of Ben Power, who I met at Headlong, held me and my plays together on many occasions through the years. I am indebted to Charlotte Knight as well as a lost friend, Dave Moore, for counsel and humour and, curiously, to the love and support of 1990s pop sensation Billie Piper.

I can feel so many people behind these plays as I reread them: some friends, some strangers. I include among the strangers my former self. I can see her bleached into the white pages behind the dialogue. I hear her tumbling through words, trying to grasp onto something real. That little girl from long ago who turned to books, desperately trying to find an answer to a question she couldn't articulate.

Maybe that's what's brought you here too. Welcome. I hope you find it.

The Sugar Syndrome

For A and for D.
I really must learn your full names.

The Sugar Syndrome opened at The Royal Court Jerwood Theatre Upstairs on 16 October 2003 with the following cast and creative team:

Dani Carter   Stephanie Leonidas
Jan Carter   Kate Duchene
Tim Saunders   Andrew Woodall
Lewis Sampson   Will Ash

Director Marianne Elliott
Designer Jonathan Fensom
Lighting Designer Chris Davey
Sound Designer Ian Dickinson
Assistant Director Maria Aberg
Casting Lisa Makin and Amy Ball
Costume Supervisor Randa Abuzaid

It was subsequently staged at the Orange Tree Theatre, London, on 24 January 2020 with the following cast and creative team:

Dani Carter   Jessica Rhodes
Jan Carter   Alexandra Gilbreath
Tim Saunders   John Hollingworth
Lewis Sampson   Ali Barouti

Director Oscar Toeman
Designer Rebecca Brower
Lighting Designer Elliot Griggs
Sound Designer and Composer Daniel Balfour
Movement Director Chi-San Howard
Costume Supervisor Molly Syrett
Casting Sophie Parrott CDG and Sarah Murray

Act One

Scene One

Dani *in her bedroom. She connects to the Internet. The sound of a modem dialling.*

Internet Welcome to Chatarama, Dani2752. Please choose a chatroom. (*She clicks.*) Chatrooms by LOCATION. Enter postcode.

Lewis *in his bedroom. He sees* **Dani** *enter the chat room.*

Internet To ensure that this forum remains friendly and fun for everyone, please report any offensive communications to our Cyclops.

Dani 17/f, wants it.

Internet *Bing.* You have . . . *Bing.* You have a message . . . *Bing.* You have a message from . . . *Bing.* You have six new . . . *Bing, bing, bing, bing, bing.*

Dani *and* **Lewis** *meet across cyberspace.*

Lewis Hello again.

Dani Hello.

Lewis Are we doing this then?

Dani Hell, yeah.

Lewis Really?

Dani Really.

Lewis How will I know it's you? What are you wearing?

Dani Good question. Dirty yet practical.

Lewis We should choose a public place.

Dani They always say that, don't they?

Lewis Or you could come here.

Dani   True.

Lewis   If you want to.

Dani   True.

Lewis   Or not.

Dani   Are you going to cut me up and put me in bin bags?

Lewis   No. But if I was, I'd say no too.

Dani   Yeah but you'd feel properly unoriginal as you did it.

Lewis   Are you coming then?

Dani   Of course I'm fucking coming.

*We are in **Lewis**' bedroom. **Lewis** and **Dani**, a little uncomfortable. He pours some wine into a glass and into a mug, which he chivalrously keeps for himself. **Dani** takes the glass and looks at it.*

A pause. They both have a little laugh at themselves.

Dani   It's still a bit weird, / isn't it?

Lewis   / It's a bit weird. Sorry, I broke the other wine glass.

Dani   Tell me straight then, am I what you expected?

Lewis   Like what?

Dani   You can say. I'm not sensitive.

Lewis   Look at you. You're hardly . . . You told the truth.

Dani   Honesty is my most attractive feature?

Lewis   Most people must lie . . . a bit. *You* don't have to. I was well relieved, I was shitting it that you might be a bloke. I couldn't believe you said yeah. You know, not in a 'you shouldn't have done' way. No reason why not, is there?

Dani *smiles and takes the tiniest of sips from her glass.*

Lewis   If you've changed your mind. I'm gonna say now, cos it's the right thing to do, we can go to the pub or something. Or you can just go. If you want. The stuff we talked about, it's all a laugh, innit?

Dani   I know.

Lewis   I've lost the plot. I'm sorry.

Dani   Do you want me to tell you what I'd like to do to you? Or I could type it out, if that helps.

Lewis *laughs, despite himself. He makes a decision, puts down his mug and kisses her on the mouth and then on the neck.*

Dani   (*gently*)   Have you been thinking about this, yeah?

Lewis (*kissing her neck, getting into it*)   Yeah.

Dani   You've been thinking about kissing me, touching me, yeah?

Lewis   Yeah.

Dani   Tell me.

Lewis (*touches her breasts*)   Your thighs, your tits. I want to lick them.

Dani (*playful*)   I've been thinking about your cock.

Lewis   Yeah? I might have exaggerated a bit on that one.

Dani (*massaging his crotch*)   Your big hard cock.

Lewis   Just so's you're not disappointed.

Dani (*puts her hand down his trousers*)   Ssssh.

Lewis *undoes his flies.* **Dani** *masturbates him. She mutters barely audibly in his ear.*

Dani   Yeah? I've been thinking about this. About touching your cock. It feels so good. Hard for me.

Lewis *tries to put his hand down* **Dani***'s trousers. She moves his hand so it's on her breast. He then puts his other hand down her trousers and begins to masturbate her. Her eyes are closed.* **Lewis** *becomes more aroused the more he touches her.*

Lewis (*quietly*)   Yeah. Oh God. Fuck.

Dani (*moves his hand away from her crotch*)   It's OK.

Lewis (*moves his hand back, he groans as his fingers enter her*)   I want to.

Dani's *eyes roll heavenward as he touches her, more through annoyance than pleasure. She closes her eyes, and winces at his over-eager touch. She takes a deep breath and lets out a sigh that could as easily be boredom as arousal. They continue to touch each other.* **Lewis** *comes after a short time.* **Dani** *withdraws her hand, sits on the bed and wipes her hand on the sheet. He slumps on to the bed.*

Dani (*acknowledging her wiping*)   Sorry. That's classy, isn't it? Having a wipe, there.

Lewis   Don't worry. They get washed soon.

Dani   'Get washed.' What, by magic?

No answer.

Dani   Washed by who?

Lewis (*reluctantly*)   My mum.

Dani (*laughs*)   Aren't you embarrassed?

Lewis (*shrugs*)   She thinks they're deodorant marks.

Dani (*disbelief*)   No, that your mother does your washing! What, she comes round and picks it up?

Lewis   Can we not talk about my mum?

Dani   I would never let my mum do that. What, does she think that people on the street are pointing and saying, 'Look at him with his crumpled shirt, sure sign of a bad mother'?

Lewis   Something like that.

Dani   Christ.

Lewis   Come here.

Dani (*makes some cursory attempt at closeness*)   Is your mum a bit mental then?

Lewis   What do you mean?

Dani   Why don't you just do it yourself?

Lewis   That would be cruel, man.

Dani   Mine's like that. We moved and they brought these two massive stone lions with them, for outside the house. A semi-detached with a tiny drive and these fuck-off white stone lions outside. And my mum didn't want the neighbours to think we were up ourselves so every Christmas or Halloween or whatever she . . . decorates them. Tinsel or witches' hats or whatever. To show we don't take ourselves too seriously. It's fucking tragic.

Lewis (*reaching out to her*)   Come here.

Dani (*leaning forward, spots something under the bed*)   Oh my God.

Lewis   What?

Dani   Don't take this the wrong way, Lewis, but, are you a virgin?

Lewis   What sort of question's that?

Dani   That's such a yes. That's a massive stack of *NMEs* under your bed.

Dani   What's wrong with the *NME?*

Dani   Nothing. Nothing. It's just a . . . you lose your virginity, you throw out the *NMEs*. Rites of passage thing. A pile of music magazines screams virgin.

Lewis   Or music journalist.

Dani (*surprised*)   Is that what you do?

Lewis   It's what I'm *trying* to do.

Dani   I feel bad now.

Lewis   You should. Using me like this.

Dani   What do you *actually* do?

Lewis   I phone people up I don't know and offer them holidays they don't want.

Dani   Cool.

Lewis   Pays the rent.

Dani   Yeah.

Lewis   Until something happens on the music front.

Dani   Sure.

Lewis   Do you do this a lot?

Dani   God, no! No!

Lewis   Sorry.

Dani   I chat a lot. I like the Internet. I like that way of talking to people. It's honest.

Lewis *laughs, not sure if she's joking.*

Dani   It's a place where people are free to say anything they like. And most of what they say is about sex.

Lewis   Yeah, there are some sick fucks. Mental to think they live round here.

Dani   I was chatting to this bloke who thought I was an eleven-year-old boy.

Lewis   Shit. Why?

Dani   He's really polite though.

Lewis   I can't believe that really goes on.

Dani   Oh yeah. But. It keeps them busy.

Scene Two

Dani *and* **Tim** *in a chat room.*

Tim   Do you like football? Who are your favourite players?

Dani   I don't like football. I'm always in goal.

Tim   Has your dad taken you to any big matches?

Dani   He's not round much.

Tim   That's a shame. Does that make you sad?

Dani (*slightly amused*)   Not really, no.

Tim   I'd be happy to take you to a match one day.

Dani   Thanks.

Tim   How's school?

Dani   I hate it. They made me move schools and I don't like anyone.

Tim   Do you miss your old friends?

Dani   I didn't like any of them either.

Tim   You're up late.

Dani   So are you.

Tim   Can you see the moon?

Dani   Now?

Tim   Yes.

Dani (*leans back to look out of her window*)   Yes.

Tim   What shape is it?

Dani   Half.

Tim   It's nice that we're both looking at the moon together.

Dani (*laughs at this, but is a little touched*)   Weirdo.

A knock on the door, **Jan** *enters with a phone bill.* **Dani** *drops down the window of the chatroom.*

Jan   Have you got the cat in here?

Dani   No.

Jan   No. Oh dear. It's getting silly now. The people next door said they saw something on the main road, but I went down and it's a badger.

No reply.

Jan   Did you have a lovely time?

Dani   Yes thanks.

Jan   What sort of party was it? (*Mischievously.*) Was it a rave?

Dani   Yes, it was a rave, Mother.

Jan   Do they have names, these friends of yours?

Dani   A lot of them do, yes.

Jan   I take it they're not as bad as you thought then, these girls?

Dani   They're just so young.

Jan   I always think there's only one thing worse than teenage boys. Teenage girls. I'll tell you one thing, we never had any of it with your brother. They kick a football about and it's all forgotten. I wouldn't go back to being your age again. Not for anything.

Dani   Great.

Jan   I'm pleased you're going out, though. That's important, isn't it? Do you know who this number is, it's costing a fortune. (*Points to the bill.*)

Dani   That's the Internet dialup number. Sorry, that's me.

Jan (*confused*)   Oh. I see. I thought it might be someone your father was ringing.

Dani   Dad never uses the phone here.

Jan   Why do you think that is?

Dani   Because he's never here.

Jan   And why do you think that is?

Pause.

Dani   Have you been drinking?

Jan   Don't be silly. Only sherry. (*As a brand new idea.*) Would you like some?

Dani   No. It's on our friends and family list.

Jan I expect it is.

Flicks through the bill.

Oh, yes, so it is. That's that mystery solved then. (*She seems a little disappointed.*) Yes, you know what it's like for us oldies, not much to report. Your brother rang to say he's joined some extreme sports society and they're all going to Cornwall for the weekend. You're going to kill me with worry, you two. It's lovely to have you home.

Dani It was just one night.

Jan No, back at home.

Tense pause.

Dani I might go to bed.

Jan Nice to be back in your own bed.

Dani'*s smile does not reach her eyes.* **Jan** *exits.*

Dani *reopens the window to the chat room.*

Tim Hello? Hello?

Dani If people knew what other people really thought of them, I think they'd kill themselves.

Tim Are you all right?

Dani I hate my mother. I hate her and I don't know why.

Tim It's only once you reach an age when you realise *why* you hate your parents that you become too polite to articulate it.

Dani I'd like to meet you.

Scene Three

A park, near a school. **Tim** *sits, fidgeting on a bench.* **Dani** *approaches and walks past, eyeing him. She pauses and lingers,* *pretending to take in a view, but can't resist shooting glances at him. Eventually, she decides to go and sit next to him.* **Tim**, *more uncomfortable, gets up to leave.*

Dani   Don't go.

Tim *stops, unsure.*

Dani   I was planning just to walk past.

Tim   You must have me confused with somebody else.

Dani (*sticks out her hand*)   I'm Dani.

Tim*'s face reveals his surprise and disappointment before he recovers.*

Tim   Well, nice to meet you, Dani.

Dani   You're quite posh.

Tim   Thank you.

He looks around suspiciously.

I'd best be off.

Dani   You're not in any trouble.

Tim   I really don't know what you mean.

Dani (*stands up*)   Well I'll just follow you until you go home and then I'll know where you live, which is worse, isn't it?

Suspicious but intrigued, **Tim** *sits back down.* **Dani** *sits down and, like a cat with a mouse, is at a bit of a loss.*

Pause.

Dani   You're young.

Tim   I think if anyone should be surprised . . .

Dani   Yeah. Sorry.

Tim   It's a boy's name.

Dani   Not with an 'i'. Come on, you knew I wasn't eleven.

Tim Can we not?

Dani Fine. We'll sit here in silence until you leave and then I'll follow you.

Tim Shouldn't you be at school?

Dani Shouldn't you have thought of that?

Tim Is this a stitch up?

Dani No. And it's college, not school. But I don't go too much.

Tim That seems a bit silly.

Dani (*mockingly*) Sorry, sir.

Tim (*smiles*) It's been a long time since anyone's called me sir.

Dani It's been a long time since anyone's told me off.

Tim I'm hardly telling you off.

A silence.

Dani So you're into boys?

Tim *sighs.*

Dani I'm a bit of a disappointment, I bet?

Tim (*a deep breath*) Actually. I'm rather relieved.

Dani You can go if you want. I was only joking before.

Tim (*considers*) I don't want you to think that I do this, that this is something I do. I've never . . . It was just our chats and . . .

Dani I know. Me neither.

Tim You should be at college though.

Dani I'm new . . . There's some real silly bitches.

Tim Won't you get in trouble?

Dani (*smiles and shrugs*) Eventually. At the moment it's a bit like, me, them, (*indicates space around herself*) eggshells.

Tim   Why's that?

Dani (*sighs but with self-mocking melodrama*)   I've not been well.

Tim   Are you sick?

Dani   Apparently.

Tim (*smiles with recognition*)   Hm.

Dani   No, I was stupid. I got a bit carried away on the not eating front. Got everyone a bit worried.

Tim   I see. You're all right now?

Dani   I spent a couple of months away in this place. Being fed.

Tim   It's not uncommon that, is it?

Dani   No, that's the thing. A bit obvious, I'm afraid. Every once in a while someone would disappear from a class and we were never supposed to ask where they'd gone.

Tim   Like Communist Russia.

Dani   Very similar, but with more Land Rovers.

Tim   Don't take this the wrong way, but you don't *look* like you've missed that many meals.

Dani (*amused by his honesty*)   You don't look like your regular child-snatcher.

Tim   Now hang on. Just because a man fancies women doesn't make him a rapist. Common sense, that's a little bit of what's required. You ought to see that.

Dani   Why?

Tim   I just think it would be good if you . . . if you saw that.

Dani *gets out her wallet and roots around. She takes out a photograph. It is of herself six months ago. She shows it to* **Tim.**

Dani   I'm not really supposed to have that.

Tim (*he struggles to look at it*)   You? Christ.

Dani   They were taken at the beginning. I think it was supposed to make me feel ashamed.

Tim   It makes me feel sick.

Dani   Really? It makes me feel fat.

Pause.

Tim (*hands it back*)   Well, you're not.

Dani   Oh, well, that's all right then. You've got a nice voice. Let me guess, unemployed actor? Late night DJ.

Tim   I used to teach.

Dani   Oooh, messy.

Tim   I have a degree and now I stuff envelopes and occasionally deliver catalogues.

Dani   Mmm. Degree in what?

Tim   Classics.

I do these evening classes in baking, don't laugh. And I offered to teach one on myths. I got really excited about that.

Dani   And?

Tim   They had to background-check me. Found me unsuitable, for an adult education class! (*Irate but appreciative of the irony.*) I mean.

Dani   You get angry.

Tim   Not often.

Dani   I do. All the time. Everyone makes me angry. Sometimes I think about just staying in bed for the whole of the day, if that didn't make me such a fucking cliché.

Tim   That sounds more like boredom.

Dani *shrugs.*

Dani   *You* interest me.

I'm past my sell-by date, am I?

Tim   Look at you. Look how you sit. Automatically covering the parts of you you think are unattractive. You're a woman.

Dani   Not your cup of tea. That's a shame because big, balding pervs really do it for me.

Tim *scowls.*

Dani   Joke. Sorry.

Tim   You may be surprised to hear that I don't need another person calling me a pervert.

Dani   I know. You're right. If we're going to do this it has to be totally without judgement. That's the deal.

Tim   Do this? You're not trying to save me, are you?

Dani   God no.

Tim   Because I've already been told. That can't be done.

Dani   When was that?

Tim   More than five years ago now. I was at one of these centres. It's been shut down now.

Dani   You were in prison?

Tim   A little.

Dani   Do I get to know what you were in for?

Tim   What happened?

Dani   Yeah.

Tim   You want me to go into it?

Dani   Not everything.

Tim   All right. Let's say you can ask me one question, anything you like but just one and I promise to answer it completely honestly. And then I get to ask you one.

Dani   Just one?

Tim   And I can't lie.

Silence. **Dani** *thinks.*

Dani   One question and you have to be completely honest. Oh, I'm torn. (*Pause.*) Honestly, am I fat?

Surprised yet amused, **Tim** *playfully hits her over the back of the head.*

Tim   You lunatic.

Dani (*giggles in acknowledgement*)   Go on.

Tim   No, no, no, I forfeit the right to a question.

Dani   Ah.

Tim   Someone needs to sort you out, Dani boy.

Dani   So they keep saying.

Tim   This place you were in. Did they shock you?

Dani   What like . . . boo?

Tim   No, they wouldn't be allowed these days. They weren't really allowed to then. It was a French doctor and you had to sign another bit of paper and then you got all hooked up.

Dani   To what?

Tim   Some electro-machine.

Dani   And they just fucking electrocute you?!

Tim   No, that's the death penalty. It's tiny, tiny shocks. (*He does an impression.*) Bzzz.

Dani   How does that help?

Tim   Pictures. A slide show of photographs of all sorts of things and when . . . the inappropriate pictures come up, bzzzz.

Dani   Inappropriate as in . . . kids.

Tim   Yes.

Dani   Dirty pictures?

Tim   A range. I don't really remember the details.

Dani   And did it work?

Tim (*considers*)   It made me want to electrocute kids.

The scream of a modem dialling up.

Scene Four

Dani *and* **Lewis** *in a chat room.*

Dani   Hey.

Lewis   Hey.

Dani   Back in the playground.

Lewis   Where have you been?

Dani   About.

Lewis   I've been thinking about you a lot.

Dani   I bet you have. Bad boy.

Lewis   Punish me.

Dani   Shall I tell you what I'd like to do?

Lewis   That's no good. I want the real thing.

Dani   Please.

Lewis   I want to see you. Please.

Dani   That could be arranged.

Lewis   When?

Dani   I'll come round. Later.

Scene Five

Dani's *front room.* **Jan** *is dressed in black gym leggings and a black sports top. When her daughter comes in she jumps up. She is like a Labrador who has been left alone in the house.*

Jan   Where have you been, may I ask?

Dani   You know where I've been.

Jan   I had a telephone call today, from your tutor. Would you like to tell me what he said?

Dani   Did he comment on my excellent attendance and ask you for my hand in marriage?

Jan   You don't have to mock everything, Dani. Believe it or not, someone has to take your life seriously.

Dani   What did he say?

Jan   I think you know.

Dani   I want you to tell me.

Jan   Why haven't you been going to your classes?

Dani   I've been going to loads of classes. But they can think again if they think I'm turning up for registrations and assemblies and General fucking Studies.

Jan   Language.

Dani   Sorry, but you should see it, the common room, these bitchy little girls on beanbags drinking their tea with both hands.

Pause.

Jan   Your father phoned to say he's working over the weekend. I didn't say anything.

Dani   What a surprise. Tell him, see if he's interested.

Jan   Of course he'll be interested. Do you know how much he's paying a term for you to swan in and out of that sixth form?

Dani   Oh well I'm sorry. I'll try harder to be value for money.

Jan   The money's not important.

Dani (*harshly*)   Then what are you *talking* about?

A familiar point for them both. **Jan** *seems to shrink a little and adjusts her clothing.*

Dani   What's with the outfit?

Jan   I've got an interview for a job.

Dani   As a ninja?

Jan   As a receptionist, actually.

Dani   At a mime school?

Jan *sighs.*

Jan (*smiles despite herself*)   At the gym on the edge of town.

Dani   Well done you.

Jan   Yes it's great. Very exciting. Free use of the facilities and all that.

Dani   I don't think they expect you to go round in sports gear all the time.

Jan (*with regret*)   I lied on the form.

Dani   Everybody lies. What, about your age?

Jan (*worried*)   No. Why? What's wrong with my age?

Dani   Nothing. Sorry. What then?

Jan   I'm supposed to have a keen and well-developed interest in health and fitness. I ticked the box.

Dani   You're going straight to hell.

Jan   Don't say that. Don't say I'm going to hell. I said my favourite exercise was Pilates. I know Madonna does it. That's it.

Dani (*quietly pleased*)   Pilates is about lengthening the muscles and building core strength, the most important element of which is controlling the abdominal belt. Hold in your stomach as if you're trying on a pair of very tight jeans.

They both suck their tummies in.

Now keep it there. Breathe from the chest . . . slowly. The top of your head is a magnet and the ceiling is made of iron, lengthen the spine. Now, you know when you're peeing?

Jan   Um, yes.

Dani   Imagine you're having a wee and you have to stop mid-flow.

Jan   Right.

Dani   Engage those muscles. Squeeze them right up. Hold that. Hold your tummy, stretch up from the spine and breathe in a slow, relaxed way from the ribcage.

Jan *focuses on all this and looks decidedly uncomfortable.*

Dani   Now you have to stay like that.

Jan For how long?

Dani   Forever, that is perfect posture. Core strength, feel the control and the focus of your body. Everything is hard and firm and deliberate.

Jan (*gives up*)   I can't do that! I have to think about that all the time?

Dani   It becomes second nature. You get stronger.

Jan   I thought it was relaxing.

Dani   Oh, it is, once you master it. You can practise the pelvic clenching and no one will know you're doing it. See. I'm doing it now, now I'm not. Now I am, now I'm not.

Jan   Righty ho. That's useful. Thank you. Now what do you want for tea?

Dani   I'm going out for dinner.

Jan   Gosh. Quite the socialite these days, aren't we?

Dani I don't have to, I'm not that bothered.

Jan Don't be silly, you go and have your fun. Is this a boy thing, or am I not supposed to ask?

Dani No.

Jan Fair enough. So it's just me then.

Dani Why don't you go into town, see Dad for a bit?

Jan He's very busy.

Dani Why not?

Jan And I don't want to leave you on your own.

Dani Really? Well, you could have fooled me.

Silence.

Jan The cat hasn't been for her food. Shall I put some more out, do you think?

Dani I don't know. Yes.

Jan You wanted her originally.

Dani I was ten!

Jan It's still a responsibility.

Dani Maybe dump her in a clinic for a few months.

Jan Now.

Dani Sorry, best not mention that.

Silence.

Jan I cried and cried after we dropped you off.

Dani Poor you. You've never asked me what it was like. I'm starting to wonder if I was ever there.

Jan I don't want to upset you.

Dani That's very considerate of you.

Scene Six

Lewis' *bedroom. He is searching for a certain album in a music collection.*

Dani   She doesn't *think* anything she doesn't *say.* It's like if she's putting something somewhere she goes, 'I'll just put that there.' Who the fuck is she talking to? Or she's driving and she's just, 'Ooh, what's he doing? I think we'll park over here.' Shut up. She's like Cassandra except her curse is to speak and have people want to beat her over the head with a hammer.

Lewis   Cassandra who?

Dani   It's a Greek or a Roman thing. She was cursed to predict the future and no one would believe her. Tim was telling me.

Lewis   Tim the chat room nonce?

Dani   I'm not sure it says that on his passport.

Lewis   Why do you still talk to him?

Dani   It's interesting.

Lewis   It's a bit sick is what it is.

Dani   He's a nice bloke. He made a good point the other day. How in history, it's always the oppressed minorities who are made out to be sick and dangerous, blacks or gays or whatever. How we need to turn them into monsters.

Lewis   What a load of shite.

Dani   We can't see it cos we're on the inside.

Lewis (*he has been trying in vain to find the album*)   Where the fuck is it?

Dani   Forget about it.

Lewis   I've always wanted to do it to this album.

Dani (*teasing*)   Look at you. You're getting well into it. Do you feel different now you've done it?

Lewis   Leave it.

Dani   Just messin'.

Lewis   I have done, other stuff, you know, with girls. I'm not a sexual cripple.

Dani (*sarcastic*)   Ah, that's romantic.

Lewis   Sorry. It's harder for blokes.

Dani   Harder to get your end away?

Lewis   You're kind of conditioned to be ignored by women. And I never wanted to play games to get girls I didn't even like to toss me off.

Dani   You can do that yourself.

Lewis   Well yes. And I did. You'll never know what it's like, cos you can go out with a short skirt if you fancy it and know you'll get attention or whatever.

Dani   Yeah but you'll never have that attention means that some pissed bloke you've never met comes up and goes 'I can smell your cunt.' (*She makes the Hannibal Lecter sound with her tongue.*)

Lewis   Was that to you?

Dani   Yeah, like the other day.

Lewis   But at least it's something. It's an acknowledgement you exist.

Dani   Fuck off.

Lewis   Something.

Dani   I'd swap in a second.

Lewis   I'd love that. I'd love you to spend one day in the life of a seventeen-year-old bloke. Hanging about listening to girls moan about how men treat them like shit and then watch them going off with the biggest wankers you've ever seen in your life, because they 'can't help being attracted to bastards'. You wonder when patriarchy's going to kick in.

Dani   Somebody's bitter.

Lewis   I'm joking.

Dani   It's just that girls mature faster than boys.

Lewis   Bollocks. That's what they said at school when all the girls in our year were going out with twenty-four-year-olds called Dwayne who deal skunk and drive clapped out escorts and treat them like shit. Because *we* were too immature.

Dani   Blimey. OK. But isn't that more or less like you and me?

Lewis   Yeah, but you don't seem younger. And I'm not a twat.

Dani   Ah.

Lewis   Sorry, that came out properly harsh.

Dani (*honestly*)   I'm not bothered.

Lewis (*cosying up to her*)   I'm not angry with you.

Dani   Good. I haven't done anything! I'm here aren't I? I'm doing my bit for the nice guys.

Lewis (*nuzzling her neck*)   You can always do more.

Dani   We can't, I've got my period.

Lewis   Oh. Cool.

Dani   It's odds of four to one, Lewis. I'm not mad keen on it myself . . .

Lewis   All right! . . .

Dani   I'm just saying.

Lewis (*in a foolish attempt to make her smile/get laid*)   Right. That's it. (*He jumps on her.*) So there's blood coming out of your vagina, eh? A likely story. How did you come up with that one? Sounds like crazy talk to me. (*He pretends to be confused and tries to unbutton her flies.* **Dani** *stops him, giggling.*) Come on, let's check this story out.

Dani   Get off, don't be gross.

Lewis   I don't mind.

Dani (*pulling away*)   That's very fucking magnanimous of you.

Pause.

Lewis   Dani . . . I know I don't know who Cassandra is and I work doing phone sales, but I'm not a bad bloke. I don't bugger children.

Dani   What's that, on your badge at work – Lewis – I don't bugger children.

Lewis   I do phone sales, a badge would be useless.

I'm going to sort it out. This music critic thing.

Dani   I know you are.

Lewis   Yeah, you know it. Come here.

Dani   You come here.

Lewis *goes over. They kiss.*

Lewis (*he squeezes her bum*)   I'll see your kiss and raise you a bum squeeze. Come on, one bum squeeze to stay in the game.

Dani *squeezes his bum, play reluctantly.*

Lewis (*throughout, he moves to be on top of her*)   Oh, she's seen it! She's staying in. Question is, is she bluffing? (*American accent.*) And here we can see, Marty, with our special under-the-table cameras that Dani the 'D-Man' Carter has a pair she's been hiding. (*He puts his hand up her top.*) Can she go all the way? Let's find out with the rest of the flop.

From her bag, **Dani**'*s mobile begins to ring.*

Scene Seven

The park bench. **Tim** *sits. He is reading the* Daily Mail. **Dani** *enters. She is carrying a plastic carrier bag with about eight 'women's' magazines in it. These should be of the* Elle, Zest *and* Marie-Claire *variety.*

Tim (*sees her, folds up his paper and puts it down*)   I haven't interrupted anything, have I?

Dani   God no.

Tim   I needed to see you.

Dani   Really?

Tim   It's a real help. Being able to talk to you.

Dani   That's what I want, I want you to be able to.

Tim   When I got out, they give you all sorts of advice . . . Do you want to know this?

Dani   Tell me.

Tim   They give you . . . numbers. Phone numbers of . . . sex lines that are particularly broadminded. You know, if you need to get something out. They do a sterling job. I called a couple of times but afterwards . . . These poor women, I thought of them in their living rooms glancing across at their kids as they listen to me . . . go on.

Dani   You don't need to feel guilty about telling me.

Tim   I feel that. I don't know why but I do feel that.

Dani   What have you done?

Tim   Nothing. Nothing.

Dani   What?

Tim (*a breath*)   Two flats above me there is the most beautiful little chocolate girl you've ever seen. Mummy's black, daddy's nowhere to be seen. She sits on the wall outside as her brothers play in the street.

Dani   A girl?

Tim   You should see her. She's lighter than her brothers. They call her Domino – I don't know, maybe that's her name. She smiles, she smiles and her eyes are luminous. But mostly she sits in a ball looking up over her knees. The longest eyelashes you've ever seen.

Dani (*confused*)   You like boys.

Tim   But she's like a little boy, a self-contained beautiful little . . . Christ. She's beautiful.

Dani   Have you got someone you can tell about this?

Tim   I'm telling *you*.

Dani   No, but. Someone real.

Tim   Yes. I could do. I don't want to be moved again. I have to take control of this. Where are they going to move me where there's no children, Hamlyn? I don't want to *do* anything.

Dani   Good. No that's good. This is the thing, I know. Every time you don't give in, you make yourself stronger. Like Jehovah's Witnesses when you tell them to fuck off. I'm a master at it, pushing down those urges, for a greater good, you know? Not doing anything has to make you feel good, the opposite of how you'd feel if you gave in, the opposite of guilt.

Tim   Innocence?

Dani   Above it all. It's just a pathetic urge. Like a dog.

Tim   But I'm not above it all.

Dani   But you're a good man.

Tim   You don't know that.

Dani (*sarcastic*)   In my vast, well-informed experience of you, you are a good man.

Tim   This is how I am. Every day.

Dani   'That's just how you are.' How convenient. So what's the point of fighting it. That's binge mentality, I've started so I may as well finish.

Tim   What do you suggest?

Dani   Every day is a blank slate. And you are defined not by your pathetic emotions and urges, but by *what you do*.

Tim   I don't *do* anything.

Dani   Good.

Tim (*looks at the carrier bag*)   What have you got there?

Dani   Recycling. Old magazines.

Tim *takes the bag and flips through all the magazines, before choosing one at random and pulling it out.*

Tim   All from this month.

Dani   Not that old.

Tim (*reaching in the bag and pulling out a receipt*)   And a receipt. From today.

Pause.

Dani   Yes.

Tim   Hmmm. Two and two would seem to equal . . .

Dani *snatches the bag back leaving* **Tim** *with the one magazine, which he examines. She hugs the bag.*

Dani   Yes, thank you . . . well done.

Tim *smiles and shakes his head as he flicks through the pages of* Shape *or something similar.*

Tim   Do they have anything but adverts in these things?

He stops flicking on a page with a black model.

Aaah. Domino has legs like that.

Dani *takes the magazine off* **Tim**, *as if to look, but smooths the page and closes it.*

Dani   It's not the same if someone's read it.

Tim   Sorry.

Dani   The smell goes and everything.

Tim   You're going to read all those?

Dani   Eventually. Not all at once.

Tim   You could read the *Iliad* in the time it would take you.

Dani   What's the point of that?

Tim   Oh, I don't know. The story that all stories spring from, expansion of the mind, understanding of myth and legend. (*Pause.*)

How much of your brain must be taken up with bollocks.

Dani   And yours. And everyone's.

Tim   But if you worked as hard at something else . . .

Dani   I've got very good at mental arithmetic.

Tim   What are your interests? What did you always want to do?

Dani   Well I've always had this dream of having a stall selling flavoured toilet paper outside dance studios.

Tim   Behave. What about when you were younger?

Dani (*thinks*)   I used to be into horses.

Tim   Aah, pony club.

Dani   Exactly. God it's so obvious. Have a horse and just get on it and gallop away, be in control of this big, beautiful animal.

Pause.

In reality though I think there's a lot of raking up shit.

Tim (*grins*)   Almost certainly true.

Dani   You just wanted to talk about the girl.

Tim   Not just. Nothing else, no, but it's a big just. I nearly spoke to her.

Dani   But you didn't.

Tim   I just want to hear what her voice sounds like. (*Smiles to himself.*) She's a little madam. At the weekend, she was sitting on the wall, with this cloth doll, she wasn't even playing with it, she was watching her brothers. One of them was bored obviously and he grabbed it off her and jammed it between the spokes of the wheel on his bike, riding about laughing at this little grinning ragdoll going round and round. So Domino, she makes a run for the bike and her brother grabs the doll out so she can't get it but she isn't even interested. She just yanks the *saddle* off the bike, pulls it right off and then calmly walks off with it under one arm and throws it into this huge skip. And you can see the brother's brain whirring and he's thinking, do I let this one go or do I crawl into a stinking skip? So he takes the doll and he holds it over the skip like he might just drop it any second, but she just sits on the wall. Isn't even bothered, so he's got nothing on her. She just taught him a lesson and the doll can go hang.

Dani   You really have too much time on your hands.

Tim (*motions to the bag*)   While you're obviously busy.

Dani   Fair.

Tim?

Tim   Dani.

Dani   What was it you were inside for?

Tim (*smiling at her words*)   What television have you been watching?

Dani   What?

Tim   Inside. Good Lord.

Dani   I'm just asking.

Tim   What are you going and asking something like that for?

Dani   You don't have to tell me.

Tim   I was very much in love. Put it that way. I did some things that I shouldn't have, for that reason.

Dani   Who was it?

Tim   We fell in love. I helped him through something and it was just one of those amazing things you read about. But his dad came round not long after. With a cricket bat.

Not used to someone his own size, little bully. I don't know what he thought I'd be like but he wasn't prepared for that. Later on the police turn up and search the place. I never saw David again, not in person.

Dani   And you were away for . . .?

Tim   Long enough. Different places. I was glad I'd been done on ABH as well.

Dani   Did you get a hard time?

Tim   That's enough about that. What about you, what about boyfriends?

Dani   God no.

Tim   They must be falling over themselves.

Dani   Don't! You sound like a creepy old uncle.

Tim   Sorry.

Dani   Thing is with boyfriends, is eventually they're going to want to take you out to dinner.

Scene Eight

Dani *and* **Lewis** *in a chat room.*

Lewis   My friends keep going on about meeting you.

Dani   Do they?

Lewis   They were ripping it out of me for you being seventeen. Cradlesnatcher.

Dani   You're only twenty-two.

Lewis   You still wear school uniform. That's not right.

Dani   No I don't. I've still got it though.

Lewis   Steady.

Dani   It's only five years. It's hardly in Tim's league.

Lewis   I'm not comparing myself to a child molester.

Dani   Don't call him that. He's a friend.

Lewis   You can't be friends with that.

Dani   I've met him. He's sweet.

Lewis   That sounds fucking stupid to me.

Dani   But it's all right me coming round yours?

Lewis   I'm not a pervert.

Dani   That's true.

Lewis *thinks.*

Lewis   I don't like you doing that.

Dani *thinks. She turns him off.*

Scene Nine

Dani*'s front room.* **Jan** *is sitting on the floor with a pile of three men's suits. The crotches of two of them lie carefully on top of one another. She is rather methodically cutting out the third.* **Dani** *enters, more buoyant than usual.* **Jan** *senses her entrance and purposefully continues to cut with more vigour.* **Dani** *eyes the situation and, after a few moments, perches on a chair behind her mother. There is a silence permeated only with the regular sound of cloth being cut. Eventually . . .*

Jan   Do we have any scissors sharper than these?

Dani (*looks to see the scissors she is using*)   Not sharper than those, no. I went to both registrations today, morning and afternoon, and I spent lunch in the library. I've read half the *Iliad*. It's rubbish.

Jan   For an essay?

Dani   Nope. Just cos I wanted to. (*Jokily, to lighten the mood.*) Cos that's the sort of student I am.

Jan *has finished cutting out the crotch of the trousers. She lays the material on top of the pile of crotches. She holds the trousers up by the legs to survey her handiwork.* **Dani** *eyes the door, it is as if she may just leave. She gets up and goes and sits on the floor next to the suits. She thumbs at one, distractedly.*

Dani   You know he doesn't wear these any more?

Jan   That's why I thought it would be all right to cut them up.

Dani *nods, aware of this speciousness. She notices her mother's outfit.*

Dani   You look nice.

This does it. A snort of derisive laughter becomes a sob and **Jan** *bows her head and quakes with tears.* **Dani** *is not perturbed by this. She is still until* **Jan** *raises her head.* **Jan** *remembers she is wearing make-up and tries to use her wrist to clean herself up.* **Dani** *passes her one of the crotches.* **Jan** *makes a motion of thanks and rubs it under her eyes. She then blows her nose on it.* **Dani** *takes it back off her.*

Dani (*considers the crotch*)   I'm not even going to say what that looks like.

Jan *laughs despite herself.*

Jan   Better out than in.

Dani   As my mother used to say.

Jan (*exhales*)   What a day.

Dani   Are you going to tell me about it?

Jan   I had my interview, went rather well actually. When I arrived in the foyer I really thought about just turning round and going straight out again. All these young, muscular boys were huddled round the desk laughing about something. One of the boys had been at school with your brother, I'm sure, Nathan Riddler, do you remember him?

Dani   No.

Jan Anyway. I said no, no, I'm going to do this and I went in and I talked about . . . Pilates and I nodded at the idea that the gym is a kind of 'third home' and that we should be a 'third family' for people, God knows who the 'second family' is supposed to be and we had a giggle about Nathan Riddler because I mentioned I used to know his mother and apparently he's a real ladies' man about the place . . . and then he shook my hand and showed me round. It's a lovely, lovely place. All wooden panelling and saunas and you can choose whatever music you want to listen to when you're on the things, you can even watch television. It really is amazing.

Silence.

Jan Dani, I don't know how to tell you this but your father's having an affair.

Dani's *unblinking response is only to raise her eyebrows very slightly.*

Dani (*surprised only by her mother's melodramatic style and not by the statement*)   Yes.

Jan I went over to the flat. I drove there, you know how I feel about driving in London. I thought I would wait for him to get home and tell him about it all. He's changed the locks. I stood in the street. In the rain. It looked so warm inside. I don't remember it being very warm. And I looked and I thought, this is one of those moments where you know what sort of a person you are. I got back in the car and drove home. (*Becoming a wail.*) And now I've ruined three perfectly good suits that OXFAM could have really done with just because I thought I should. You don't seem very surprised.

Dani I'm surprised that you're surprised.

Jan I'm not surprised. I'm just . . . I'm really shocked.

Dani He comes home every other weekend, if that. I have no memory of you two sleeping in the same bed.

Jan Your father snores.

Dani It was never like on TV, so . . .

Jan   Life isn't like TV.

Dani   That's the conclusion I came to.

Jan (*self-righteous*)   And now, after everything. This is how he repays me, sneaking around with some thirty-something tart.

Dani   I thought there must be some kind of . . . arrangement.

Jan (*stares at her bleary-eyed*)   What world have you been living in?

Dani   This one.

Jan   Sssshhh. Listen to how quiet it is.

After a moment, the house phone rings. They both jump and then look at each other. **Dani** *goes to get it.*

Jan   I don't want to speak to him.

The answerphone answers the call.

Jan (*on answerphone*)   Hello, you've reached the Carters, please leave a message and we'll call you back!

Gym Bloke   Ur, hi. This is a message for Jan Carter? This is Fitness United. Sorry to have to tell you that, thank you for coming in but we really, we needed someone with IT skills, cheers. Sorry. Bye.

Jan (*pause*)   Look. (**Jan** *beckons* **Dani** *to come and look over at her face. She pulls the skin taut around her mouth.*) I saw myself in the mirrors. No matter how much you pull, they don't go away. I can't even get a job at a place where my son's schoolfriend would be my boss. My husband has an 'agreement' with me I never knew about, even the cat's disappeared.

Dani   She's always wandered off. Someone else is feeding her, that's all.

Pause.

Jan   Bloody good sense of humour, that cat.

Dani   Come on, Mum. Did you even go round there?

Jan   Of course I did.

Dani   Are you sure? Because you're back suspiciously early for someone who had an interview at two and then drove to London and back.

Jan (*horrified*)   How can you think that?

Dani   Fine, whatever.

Jan   Don't whatever me young lady. I was suspecting your father of having affairs while you were in nappies.

It's very complicated. I have a great deal of respect for your father.

Dani   Dad's a cunt, Mum. He's always been a cunt.

Jan   Dani!

Dani   You've been married to the man for twenty-five years, you must know this.

Jan   How can you be so ungrateful? Don't speak about your father like that.

Dani   He gets away with murder everywhere. THIS ISN'T NEW.

Jan (*hits her clumsily, she hasn't done that in a long time*)   You silly spoilt . . . girl. Everything you have is thanks to your father, everything you've thrown away and all the people you've upset and he's never once complained about it.

Dani   About what? Complained about what? Throw money at it. Do whatever it takes, so that you never have to deal with the fact that it might just be YOUR FAULT!

Jan   Get out.

A moment.

Dani   Fine.

Jan   If that's how you feel you can get out.

Dani   Not a problem. (*She dramatically picks up her bag.*)

Jan   No. Don't, Dani.

Dani (*preparing to leave*)   You wear me away, Mum.

Jan   I meant the room.

Dani   I'm around you and I feel like I've had a layer of skin removed.

Jan   I know. Spare a thought for me, Dani. You can't imagine how it is to give up half your life to people who don't even like you.

Dani *leaves*. **Jan** *looks around the room, searching for purpose.*

Act Two

Scene One

Tim's flat. It is small and poorly decorated, as if the landlord stores all the furniture that does not match here. There is a freshly baked Victoria sponge cake on the side. **Dani** is standing in the doorway with two bags, surveying the interior. **Tim** looks at her bags a little dismally.

Dani   Should I take my shoes off?

Tim   If you want to.

Dani   OK. No, I'll keep them on.

Tim *nods. A pause.*

Tim   Let me. (*He takes* **Dani**'s *bags off her and ushers her in from the doorway. Then, rather impotently, he puts the bags down only a few yards from where she has been standing.*) I could sleep out here if you wanted. If you wanted my bed.

Dani   Don't be daft. I don't know how long I'll need to stay.

What's with the cake?

Tim   I baked it. For my class. You've got to have a hobby.

Dani (*laughs, this defrosts the situation and they both relax a bit*) Yeah, you've got to have a hobby.

Tim   Would you like some?

Dani (*automatically*)   No. Thanks. I didn't know who to call.

Tim   Do you think it's a good idea to have left her on her own? If she's just found that out?

Dani (*rolls her eyes*)   But this is it, she hasn't. She's known for bloody ages, just like everything else. Now it's convenient for her to be like, oh my family have left me, oh our cat's found another home, oh how did this all happen when I wasn't looking?

Tim   You're a bit harsh.

Dani   Try living with it. What are you going to do with that cake?

Tim   Do?

Dani   Well you can't just leave it sitting there.

Tim   Eat some of it. Take some in to the class. Do you want a bit? If you're staying in my house it's my rules – let them eat cake.

He cuts two slices of the cake.

Don't mind fingers. (*He passes her a slice.*)

Dani *salivates at the smell.* **Tim** *tucks into his piece, considering the texture.* **Dani** *stuffs the cake into her mouth and chews it aggressively. She devours the rest of the slice.*

Tim   What do you think?

Dani   It'll be fun, me staying here.

Dani *goes and cuts herself another slice of cake and eats it. She cuts more thin slices off and eats them during the following conversation. When she speaks with her mouth full she can repeat herself, as one would. The more she eats and as the conversation proceeds she gets more hyper and excited.*

Tim (*teacher-like*)   You're going into school, though, on Monday.

Dani   College. And I have been. I've been brilliant lately.

Tim   And your mum knows where you are? I don't want her to be worried.

Dani   She'd be more worried if I rang her up and told her. Stop fussing!

Tim   Fun, then?

Dani   Yeah.

Tim   I've got Pictionary.

Dani   Fuck Pictionary. When was the last time you went out? I mean properly.

Tim   When was the last time *you* went out?

Dani *(shrugs)*   I feel a bit weird.

Tim   Like what?

Dani   I don't know. We should *get involved*, Tim, *do* some stuff. Do you want to go bowling?

Tim   No, I don't want to go bowling!

Dani *(temptingly)*   There'll be kids there.

Tim   You're supposed to be helping me, you're supposed to be my support.

Dani   Exactly.

Shit, no, I've just had a kick-arse idea!

She begins to roll up the skirt she is wearing.

Dani   Oh yes. Do you have a shirt and tie?

Tim *(indicates his bedroom)*   In the wardrobe. Are we going somewhere posh?

Dani *gleefully skips into the bedroom.*

Dani *(off)*   Oh my God! Look at your collection of dad rock! I love it. Can I put some on?

Tim   I resent the term 'dad rock'. It's classic rock with acoustic roots. What are you doing in there?

Paul Simon's 'Down by the Schoolyard' is heard from the bedroom.

Dani   We're going to do a little experiment.

Tim   Oh God.

Dani   You'll see.

Tim *smiles at the tune. She bursts out of the bedroom, doing up a man's white shirt and with a tie loose round her neck. She proceeds to tie up the shirt in a knot at her waist and to tie the tie. Meanwhile:*

Tim   I'm not going to shag you.

Dani   I don't want you to shag me. Jesus. You only have one tie so we'll have to share it. How come you only have one tie?

Tim   I only have one neck and I'm not often in court. Where are we going?

Dani   You'll see.

Tim   Should I change?

Dani   Not unless you've got little shorts and a cap. (*Pause.*) That are yours.

Tim *shakes his head.*

Dani   Thank God for that.

She gets a brush out of her bag and brushes her hair while she has a little dance. **Tim** *watches her.*

Tim (*fondly*)   You're a lunatic, you are.

Dani   How do I look?

Tim   Like a stripper. No offence.

Dani   No, no. That was the look I was going for.

She continues to dance and gets him to copy her. He does, self-consciously.

Dani   There we go. Get any stuff you need.

Tim (*does a silly salute*)   Testicles, spectacles, wallet and watch.

She dances round him, grabs more cake and eats it as she dances.

Dani   Come on then, this'll be great.

Dani *takes him by the hand and they exit. She runs back in, grabs a chunk of cake, and then exits again.*

Lewis *is on his computer. He is writing an email.*

Internet   To Dani2752@demon.co.uk

Lewis   Dani. You absent bitch. I miss you. It's been six days, man. I'm sounding a little bit mental, which I don't like. I rang you again and no answer. I get the feeling you're actively not ringing me now. What if you're dead? How would I ever find out? No one would think to call me. I'd just sit here forever looking at this screen.

You don't even have to call, you could just email me to tell me why you're not calling. At least then I'd KNOW.

I can't think about anything else, you've taken over my brain. Every part of me is willing that little gold envelope to appear. Send and receive. Send and receive. But when it does its always nubile young Russian girl-on-girl action. Still.

The clock tells me it is far too late for anyone to be calling anyone. I tell the clock to shut up, what do you know, you're a fucking clock.

I apologise to the clock. It has always been there before when you've written and may be a lucky charm.

I think you're lovely. Sometimes I want to smash your face in, like now, to remind you I'm here, but I think you're lovely. Will you not just write a little? Just to keep me going? Cos I just keep imagining what you could be doing and it's sending me mental. I'm sorry but it is. I miss you. Obviously in a manly, independent, not bothered way. But I do.

He sighs.

Internet   Save as draft.

Scene Two

Three o'clock in the morning. **Tim's** *flat.* **Dani** *is lying on the floor, worse for wear.* **Tim** *is sat in an armchair, happily drunk. There is an open bottle of wine with one glass which* **Tim** *drinks from. A pizza box with only a few crusts left in it lies on the floor next to the empty plate that the cake was on. Another dirty plate with cutlery and a container of salt. Bizarrely,* **Tim** *is holding a modern child's Etch A Sketch of the kind that comes with a pen for drawing on the screen and a sliding knob to clear the picture. He has drawn on it a knife with some butter on it, the devil, a pointing hand and a gnome.*

Dani (*giggling*)   I *don't* fucking *know.*

Tim   You're so nearly there! You've got the knife spreading something on . . .

Dani   The devil.

Tim (*nodding*)   And the hand's saying 'you' and this little fella here. (*Pointing to the gnome.*)

Dani   The dwarf.

Tim   We agreed he was a gnome.

Dani   Spread on the hell gnome. Margarine on Satan's hand gnome.

Tim   For God's sake!

Dani   Butter the devil you gnome.

Tim   Yes!

Dani   Butter the devil you gnome?

Tim   Better the devil you know!

Dani   You penis.

Tim   Undefeated.

Dani *grabs the Etch A Sketch and writes 'TIM IS A NOB' on it and shows it to him.*

Dani (*as a child*)   I'm hungry.

Tim   You've eaten everything in the house.

Dani   Take that back.

Tim   It's true. God, you don't do things by halves, do you? I've got some crackers.

Dani (*turning over*)   Crackers are shit. Can't you make another cake?

Tim   I *have* got some cake mix in the fridge, for a chocolate cake.

Dani *'s eyes light up. She jumps up.*

Dani   Wicked!

Tim   I'm in no state for baking.

Dani   That's fine, that's fine.

Dani *is already running out to get the mix.*

We hear her whoop with delight on finding the mix. She re-enters with a large plastic bowl of chocolate cake mix and a big spoon.

Dani   See, isn't this fun? (*With the random clarity of the very pissed.*) Shit, where's my phone?

Tim   You gave it to me to look after. (*He rummages in a pocket and pulls out Dani's mobile.*)

Dani   Did I? I'm brilliant.

Tim (*chucking it to her*)   You said it ruined the line of your outfit.

Dani (*she looks at the screen.*)   Seven missed calls. Blimey. I'm well loved.

Tim   Bet they're all from your mum.

Dani (*goes through them*)   Yeah and bloody Lewis.

Tim   Who's Lewis?

Dani   God bless him. I think he's a bit obsessed with me. Bit of a geek, that's all. Jealous?

Tim   Desperately.

Dani   So come on. Tonight. I thought you'd be wandering round like a dog on heat.

Tim   Did you really?

Dani   I don't know.

Tim   It was all a bit . . . ridiculous. Does that happen every week?

Dani   Yeah, a thousand grown ups pay fifteen quid to dress in school and go dancing to 'Love Shack'.

Tim   I should get out more.

Dani   At least you're honest about it. Not like all those blokes there drooling over little girls where it's safe, where it's allowed.

Tim   Come on, and you don't love it? That's the whole point.

Dani   I remember when we'd come out of school and we'd roll our skirts up, because they bloody measured them when we came in every day. And we'd walk down to the train station and the looks we'd get.

Tim   Exactly. You girls. You know.

Dani (*laughing*)   One time, the path out the back of school. Some bloke had left a trail of passport photos of his genitals. With a hard on, all down the path to the station. It was hilarious.

Tim   No!

Dani   Straight up. It was just the thought of this bloke paying, like five quid, and clambering into the photo booth with his trousers round his ankles.

Tim   Adjusting the stool height?!

Dani   Exactly. And cutting them up and then leaving a trail! We picked them up cos, you know, we didn't want the little girls finding them.

Tim   Did you tell anyone?

Dani   No, no. I think we were like . . . here we are, the top two percent of the country at this private school, always being told we could do whatever we wanted if we put our mind to it . . . and here's this bloke who hasn't even got the guts to flash at some kids in person. So, leave him be. (*She laughs.*) Poor sod, we thought it was funny.

Tim   Worse thing you can do to a man, that. Laugh at him.

Dani   Then don't leave photos of your penis all over the street!

Tim   They'll be laughing on the other side of their face, if I get hold of them. That's what he'll have thought. Worst thing you can do.

Dani   Well lucky bloody you. If laughing's the worst thing that can happen to you.

Tim   You should have told someone.

Dani   Just saying. I thought all you lot would stick together.

Tim   'You lot.' Not me. No one normal likes to hurt anyone, certainly not children.

Dani (*incredulous*)   You just fancy them.

Tim   I have a preference. It would be strange if, say, you only liked men with blue eyes. But it shouldn't be made illegal. You shouldn't be beaten up over it.

Dani   That's not the same.

Tim   I'm not doing it any more.

Dani (*grabs the bottle of wine and raises it*)   To not doing it any more.

She drinks from the bottle.

Tim   Do you want me to get you a glass?

Dani (*considers*)   What's the point?

She tops up his glass.

Dani   So do you have, you know, a lot of stuff to look at?

Tim   Dani!

Dani   I'd be interested to see, that's all. (*Looks about.*) Is there a hidden room?

Tim   No.

Dani   You must have something, all blokes do. (*She becomes more serious.*) I was terrified when I found my dad's. I couldn't get the picture out of my head of him, this big, cross man, going at it over these silly photos.

Tim   Top shelf material?

Dani   Must have been. I remember thinking how pretty the women were, that didn't bother me at all. But I couldn't sleep cos some part of me thought when the magazines ran out he'd come up those stairs. Because suddenly I didn't know my dad any more. Something controlled him.

Tim   Did he ever come up the stairs?

Dani   Course not. Fat bastard couldn't be arsed. Go on, show us. Look, I'll show you mine. I've never shown anyone this before.

Dani *crawls over to one of her bags and roots around before pulling out her 'Thinspiration' book. The pages, crammed full of celebrity and model shots, are slightly tattered.*

Tim (*taking it*)   What's this?

Dani   Stuff.

Tim *flicks through some of the pictures, resting on one with an article stuck in.*

Tim (*reads out in a silly voice*)   Tips for the party season: If a buffet's being laid on, eat *before* you go so you can enjoy just a few healthy snacks. Nothing will tempt you to break your diet like turning up at a party starving hungry!

Dani (*ironically*)   Good point.

Tim   Always finish your glass completely before filling up again.

Dani (*has a swig of wine*)   Not a problem.

Tim   That way, you'll be certain how many calories you've drunk!

Dani   Wahey!.

Tim   Always carry a toothbrush to purge with. Otherwise you'll scrape your knuckles on your teeth.

Dani   That's something else. That's from a different thing.

Tim (*chucks the book dismissively*)   I can't connect you with this. You want to get rid of this. Burn all this stuff. Blank slate.

Dani   Is that what you've done?

Tim   I keep letters. Personal things. If I wanted other stuff, you just have to look around. That's what assures me I'm not a nutter, you just have to look around you.

Dani   I know. I know.

Tim   They said to me, we've no way of knowing. It's totally up to you. There's only so much *we* can do.

Dani   That's true though.

Tim   Aye. Yes.

Dani   Because it's in *your* head.

Tim (*conspiratorially*)   I don't think it's dirty. I don't know when it's bad.

Dani   You have to have a line.

Tim   For the fantasy?

Dani (*lets the remainder of the cake mix fall from the spoon as she speaks*)   I have a fantasy. Where I can take a trowel and run it down the inside of me (*she motions downwards from just below her breasts to the bottom of her belly*) and it will all curl off and flop out of me.

Tim (*after a moment*)   I was supposed to alternate. One day, 'normal' fantasies, the next day, 'abnormal' fantasies.

Dani (*smiles*)   Ha! Protein, carbohydrates, protein, carbohydrates.

Tim   Phase them out.

Dani   Phase them all out.

Tim   Trouble is, masturbation doesn't take direction very well.

Dani   With me, I can't (*mock embarrassed, makes a half-hearted wanking gesture*), you know, unless I've had a good day, eating-wise.

Tim   Do you?

Dani   It's a kind of a reward. But I haven't in ages. You can't have sex with someone who disgusts you, can you?

Tim   But you're so lovely.

Dani   Bless.

Tim   (*rubs his eyes*)   It's too late for this.

Dani   I feel sick.

Tim   I'm not surprised. You daft thing.

Dani   I don't want to go to bed.

Tim   Really? I look forward to it all day.

Dani   I want to talk about things, not the way we talk to other people. Like when you told me about that girl upstairs. I liked that.

Tim   I haven't seen her.

Dani   You want to know the dirtiest thing I ever did?

Tim   (Christ, Dani.)

Dani   When I was little I used to smear butter all over my knickers and take the cat to bed with me.

A pause.

Tim   No wonder it's buggered off.

She giggles. He giggles. They both dissolve into childish sniggering at themselves.

Tim   . . . And relax.

What are you like?

Dani   What are you like, more like.

Tim   I'm knackered.

Dani   Can I put some music on? I'm going to have S Club fucking Seven in my head all night.

Tim   Nothing heavy. Time-for-bed music.

Dani *wanders out to the bedroom.* **Tim** *stands up and surveys the mess. He winces at his own drunkenness.*

Tim   Sleeping bag.

Tim *goes off to the kitchen. Bob Dylan's 'A Simple Twist of Fate' begins from the bedroom.* **Dani** *comes back in. She has a baggy T-shirt of* **Tim** *'s. She takes off her shirt and quickly puts the T-shirt on.* **Tim** *re-enters with a sleeping bag and a pint glass of water. He sees her pull her bra off though one sleeve.*

Tim (*impressed*)   The things I'll never know.

Dani *smiles. He offers her the glass, she takes it and has a sip.* **Tim** *carefully puts the sleeping bag down.* **Dani** *puts the glass down. A moment.* **Tim** *grandly puts his hand out as an invitation to dance,* **Dani** *jokily curtsies and accepts. They dance, slightly awkwardly as they only have a small area of clear floor, but both smiling.*

Tim   This is my sort of dancing, eh. I must be getting old.

She rests her head against his chest. He raises his hand to pat her hair, **Dani** *reacts by raising her head. Their faces are close. She looks up at him – her gaze flicks down and then up again.* **Tim** *stops dancing and* **Dani** *moves her arms to around his neck. She kisses him. He lets her for a little while and begins to kiss her back before pulling away.* **Tim** *takes one of her arms from around his neck and steps away. He kisses her hand, leans towards her and whispers something like 'sleep well'. He then picks up and moves the sleeping bag for no apparent reason and goes into the bedroom.*

Dani *seems to be waiting to see if he will re-emerge. He does not. She surveys the room. She begins to solemnly unpack the sleeping bag but stops. She gets on her knees to pile up the dirty plates and puts the pizza crusts into the empty box. She eats one. She then licks the plate that the cake was on. She looks at the bowl with some cake mix left. She puts her 'Thinspiration' book back in her bag and then, sadness giving way to determination, she pours a con-siderable amount of salt into the pint glass full of water. She swirls it around and looks at it. She stirs it with the end of the cake mix spoon. Quickly and without ceremony she takes a massive gulp of the salt water, and then another. Instantly, she retches and vomits* *copiously into the bowl. It is done with quiet practicality. She sits back and takes a big, cleansing breath.*

Voicemail   You have two new messages. Beep.

Lewis   Hi, urm, I don't know if you got my message because there was a weird beep halfway through so I thought I'd call to say I rang. OK. Bye. Oh, it's Lewis by the way.

Beep.

Hi, urm, this is Lewis. Just wondering what you're up to. Urm. You've got my number, I think. Bye.

Another beep.

Scene Three

Tim's *flat, the next morning.* **Dani** *has gone, as have her bags. The bowl has been cleared away but the rest of the mess is still there. The sleeping bag has been used. There is an authoritative knock on the door. Eventually,* **Tim** *emerges in a dark green dressing gown, looking decidedly unwell and disorientated. He surveys the room. There is another knock.*

Lewis (*off*)   Hello? I'm looking for Tim.

Panicked, **Tim** *immediately goes to a cupboard where there is a (old) laptop and laptop charger. He puts them both inside the sleeping bag, the closest thing to hand, rolls the sleeping bag up and puts it back into the cupboard. Underneath where the sleeping bag lay* **Tim** *finds* **Dani**'s *'Thinspiration' book which he also hurriedly hides. He then goes into the bedroom and scurries back in with a cricket bat. During:*

Tim   Who is it?

Lewis (*off*)   Does Tim live here?

Tim   Who is it, please?

Lewis (*off*)   I'm looking for Dani.

Tim   She's not here.

Lewis   Can you let me in, mate? I want a word.

No answer.

Lewis (*off*)   I can stay here all night.

Tim   Fine. Hang on, mate.

Tim *opens the door to* **Lewis**, *holding the bat as nonchalantly as possible.* **Lewis** *is taken aback by the size of him and the bat.*

Lewis   There's no need for that.

Tim   I'm sorry. Bad area, round here.

Lewis   Yeah, I saw.

Tim   Is Dani all right?

Lewis   You tell me.

Tim   I'm not sure what you mean.

Lewis   Look mate. I know all about you and unless you want your neighbours to know and all, I'd let me in.

Tim   There's no need for *that*.

Tim *ushers* **Lewis** *in.*

Lewis   I've been up and down this block looking for you.

Tim   Oh yes?

Lewis   You must be the only person in this building without tattoos.

Tim (*suspicious*)   I'm not that easy to find.

Lewis (*looking round with distaste*)   Dani said where they were making you stay.

Tim   That's thoughtful of her. I've lived in better places.

Lewis   I've shat in better places.

Tim   Well, lucky old you. Is there something I can help you with?

Lewis (*eyeing the bat*)   I've got a couple of points to make and it's better for you if it's said here, in private.

Tim   It's not Lewis, is it?

Lewis (*taken aback*)   Yeah.

Tim   Dani's told me about you. Hello.

Lewis (*thrown off*)   Hello. Oh. What's she said then?

Tim (*goes and props the bat against the wall*)   She talks about you a lot.

Lewis   That's ironic cos she talks about you all the bloody time and all.

Tim   Would you like a cup of tea?

Lewis   No. Cheers. I don't drink tea.

Tim   Really? I couldn't live without it.

Lewis   Warm dishwater.

Tim   Ah. No one's ever made you a really good cup of tea. Do you mind if I sort myself out a bit?

Lewis   No, sure.

Tim *exits to the kitchen/bedroom area.* **Lewis** *stands, looking around. He eyes the cricket bat. He goes over and picks it up, feels the weight of it. He practises a swing, he is obviously unused to holding one.*

Tim *comes back wearing trousers and a shirt, he is doing up his flies.*

Tim   Are you sure you don't want a drink?

Lewis (*frowning. This is not going as planned.*)   No, you're all right.

Tim   Sorry about the mess.

Lewis   Yeah.

Tim   She's really not here.

Lewis   Yeah, look, thanks there's a couple of points I want to make. I know what you're about and, honestly, that makes you messed up in my eyes and . . .

Tim   Oh you know what I'm about, do you?

Lewis   As much as I need to know.

Tim   And what's that?

Lewis   I don't know if you're reformed or whatever now, that's not my business. Well it is if you're not, it's everybody's business. Society. I don't want to call you a pervert in your own home, but that's what a lot of people would call you.

Tim   Was that what you came over to tell me, that you didn't want to call me a pervert in my own home?

Lewis   I came to ask . . . I think you should stay away from Dani.

Lewis *eyes the cricket bat.*

Tim   Sorry about that, you can't be too careful.

Lewis   I bet you can't. (**Tim** *nods.*)

She's a nice girl, Dani. And I've got to be honest. I don't know what's gone on with you two . . . (*He trails off deliberately, waiting for* **Tim** *to correct him.*) It's not right.

Tim *is deliberately silent.*

Lewis   I worry about her. She's the sort of girl who puts herself in dangerous positions . . .

Tim   Are you fucking her, Lewis?

Lewis   What?

Tim   It's a simple enough question. Come on, now, blokes together.

Lewis   Watch your mouth.

Tim   That's what you came round here to ask *me*, wasn't it?

Lewis   I'm worried about her.

Tim   Oh, forgive me.

There is a tense silence. .

Lewis   That is one of the things I'm worried about.

Tim   Ah.

Lewis   Don't make out like I'm predictable. It's fucking rank, man, that's how I feel if I'm honest with you. To have feelings like that for kids and that's not on and that's the law and nature and everything and I don't want Dani to be around . . . that.

Tim   You don't think that's the safest kind of man for an attractive young woman to be around?

Lewis   I fucking doubt it.

Tim   If you're concerned about Dani, then that's commendable. But she's a bright, lovely girl. She'll do what she wants.

Lewis   So, have you then?

Tim   No, Lewis, you win. I haven't touched a hair on her head. Or anywhere else. So you can take your adolescent hormones and dis-appear off and watch *Buffy*. I'm tired.

Lewis   You smug cunt. You ever had to wash the spraypaint off that door? Or do you just paint over it? Is that easier?

Tim *makes a very subtle movement or looks in the direction of the bat.*

Tim   Goodbye, Lewis.

Lewis (*making it clear he is leaving*)   Leave her alone, eh? I could tell everyone in this place about you. I could write it large all over this place.

Tim   I know, Lewis, you could. And I'm terrified cos I've got just so much to lose.

A moment. **Lewis** *leaves.*

Tim *sits, unsettled.*

Scene Four

The park. **Tim** *sits with* **Dani** *next to him. She has her head in her hands.*

Tim   I don't know what you expect me to say.

Dani (*wincing*)   I'm so sorry. Oh God. I'm so embarrassed.

Tim   I'm not a curiosity you know, to tell your friends about.

Dani   I'm so sorry. I'll kill him. I never thought . . .

Tim   Why would you tell people?

Dani   Just him. I was . . .

Tim   What?

Dani (*regressing and admitting*)   I was showing off.

Tim   Danielle.

Dani   I didn't think he'd ever go looking for you. I jus' . . . mentioned the flats, you can see them from his.

Tim   That's comforting. He could tell . . . anyone.

Dani   It's my fault, I know.

Tim   No. This was always going to happen. This is how it goes.

Dani   Don't say that. He's no one, he won't do anything.

Tim   Every knock on the door. Every shout at the window.

Dani   He wouldn't say anything.

Tim   It's exhausting.

Dani   I'm an idiot. (*Pause.*) You're still speaking to the idiot though.

Tim   I do have things I shouldn't have.

Pause.

Dani   OK.

Tim   On my computer.

Dani   You never said.

Tim   I was embarrassed.

Dani   Just delete it.

Tim   You can't delete anything. Not completely. I can't get done now for some rubbish I've never even looked at.

Dani   I asked and you never said.

Tim   They're not even real anyway these days.

Dani   What aren't real?

Tim   You know . . . superimposed.

Dani   Oh. Airbrushed.

Tim   Exactly.

Dani   You could have told me.

Tim   I know. There's no one else in the world I could have told.

Dani   I'd never mess this up on purpose.

Tim   I know. Dani, will you look after it for me?

Dani   Your computer?

Tim   Would you take it?

Dani   OK. What's on it?

A silence.

Dani   Don't worry. I've seen all that stuff. They look like perfume adverts. (*Pause.*) The other day I saw this personal ad in the paper. Lonely woman needs company for her and her blond blue-eyed son. I saw it how you would see it. You know, how it's everywhere for you.

Tim   It is.

Dani   How everyone tells you to get well but they're all working to keep you ill.

Tim   That's exactly it. I'm doing fine. I'm completely in control and then . . .

Dani   I understand completely.

Tim   Do you believe in God, Dani?

Dani   Course not, who believes in God?

Tim   I wondered if that's why you don't judge me?

Dani   I just think we should work on ourselves first, you know?

Tim   What was it like before I met you? I can't remember.

Dani   Very dull I'd've thought.

Tim   There's that smile. Silly girl.

Dani   Yeah.

Tim   You made a right mess of my flat.

Dani   *We* did. It wasn't just me.

Tim   But I cleared up.

Dani   I was wankered.

Tim   Here. I've got something of yours.

He gets her 'Thinspiration' book out and gives it to her.

Dani   Oh God!

Tim   I thought you might miss it.

Dani (*hugs it sarcastically*)   How could I forget my Bible?

Tim   Are you coming back to the flat then?

Dani   Sure. Why?

Tim   For the computer.

Darn   Oh, yeah.

Tim   Some day, Dani, I'm going to take you to the best restaurant in town and we'll eat ourselves silly. I'll propose and we'll argue about what to call our kids. I'll want to give them stupid names from literature and I'll go out in the middle of the night to get you gherkins and ice cream when you're pregnant and all stuff like that.

Dani   And when people ask us how we met, we'll just give each other a knowing look.

Tim   Yes! Exactly that.

Dani   You mad git.

Tim   Come on, then.

Dani   I'm good for you really though, aren't I?

Tim   Hey. I had to scrape your vomit out of that pudding bowl.

Dani   Aah. This is what it'll be like when we're married.

Tim *exits.* **Dani** *trots out after him.*

Scene Five

The Carters' front room. **Lewis** *perches, slightly uncomfortably, taking in the room.* **Jan** *comes in from the kitchen with a plate of toast.*

Jan   Are sure you won't have bacon or anything with it?

Lewis   No that's fine, thank you, that's great.

Jan *hands him a glass of something, probably squash. She watches him eat the toast.*

Jan   I tried to phone her but it's switched off.

Lewis   I know.

Jan   She should be back. She knows you're coming, does she?

Lewis   I left her a message.

Jan   At least this way I get to meet you. It's impossible to get anything out of her, Lewis, it really is. I bet your mother doesn't have to force everything out of you, does she?

Lewis   Don't know really.

Jan   No. She shouldn't be long. Cos you know each other from . . .?

Lewis   I live near.

Jan   Oh yes. I'd hardly know. Not the friendliest area I've ever lived in, I have to say. Everyone stays in their little boxes.

Lewis   It's commuter-ville, innit.

Jan   I suppose (that's it) . . .

Lewis   But you don't know what goes on behind closed doors. I tell you there are sick people round here, you don't want to come out of their box, I tell ya.

A moment.

I love toast.

A moment.

Dani (*to* **Lewis**)   Lewis! Hello.

Lewis   All right?

Dani (*to* **Lewis**)   How did you find my house?

Lewis   The lions outside. They've got football scarves.

Jan (*helpfully*)   It's for the World Cup.

Dani   Right. Good.

Lewis   I left loads of messages on your phone.

Jan (*to* **Dani**)   He is a friend of yours?

Dani (*to* **Jan**)   Yeah, yeah.

Jan   I'll leave you to it, shall I? Unless you want more toast or anything?

Dani   No.

Lewis   No thanks.

Jan *exits.*

Dani   Christ, worlds colliding. Fuck, Lewis! Have you been round town looking for stone lions? You mental.

Lewis   I wanted to see where you live.

Dani   Oh my God. And that doesn't strike you as strange?

Lewis   You could have just phoned me.

Dani   You've got no right!

Lewis   Why didn't you call?

Dani   Maybe because you're quite obviously a psycho.

Lewis   I was worried.

Dani   You don't just turn up . . .

Lewis   I left you messages. I've just come round your house.

Dani   At four o'clock in the afternoon. You should be at work!

Lewis   I've jacked it in. I'm sick of calling people up when I know it's something they don't want. I'm gonna take the critic thing seriously. I'm gonna do work experience.

Dani (*amazed that he thinks she should care*)   Bothered!

Lewis   I'll go then, if you want.

Dani   No! What right do you have to go round and threaten Tim? You don't even know him.

Lewis   You do, do you?

Dani   Yes I do! I've been trying to help him and you turn up on his doorstep like some kid who's had his toy taken away.

She has been holding the laptop all this time. She makes some sort of a move to put it down.

Lewis   Is that yours?

Dani   No it's not mine! What made you go round there?

Lewis   It's not his, is it?

Dani   Mind your own fucking business!

Lewis   Oh, Dani, there could be anything on there.

Dani   I know what's on it.

Lewis   Like fuck. What a bastard. You could get properly done.

Dani   This has NOTHING TO DO WITH YOU.

Lewis   Dani, I care about you. I went round there cos . . . I love you.

Dani   Don't. Talk. Shite.

A pause.

You love me. You don't even know me.

A pause.

Let's be honest, you met me to have sex and that's wonderful, that's simple, that's clean, I liked that. I wanted to help you. Just like with Tim. He needs fixing. You needed a shag, Lewis, let's be honest, that's what you were after.

Lewis   That's bollocks. I never used you.

Dani   I never felt used. Just useful.

Lewis *stares at* **Dani**.

Lewis   You're not right in the head.

Dani   Oh! Don't you think I've been told that before?

Lewis   I don't know. I didn't have you down as this selfish.

Dani   Selfish my arse! I've done everything for you. The moaning and the sighing cos you can't get off unless you think I'm getting off. That's sweet. But it just means I have a sore cunt as well as a sore wrist.

A horrible pause.

Dani   It's not my fault you decided to get so *involved.*

Lewis (*he stares at her*)   You little girl. People are gonna feel stuff, Dani.

Dani   You should be grateful. You're one of those mangy male lions, Lewis, who'll be on the edge of the pride forever, getting angrier and angrier.

Lewis   You think you see everyone for what they are and no one can see you. I see you, Dani.

Dani   Oh do you?

Lewis   Yeah. You've had me wrong. I never wanted your pity. You can stick it up your arse.

Dani   Yeah, well, you can stick your tiny penis up your arse.

The weakness of **Dani***'s remark hangs in the air.* **Lewis** *leaves, his final look at her is one of pity.*

Lewis *exits.* **Dani** *sits, sulking and confused. Her curiosity draws her to the laptop, which she opens and turns on.*

She clicks on icons on the computer, revealing images which we cannot see. She clicks a couple more times to reveal different images. She is shocked but entranced. An audio file is opened. The sound of a young boy, eight or nine, screaming in terror and begging through tears for it to stop. It is chillingly real. **Dani** *is appalled and deeply shaken by the monstrous sound. Her frantic clicking does nothing and she is forced to slam the lid of the computer to halt the screams. She is on the verge of tears.*

After a moment, **Jan** *gingerly enters.*

Jan   He's gone, has he?

Dani *nods.*

Jan   Oh darling. Can I help?

Dani (*shaking her head*)   Thank you.

Jan   I don't mean to be insensitive but I think you're best out of that.

Dani   There wasn't anything (to be out of) . . .

Jan   No, course. That's fine. Your friends are really welcome to come round the house, you know that. He was a funny one though.

Dani (*there is some comfort in her mother talking*)   Sorry.

Jan   He's all right, is he?

Dani   I don't know, Mum.

Jan   I'm always worried about kids like that. Is he involved with drugs and things?

Dani   No.

Jan   I won't be angry.

Dani   No.

Jan   You might not know, of course.

Dani   No.

Jan   I sympathise with all that. Growing up now.

In the war, you could save up your tokens, get a big joint of meat or something. But for one token you could get sweets, sugar. And everyone used to do that. Because it made you feel better instantly. And when you could die suddenly, bombed any minute, that's what people would do. So there were all these stores of meat waiting for families to come and get them with all their tokens. But they never did, they got the sugar.

And I'm sure that's how it is with drugs. There but for the grace of God.

A pause. **Dani** *has been reflecting.*

A moment.

Dani   You said I was doing it out of spite.

Jan   What?

Dani   Before you sent me away.

Jan   I don't remember that.

Dani   We were in here. 'You're doing it out of spite' and you spat on me, here. (*She points to the side of her mouth.*) Accidentally. 'You're doing it out of spite.'

Jan   I thought you were for a while.

Dani   'Just eat something, you attention-seeking cow.' That's what you said.

Jan   I would never say that.

Dani   You did.

Jan   That's not the kind of thing I'd say.

Why did I catch you eating . . . that stuff then, if it wasn't for attention? There's always bread or pasta . . .

Dani (*quietly disgusted*)   It was a protein day.

Jan   You see. How am I . . . What am I supposed to do?

Do you hate me?

Dani   Do you hate me?

Jan (*a small smile*)   A bit.

Dani *laughs. A moment.*

Dani (*smiling*)   Oh God.

Dani's *gaze falls on the laptop. Her mother sees it.*

Jan   Whose is that?

Dani   It's no one's.

Jan   It's not yours.

Dani   No, I have to get rid of it.

Jan   I'm not having stolen goods in my house.

Dani   No, please, don't worry.

Jan   Of course I worry. That's what I do.

Dani Did you see? The cat's back. She was outside cleaning herself like nothing's happened.

Jan Aaah, is she? Shall I get her?

Dani Yeah, get her. Bring her in.

Jan *exits, in search of the cat.*

Dani *glares at the laptop. She takes a deep breath. She opens it, sadly. She gets her 'Thinspiration' book out of her bag and opens it, looking at it one last time. Slowly, almost as if to see what will happen, she takes a lighter to the corner of the book and watches a flame lick up the side of the book, devouring the pictures. Never allowing it to get out of hand, she puts the book on the keyboard of the laptop and pours the squash from* **Lewis'** *glass all over the book and computer. She then tightly closes the lid and puts it to one side. She turns and waits for her mother who she can very vaguely hear returning. 'You're a good girl aren't you? Where have you been? Mummy's been worried, who's a naughty pusscat?'*

Enron

Enron premiered in a Headlong Theatre, Chichester Festival Theatre and Royal Court production at the Minerva Theatre, Chichester, on 11 July 2009. The first performance in London was at the Royal Court Jerwood Theatre Downstairs, Sloane Square, London, on 17 September 2009. The cast was as follows:

News Reporter	Gillian Budd
Lehman Brother, Trader	Peter Caulfield
Security Officer, Trader	Howard Charles
Trader	Andrew Corbett
Claudia Roe	Amanda Drew
Congresswoman, Business Analyst, Irene Gant	Susannah Fellows
Arthur Andersen, Trader	Stephen Fewell
Lehman Brother, Trader	Tom Godwin
Andy Fastow	Tom Goodman-Hill
Lou Pai, Senator Hewitt, News Reporter, Prostitute	Orion Lee
	Eleanor Matsuura
Ken Lay (Enron Chairman/CEO)	Tim Pigott-Smith
Ramsay, Trader	Ashley Rolfe
Jeffrey Skilling	Samuel West
Daughter	Cleo Demetriou, Ellie Hopkins
Lawyer, Trader	Trevor White

All other parts played by members of the company.

Director Rupert Goold
Designer Anthony Ward
Lighting Designer Mark Henderson
Composer and Sound Designer Adam Cork
Video and Projection Designer Jon Driscoll
Choreographer Scott Ambler

Enron transferred to the Noël Coward Theatre, London, on 16 January 2010, and opened on Broadway at the Broadhurst Theatre on 27 April 2010, presented by Matthew Byam Shaw, Act, Caro Newling for Neal Street, Jeffrey Richards and Jeffrey Frankel.

Prologue

The eerie, mechanical sound of singing. It is the word 'WHY' from Enron commercials.
Three suited individuals enter, finding their way with white sticks. They have the heads of mice.
Over which, the commercial's voice of:

Jeffrey Skilling (*V.O.*)   Enron Online will change the market. It is creating an open, transparent market place that replaces the dark, blind system that existed. It is real simple. If you want to do business, you push the button. We're trying to change the world.

The three mice-men have wandered across the stage, feeling their way with the sticks. Perhaps one turns and seems to stare at us.

A single bright light sharply illuminates **The Lawyer.**

Lawyer (*to us*)   I'm a lawyer and I'm one of the few who makes money in times like these. When businesses fail, when unemployment rises, marriages break down and men jump to their deaths. Somebody. Divides up. The money. At times like this we're exposed to how the world really works. (I could explain to you how it works but, I don't have the time and you don't have the money.) Every so often, someone comes along and tries to change that world. Can one man do that? We look at some and pray to God they can't. But, when things get desperate, we find ourselves 'A Great Man', look up to him and demand he change things.

Hypocrites. Within every great man there's a buried risk. The guy I know tried to change the world was the man behind the corporate crime that defined the end of the twentieth century, and cast a shadow over this one. Now as a lawyer I choose my words carefully. So when we tell you his story, you should know it could never be *exactly* what happened. But we're gonna put it together and sell it to you as the truth. And when you look at what happened here, and everything that came afterward, that seems about right.

Here, in the beating heart of the economic world: America. In the heart of America, Texas. And in the heart of Texas, Houston. There was a company.

Act One

Scene One – Mark to Market Party – 1992

A PARTY in a small office at Enron. Present are:

Employees *drinking champagne.*

Claudia Roe – *a blonde woman (40) in a short skirt – enters. She sticks close to:-*

Ken Lay – *an easy, short, convivial man (60s), greeting and acknowledging every employee with practised southern hospitality.*

Andy Fastow *is a nervy, lupine guy, circling, with an unsettling grin (30s).*

Fastow *is on the outskirts, of the group of* **Employees**, *ingratiating himself.*

Roe *and* **Lay** *sweep around the room.*

Employee (*to* **Roe**)   I loved your speech, by the way.

Employee 2   Really great speech.

Roe   Oh, thank you so much.

Fastow   Quite a party.

Employee   I beg your pardon?

Lay   (How you doing. Good to see you.)

Fastow (*one eye on* **Lay**)   Just. It's great news. About mark to market.

Employee 2   Oh, the accounting system.

Employee   We just came down for the champagne.

Elsewhere:

Roe   Should we expect a speech from you, sir?

Lay   No, Claudia, I don't think we need ourselves another speech right now. Informality. Colleagues enjoying themselves.

Back at the group **Fastow** *is trying to break into:*

Fastow   Look, even Ken Lay's here.

Employee   Yeah.

Fastow   You think he plays golf?

Employee   I don't know(!)

Lay *magnanimously greets another couple of starstruck* **Employees.**

Fastow   Where's the guy who put this thing together?

Employee 2   What do you mean?

Fastow   Jeff Skilling.

Employee   Never heard of him.

Fastow   The mark to market guy.

Employee 2   No idea.

Fastow   Maybe he's not a big party guy.

Employee   Maybe you'd get along(!)

Fastow   Actually I always thought we would.

Lay   Have I met the mark to market guy?

Roe   Jeff Skilling. I don't know where he is.

Lay   I've only got a half hour here. Make sure I shake his hand.

Outside the party, **Skilling** *straightens his suit, his hair. He's a bespectacled, overweight, balding accountant. He takes a deep breath.*

Skilling *enters the party and finds himself a drink for confidence.*

Fastow   You can't get Lay away from Claws there. It's like she's his carer.

Employee Why don't you go talk to him?

Fastow Yeah. You think I should?

Employee I think you should.

Fastow He's just a guy, I'm a guy.

Beat.

Fastow Yeah. This is how things happen.

Employee You go girl(!)

Roe (*noticing* **Skilling**)   There he is.

Roe *goes over to collect* **Skilling.**

Fastow *strides over to introduce himself to* **Lay.**

Roe Jeff, come over. Ken Lay.

Skilling 'Hi, how are you?'

Roe (*sarcastic*)   'Hi, how are you.'

Ken Lay.

Fastow Hi there, Mr Lay.

Lay You're not Jeff Skilling, / by any chance –

Fastow No sir, I wish I was, I'm Andy –

Lay Andy, Andy Fastow.

Fastow Yes sir!

Lay I make a point of knowing people, son.

Roe *drags* **Skilling** *over to* **Lay.**

Roe Ken –

Lay *slaps* **Skilling** *on the back.*

Lay Here's the guy! Jeffrey 'mark to market' Skilling. You know Claudia. Our star abroad.

Skilling I believe I may have seen her in *Vogue*.

Roe   That was cropped from a profile in *Forbes*.

Lay   One of the fifty most powerful women, wasn't it?

Roe   I don't recall.

Skilling   Most powerful *women*?

Roe   Number fourteen.

Skilling   I remember. There was a great bit on Oprah and her dogs.

Roe   We were talking mark to market.

Skilling   I think one of her dogs was at number twelve.

Fastow   I just wanted to say congratulations – mark to market, much more appropriate, much more transparent. Exactly the right thing.

Skilling   Thanks. Are you –

Fastow   Sorry. Andy, Andy Fastow, you hired me –

Roe   This new accounting system, Jeff, you think it's worth celebrating?

Skilling   Well don't you?

Roe   I'm not an accountant.

Lay   You settled for fourteenth most powerful woman in the world.

Fastow   Mark to market is the accounting system for all the big investment banks / on Wall Street.

Roe   Yes. But *we* are a gas and oil company.

Fastow   No, you see –

Skilling   We're an *energy* company.

Lay (*gesturing to staff*)   I've been explaining mark to market, people get all tied up in knots.

Skilling   Seriously?

Lay   In what sense?

Skilling   There are people at this party who don't understand *the idea?*

Fastow   Mark to market lets us show the future / profits / –

Lay   / We know.

Skilling   / I know.

Skilling   My people have worked their asses off to get the SEC to understand and approve this –

Roe   And it's very much appreciated.

Skilling   Everyone gets mark to market here, right?

Fastow *exhales and glances at the group of* **Employees** *who had teased him.*

Fastow   I've talked to some people, I don't know …

Skilling   I've got slides I can bring down.

Roe   No.

Skilling   It doesn't kill you? Everyone standing around celebrating their ignorance –

Roe   It's not a celebration of ignorance, Jeff, it's a party.

Skilling   These people are getting *paid.*

Skilling *takes* **Fastow**'s *glass and clinks it to get everyone's attention. It's a surprise – any speech would be deemed to be* **Lay**'s *job.*

Skilling   Hi. Hi. Everybody. For those who don't know, I'm the reason you're here. I said I would only join this company if we started to use Mark to Market. What does that mean? Anybody? Well, it's a way for us to realize the profits we're *gonna* make *now.* If *you* have an idea, if you sign a deal, say that we're gonna provide someone with a supply of champagne for the next few years at a set price, every month whatever – Then that definite *future income* can be valued, at market prices today, and written down as *earnings* the moment the deal is signed. We don't have to wait for the grapes to be grown and squashed and … however the hell you make champagne.

The market will recognise your idea and your profit in that moment. And the company will pay you for it. If you come up with something brilliant – You know, life is so short. If you have a moment of genius, that will be rewarded now. No one should be able to kick back in your job years from now and take all the credit for the idea you had.

Fastow   They'll have to have their own ideas.

Skilling   Right. This guy gets it. Any questions? Anyone not understand? Okay, well. Have a party.

Skilling *turns and walks back to* **Lay**, **Roe** *and* **Fastow.**

Roe   Nicely done.

Skilling *downs his drink.*

Skilling   I should have brought the fucking slides.

We see projections of the joys and stability of the 1990s:

Bill Clinton, the break up of the Soviet Union, Microsoft, the Internet and the rise of the home computer and Intel, Friends, *Nelson Mandela's election, images of Arnie in* Terminator 2.

An **Employee** *comes forward to speak to us.*

Employee 3 (*to us*)   The nineties. It's a time of little conflict internationally, the fastest growing economy there *has ever been*. And the fashions are pretty good too. There's a new administration; a president who plays the saxophone. He's a Democrat but he understands the South.

It feels, genuinely, like the most exciting time to do business in the history of the world. There's a feeling that the people who are gonna change things aren't in parliaments or palaces, but in corporate boardrooms all over the United States of America.

Scene Two – Afterparty

In a corporate boardroom, high up, **Skilling** *and* **Roe** *finish having clothed, quick sex.*

Roe   I've been thinking about mark to market.

Skilling *laughs at her immediate switch to professionalism.*

Skilling   That's ... concerning.

Skilling *is doing his pants up.* **Roe** *is pulling her skirt down and straightening herself.*

Roe   Essentially, we are deciding what our own future profits will be.

Skilling   No. The market is. You want to have this argument *now?*

Roe   All I said is we get to decide the profits. Why would that be anything but a good thing?

Skilling   Right. But you're wrong.

Roe   Spiky. Look at you! Look at your face!

Skilling   What?

Roe   You just changed is all.

I'll bet you *were* a real serious kid. My oldest is like that.

Skilling   Not ... really.

Roe   You know, I read that it's better to hire people who were bullied at school. Cos they want it more. They've got in-built competition.

Skilling   I wasn't bullied! I got things quicker. When you get things quicker. You begin to resent people who don't.

Roe   You thought you were special.

Skilling   No, hey, I was drunk when I told you that stuff. I don't want to get on the couch about it.

Roe   Oooh! 'Whatever.'

Skilling   You know what, we accept that some people are prettier than other people and their lives are probably easier and we accept that some people are funnier – ... But if you're smarter. You're supposed to walk around like you're shamed by it. Like everyone's viewpoint is equally valid. Well it's not, some people are fucking idiots.

Roe (*laughs*)   Not here.

Skilling   No, not here. Exactly.

They look out a window over Houston.

Skilling   I love a work place at night. No banality.

Roe   Before the market opens. The world waiting.

Beat.

Skilling (*to* **Roe**)   We need to talk about a thing.

Roe   Ohh(!) Ken told you.

Beat.

Skilling (*lying*)   Yeah.

Roe   Yeah. I like how you bring it up *after* you screwed me /

Skilling   / What did he say to *you*?

Roe   I'm not gonna break that confidence. But if you think when I'm president, you're getting special favours –

Skilling   Wait, Rich is leaving?!

Roe   No. Shit. Yes.

Skilling   You're getting *President*?!

Roe   You said you knew.

Skilling   No! /

Roe   You are a real son of a ... I can't / believe –

Skilling   / I was gonna say Susan and I have separated.

Beat.

Roe   Oh my god!

Skilling   Rich is leaving Enron?

Roe   Do I need to feel guilty?

Skilling   Has Lay offered you the job?

Roe   I can't be the cause of a *marriage* break up –

Skilling   / I can't believe he's going.

Roe   We've only had sex three times.

Skilling   Rich is leaving(!) And it's four times.

Roe   Yes Rich is leaving. And I had sex with you three times.

Skilling   That is wrong but –

Roe   One, South America. Two, after the SEC announcement – three –

Skilling   / You forgot the plane.

Beat.

Roe   How are you defining sex?

Skilling   Sex. Penetration.

Roe   We did not have penetrative sex on the Enron jet! We fooled around. I went down on you.

Skilling   That's penetration! I was penetrating your –

Roe   Oh my god, well if you want to throw that in … (!)

Skilling   I don't want to throw anything in(!) – it doesn't matter, nothing will be penetrated anymore.

Roe   When did Susan leave?

Skilling   Has he offered you the job?

Roe   That's none of your business. When did your wife leave?

Skilling   *I* left. She *left*. But I – *left*.

Roe   I hope I'm irrelevant.

Skilling   You are entirely irrelevant.

Roe   Good.

Beat.

Skilling   Will I have to call you Madam President?

Roe   Come on, how old are you?!

Skilling   I'm forty-two.

Roe   Yeah.

Skilling   Oh god.

Roe   Stop it. You're Harvard, you're McKinsey, you're running a whole division. You're just having a mid-life / – (crisis)

Skilling   It's not that.

I've been thinking. Waking up at night with all these ideas. Ideas for here.

You know, maybe every extraordinary thing that's ever happened was conceived by a man alone in a room at four in the morning.

Roe   Oh, really? I think most acts of depravity too.

Look, don't get all … I'm sure you got ideas. I'll talk to Ken –

Skilling   He doesn't get me. I didn't grow up on a farm.

Roe *smiles.*

Roe   And you're a godless atheist.

Skilling   I'd like to be the other thing. Be nice.

Roe   It is nice.

She picks up her underwear and puts it in her handbag.

Roe   You gonna go home?

Skilling *shakes his head.*

Skilling   No. I'm going back to work.

She eyes him.

Roe   As an addendum, can I just say, previously you had an incentive equal, I believe, to mine for not disclosing this. I'd like to stress that this and the other three occasions, or four if you're gonna be a high school girl about it, are not to be discussed or recounted at any future date. And it will not happen again.

Skilling   Wow.

Roe   You got a Kleenex. I appear to be running.

Skilling *gets a tissue out of his pocket.* **Roe** *takes it and gently wipes all the way up her inner leg, wiping off the ejaculate that has run down her thigh.*

She tosses the Kleenex away deliberately casually and confidently strides from the office.

Scene Three – Ken Lay's Office – 1996

Bill Clinton (*on screen*)   I did not have sexual relations with that woman, Miss Lewinsky. I never told anybody to lie. Not a single time. Never.

News footage of the stories dominating American screens:

The OJ Simpson trial, Microsoft, Supermodels, the divorce of Charles and Diana, and other distracting and comprehensible news items.

In another office, **Ken Lay** *sits with* **Roe** *and* **Skilling** *sat before him.*

Lay   What is Enron? In the past, folks thought that the basic unit of society would be the state, or the church or lord help us, the political party. But we now know it's The Company. And the family. And those two things should be the same. A place where a group of like-minded individuals work for the betterment of themselves and for those they love. I believe in God, I believe in democracy and I believe in the company. Now I think it's right for Rich to be leaving, I think it's the right decision. It does put me in the position of needing myself a president.

Skilling   Yes.

Roe   I imagine you'd want to indicate that Enron is not an old-fashioned, macho place to work.

Skilling   'Macho'. That's subtle.

Lay   Where is our company going?

Pause. **Lay** *leans back.*

The competitors look at each other. Dual dialogue.

Beat.

Roe   Ken, before he talks over me here I wanna say –

I don't know how aware you are of people's reputations but Jeff is not a people person –

He doesn't have the skills to manage people effectively –

Skilling   I want to build a trading floor –

A different sort of company. Hire the best graduates, if they're not top two per cent we don't want 'em. Make Wall Street look like Sesame Street.

Roe   He has trouble relating to others. He doesn't remember names. He called a client stupid.

Skilling   What client?

Roe   Fan Bridglen.

Skilling   I have no idea who that is.

Roe *makes a 'see?' gesture.*

Skilling   You're a politician, Claud. I've never claimed to be.

Lay   Some of my best friends are politicians.

You wanna build a trading floor?

Skilling   Yes sir.

Lay   For trading?

Skilling   Ask me what I want to trade.

Lay   What were *you* gonna say, Claudia?

Roe   My vision. The international energy company. Enron: delivering gas and oil to the world.

Skilling (*spits it*)   That's a parochial vision.

Roe   *The world* is?

Ask me. What. I would trade.

Skilling

Lay   What do you see us trading, Jeff?

Skilling   Energy.

Roe   Brilliant(!)

Skilling   Sure, we make it. We transport it. We sell it. Why don't we *trade* it? You gotta pull back and look at this thing from above. Why do we even have to deliver the gas at all?

Roe   We're a gas company, Jeff.

Skilling (*to* **Lay**)   If we got a customer wants a steady supply of natural gas and we don't have a pipeline near them, what do we do?

Lay   We buy the gas from someone who does have a pipeline there and we charge the customer a little more than we paid for it.

Skilling   So let's always do that. Buy from someone, sell it on. In. Out. Without ever having to deliver the gas or maintain the pipeline. We can send energy through the air in nothing but numbers.

Roe   We should be focusing on building more plants.

Skilling   God, if you could hear yourself. 'Build more fucking powerplants'. No imagination, go crazy – What about wind farms or hydro –!?

Roe   *Wind farms?!* I'm sorry I though I was the only woman in the room.

Skilling   We don't need the hard stuff.

Roe   India, Africa – huge power requirements in the future –

Skilling   That will take *years!* You really want to pay for people to go build pipelines along disputed borders, tribes with AK47s. You want that fucking *mess* –?

Roe   I think in the most volatile areas in the world it might be worth controlling their energy supply, yes.

Skilling   Scratching around in the dirt. I'm not talking about pushing on an industry already in place. I'm trying to tell you … Ken, you've seen some changes in business since you started.

Lay   Sure. I'm as old as the plains.

Skilling   Well it's time to evolve again. We *have to. America doesn't have the natural resources anymore.* Not really. And that's good, that's fine. We have intellectual capital and the best of it in the world. Look at the societies that *do* have the raw materials, how modern do they feel, really? Then take a landlocked, barren country like Switzerland. What do they do? They invent *banking.*

We should be coming up with new ideas. About everything. Employ the smartest people we can find. Have 'em free to look at whatever they want – less structure, less routine, let people's minds work, free from the old assumptions about what this company is.

Roe   Sounds like hippy talk to me.

Skilling   I'm not gonna patronize you by pretending you believe what you just said.

Lay   You've got one idea about trading.

Skilling   I got plenty of ideas. Mark to market, energy trading, that's just the beginning.

Roe   I can push through natural gas deals we already have experience of. All over the world. You want power? Enron. India? Enron. South America? Enron.

Skilling   Countries are meaningless.

It's all going to be virtual. Oil and land run out.

Roe   In which case, don't you think it's worth being the only people in the world with power plants?!

Skilling   There's a whole, glistening, clean industry above what you're talking about that no one's even thought of yet.

Roe   Except you(!)

Silence. **Lay** *leans back.*

Lay   You see, I'm like Claudia. I like holding things – you know. In our daddy's day, a man worked and he saw himself in his work. If he made a table, he saw himself in the table he made. It was part of him, and he of it. I *am* oil and pipelines.

Skilling   My father was a valve salesman. I didn't want to grow up to sell valves. Tiny pieces of something bigger he never saw. There is a dignity to holding something, Ken. But your daddy was a Baptist preacher. There's a dignity to giving people something they *can't* touch.

Roe   Suddenly you have a 'calling'. Well, I find it distasteful.

Skilling   I don't want to work for you. I feel I gotta say if Claudia takes this job I won't be staying.

Lay *considers the younger man and his presumption.*

Lay (*to* **Skilling**)   I think you should step out.

Skilling *tries to maintain his dignity and leaves.* **Lay** *takes* **Roe**'*s hand.*

Lay (*to* **Roe**)   You know, you were always my favourite. But I'm offering Jeff the job.

As **Roe**'s *dreams are shattered,* **Skilling**'s *dreams are made real.*

The transformation of Enron. From discrete, regular offices, **Skilling** *and* **Lay** *oversee it becoming an open plan, free, shiny expanse.*

It should feel like a physical liberation; a clearing of clutter.

Lay (*to us*)   Henry Ford. There's a man folks think revolutionized things. He did not. He took people out of the equation. Of which I do not approve. No, the man who ought to be remembered is Alfred P. Sloane – Head of General Motors and a great philanthropist. There was a time when the cost of the automobile meant that most Americans could never afford one. And General Motors felt there must be a way to open up that market. Over at Ford, Henry didn't care. Ford felt that only a man who'd saved every single cent for a car deserved one. And if he had not the money, he should not have the car. Never mind that meant the automobile was only available to the very rich. Now Alfred P. Sloane said, well hang on a minute, if a man will pledge to pay the full amount of the car in installments, over time, we will provide him with one. And when we do, he will use that car to travel to a place of work, where he will make more money than he might otherwise, thus he will use that very car in his effort to make good on his promise. And in such a way the common man was given access to the automobile. And in such a way General Motors overtook Ford as the most successful and profitable company in America. And in such a way, the world was changed.

Today I am pleased to announce the appointment of Jeffrey Skilling to the post of President of the Enron corporation.

They shake hands.

Skilling *looks down at the Enron he envisioned beneath him; glass, reflective surfaces, futuristic design, open spaces, a huge trading floor.*

Scene Four – An Orgy of Speculation

Skilling   Let's trade.

Magical music.

Above us somewhere, there is a twinkle of gold. And then another of silver somewhere else. And then more, commodities like stars in the sky.

The sound of singing, each their own different song. It builds to an atonal babble of commodity prices and bids. It's a musical cacophony of the trading floor. Over time, the voices all conjoin to meet at a pure, single note. It is beautiful.

Voices (*sung*)   Gold. Up twenty-five.

The gold glints somewhere in the auditorium.

The voices and notes become an atonal mess again. Eventually blending to everyone singing a single note and price.

Voices (*sung*)   Aluminium. Down one.

A shimmer from aluminium.

And again the clamor builds up before finding a commodity value in one distinct harmony.

Voices (*sung*)   Natural gas. Up five seventy-one.

Voices   Orange juice. Down fourteen.

They split again into babble.

Voices   Pork belly. Up seven twenty-four.

*This empty, beautiful purity in **Skilling**'s head is interrupted by the reality of the **Traders**' arrival.*

*The **Traders** flood the stage. The stock price rises.*

The chaos, the physicality, the aggression and shouting of a trading floor. This simmers to doing deals, buzzing, on phones and computers making money. Overlap is fine.

A melee of sound and trading and speculation into –

Trader 5   I'm waiting on a call from Louisiana. Are you in play?

Trader 3   Speculation confirmed.

Trader 6 Spread's widened.

Trader 3 Another bid. What's the market doing?

Trader 5 What's the market doing?

Trader 7 Crude is up.

Trader 5 Gimme price.

Trader 7 Twenty-three.

Trader 1 Yes!

Trader 4 If market closes below twenty-one, this guy's fucked

Trader 1 I really am.

Trader 1 I lose a million.

Trader 6 Hey, it's *at* twenty-three –

Trader 2 *For now* …

Trader 7 Dropping!

Trader 1 Oh fuck. I'm gonna lose a million dollars. Fuck.

Trader 3 Hey, market's not closed yet.

Trader 5 There goes your bonus.

Trader 1 Bonus ain't shit. I just don't want Jeff Skilling up my ass.

Trader 6 Chill, dude. Skilling gets it. He's a fucking trader, man.

Trader 3 You've drunk the Kool-Aid.

Trader 5 Tell him about last week.

Trader 6 Oh yeah. You were in Dallas.

Trader 4 Is this the shit with me?

Trader 6 Look at this kid, twenty-six years old – hey, you tell it.

Trader 4 So I had a big loss.

Trader 1 How much?

Trader 4   I got down twenty million / dollars.

Trader 6   Twenty million.

Trader 4   In one day.

Trader 5 *whistles the loss.*

Trader 4   It's not a good day.

Trader 5   And it's the day Jeff's coming down to visit the floor.

Trader 2   He's pacing and crying around the place.

Trader 4   It was twenty million dollars!

Trader 2   'It was twenty million dollars!'

Trader 5   Any Wall Street Bank'd push him off the roof then check his teeth for gold.

Trader 2   We thought it was hilarious.

Trader 4   You did, I remember that.

Trader 6   And Skilling's heard about the loss.

Trader 2   Sure he has.

Trader 4   There's nothing Skilling don't know. And he comes in, he makes a bee line for my desk and everybody watches.

Trader 2   He goes over and he puts his arm round this fuck, and he says, what does he say?

Trader 4   He says, 'Only people prepared to lose are ever gonna win.' And he slaps me on the back and he leaves.

Trader 5   Slaps him on the back.

Trader 4   And he leaves!

Trader 2   True story.

Trader 4   And that's Jeffrey fucking Skilling.

Trader 2   Hey, anyone invited to Mexico here?

Trader 5   For what?

Trader 2   One of Skilling's death weekends, man! Rolling jeeps and motorcycles and wotnot. Someone's gonna fuckin die /

Trader 5   That is the coolest thing.

Trader 2   And Fastow gets to go. Lapdog motherfucker.

Trader 7   Going up!

Trader 4   You seen that double breasted douchebag? Thinks he's Sinatra.

Trader 2   What the fuck Skilling see in the guy?

Trader 3   We're going into electricity, a whole new market and you get Fastow to run it, I mean, really, *Fastow*?

Suddenly, **Fastow** *enters, all smooth self-importance. All the* **Traders** *react mockingly.*

Trader 5   Oh jeez, here it is.

Fastow   Yeah, hi. You gotta help with some figures. The electricity retail market.

Trader 3   You're kidding right? We're closing deals here.

Fastow   I'm here on behalf of Jeffrey Skilling.

One of the **Traders** *makes a 'whoo' noise.*

Trader 2   We don't have shit on your retail markets. We're traders.

Fastow   Just get me whatever numbers you've got on electricity suppliers you trade with, that's your fucking job.

Trader 2   No, that's your fucking job and you're asking me to do it.

Skilling gets that, right?

Fastow *goes for* **Trader 2,** *physically. He gets right in his face, aggressively.*

Trader 5   Crude down six.

Trader 1   Fuck, man!

Fastow   I don't have time for you to be whoever the fuck you are!

Trader 2   Is this guy serious?

Fastow *touches him.*

Fastow   I'm very serious.

Trader 3   Whoa whoa whoa.

Trader 2   Get your fucking hands off me.

Trader 2 *shoves* **Fastow. Fastow** *falls to the floor. Pandemonium.*

Trader 3   Come on, Fastow, you'll get destroyed.

Trader 3   *moves in to break it up.*

Fastow *is pulled away.*

Trader 1   Oh god, crude's falling.

Trader 5   You're gonna take it in the ass.

Fastow   I want that recorded!

Trader 3   I gotta fine you for that.

Trader 2   Fuck, Clem.

Trader 3   That was physical on the floor.

Trader 2   But it's Fastow!

Trader 3   I gotta take two hundred.

Fastow *watches, pleased.* **Trader 2** *reaches into his pockets and doles out a whole heap of bills on the floor.*

Trader 2   Take *five* hundred. Cos I'm gonna fucking finish.

Trader 2 *swings around and goes for* **Fastow**, *who, not expecting this, scrambles out of the way to the other side of the space. Other* **Traders** *mock and physically berate him. One shows him his penis.*

Fastow   (That's illegal.)

As **Fastow** *beats a hasty retreat he tries to maintain some dignity.*

Fastow   I'll remember that when I'm CFO.

Fastow *exits.*

Trader 2   Did everybody see that?

Trader 4   Big hat no cattle, muthafucka.

Trader 3 (*genuinely staggered*)   Is it me or did that guy just come in here and say, tell me how to sell electricity?

Trader 5   I think he did.

Trader 3   Unbelievable. Hey, market closing!

The bell rings for end of trading.

Trader 1   This is it, this is it!

Trader 4   What's the price?

Trader 5   Someone call it!

Improvisation of trading at its highest pitch.

Market closes.

Trader 4   Boom!

Trader 1   COME ON!

Trader 1 *is delighted, sweating, filled with testosterone and joy.*

Trader 4   You're one lucky fucking cock-sucking cash-loving son of a bitch!

Cheers.

Trader 1 (*to us*)   I wish you knew. You're right, you were right, it's there in a number, right in front of you and no one can dispute it. This is the purest place to work in the world. You know where you come if you're top of your class? Here. You know where Wall Street wishes it was? Here. We don't just play the game, we are the game. There's you and the guy on the other end of the deal, and who can move faster and who can move smarter. But it's not just up here. There's something … primal. Closest thing there is to hunting. Closest thing there is to sex. For a man, that is.

Lights of commodity prices over the faces of all the traders, a sea of figures.

Alan Greenspan (*on screen*)   (Clearly, sustained low inflation implies *less uncertainty* about the future, and lower risk premiums imply *higher prices of stocks and other earning* assets. But how do we know when *irrational exuberance* has unduly escalated asset values ...) irrational exuberance ... irrational exuberance ...

Scene Five – Trimming the Fat

The sound of motorbikes revving, screeching brakes, the hum of manly pursuits.

Split scene.

Below:

Enron gym.

Skilling *is on a running machine, in sports clothes. He's pushing himself and relishing the physical challenge.*

Above:

Ken Lay's *office.* **Lay** *and* **Roe** *are meeting.*

Below:

Fastow *enters the gym with trepidation in a suit.*

Skilling   Andy Fastow.

Fastow   You want me to go wait somewhere?

Skilling   This is the meeting. Get on.

Skilling *gestures to running machine beside him.*

Fastow, *nervous, takes off his shoes and jacket and gets on the machine.*

Skilling *immediately ups it to a run for* **Fastow**.

Fastow   I'm sorry I screwed up Electricity.

Skilling   Yeah you have. You know I was supposed to announce it on the tour today?

Fastow   Yeah. I tried, I really –

Skilling   I heard you got aggravated on some trader?

Fastow   I –

Skilling   They'll do that to ya.

Fastow   I won't be mocked.

Skilling   Is that right?

Skilling   *can't help smiling a little. He ups* **Fastow***'s speed, along with his own.* **Fastow** *tries to keep up.*

Skilling   You ever read those business books, how to win friends and ... the seven secrets of highly effective people and stuff like that –

Fastow   Yeah, I –

Skilling   Don't. It's bullshit. Read Dawkins, *The Selfish Gene*?

Fastow   I don't know it –

Skilling   Guy named Richard Dawkins. Read Darwin.

Fastow   Am I getting fired Jeff?

Skilling   By rights you should be out. I got this company running on Darwinian principles.

Skilling *ups* **Fastow***'s speed again.*

Fastow *redoubles his efforts.*

Fastow   Please don't fire me!

Skilling   Charles Darwin showed how an idea can change the world. Now we understand our own nature. And we can use that.

Fastow   Use it for what?

Skilling   For business. Business *is* nature.

Fastow   Like self-interest and competition?

Skilling   Exactly. Money and sex motivate people, Andy. And money's the one that gets their hands off their dick and into work.

Above:

Roe   I don't know if I can work under this regime, Ken.

Lay   Come on now, Claudia.

Roe   I mean it.

Lay   I don't like this fighting. This is a family!

Roe   Well families fight! And Jeff doesn't listen to anyone.

Lay   He could learn something from you in charm, I'll give you that.

Roe   How am I supposed to run a division where ten percent of my people are cut every time we have an evaluation?!

Lay   It's the bottom ten per cent.

Roe   Who don't get replaced! Or they get replaced with really smart twenty-year-olds with no idea what's going on!

Lay   It's a strategy! Gimme a break, Claudia, you gotta be nice to me today. It's my birthday.

Roe   It is? Well, happy birthday, Ken.

Lay   Fact I got a card from an old friend's son.

Lay *passes it to* **Roe.**

Roe   'Happy birthday, Kenny Boy! Now you're really old! Call me sometime. From *W.*'

Lay   He ain't got the manners of his daddy. But I think we got a shot at the White House with him. Stick around, it's gonna get interesting.

Below:

Skilling   Run you fucker!

Fastow   I'm gonna have a heart attack.

Skilling   That's cos you're weak.

Fastow   I'm sorry I fucked up electricity!

Skilling   What did you say?

Fastow   I'm sorry I fucked up electricity!

Skilling   I can't hear you!

Fastow   I'm sorry!

Skilling *presses the stop button on* **Fastow***'s running machine, hurling the younger man from his treadmill.*

As **Fastow** *regains his balance and composure as* **Skilling** *calmly slows his own speed.*

Skilling   Never apologize, Andy.

Skilling *gets off his machine.*

Skilling   Fact is, it's not all your fault.

An exhausted **Fastow** *agrees physically while he pants.*

Skilling   Electricity's an industry with no competition, no natural selection. The fact is retail is never gonna make money until electricity gets deregulated.

Fastow   Yes! Deregulate electricity and that market's ours.

Skilling   That's what I'm looking for. It's a political decision though. Ken's dealing with it.

Fastow   That's great. So I can keep my job?

Beat.

Skilling   Are you smart, Andy?

Fastow   Yeah, I am.

Skilling   I'm fucking smart. And I like guys with spikes. I didn't know you had any til I heard about you taking on a pack of traders.

Now that takes a special kind of stupid. But also balls. You started in finance?

Fastow   Yeah.

Skilling   Let's get you back there. I know your background, you're an abstracts man. Securitization. Risk assessment. I never met anyone less suited to retail in my life. Let's get you down in finance. Where you can keep away from people.

Fastow   Thank you. Yeah! I won't let you down!

Above:

Lay   What is it you want?

Roe   I want to build a power plant in India.

Lay   India? Nobody's in India.

Roe   You wanna be the first? Jeff won't go for it, he doesn't even think outside the States. One power plant.

Lay   'One power plant!'

Roe   It's India, Ken. The size of it. Don't you want some skin in that game?

Beat.

Lay   Okay, let's get into your power plant.

Roe   I knew I could come to you.

Lay   I understand your concerns about Jeff. But look, we got the stock analysts coming in today to rate the company. Let's see what Jeff Skilling means for the share price.

As **Lay** *says 'share price' the share price' is revealed; a figurative representation of the company's worth, represented by light some-where on stage.*

An **Analyst** *enters and speaks to us.*

Sloman (*to us*)   An analyst rates a company's stock to the out-side world. We're go-betweens. The first port of call for someone looking to invest their money. Where's safe? Where's profitable? We'll rate a company at 'Buy', 'Sell' or 'Hold'. Why trust what we think? Well. We know the world, we're from the world. We're employed by the biggest investment banks and brokerage firms so we know how it works. You need access to hear the rumours, to get the skinny. It takes years to get access, to build up knowledge. A company needs customers and good press maybe, but if it really wants to thrive? It's us they need to impress.

The **Analysts** *are* **Sheryl Sloman** *of Citigroup,* **JP Morgan** *and* **Deutsche Bank**. *All follow* **Skilling**, *enraptured.*

As he walks around the space, various employees approach **Skilling** *with contracts for him to approve and sign. He smoothly signs though barely looks at them, treating them like autographs.*

Skilling   Ladies and Gentlemen, Enron is a new kind of company. You want to see the next big thing? It's in the minds of one of these people. We're not just an energy company, we're a powerhouse for ideas. No other company lets people work as freely and creatively as we do. If you hire only the most brilliant people you can create new industries, new economies and reinvent the old ones. The league we're in? We're not the Houston Oilers, we're not even the Dallas Cowboys. We're the whole damn NFL.

The **Analysts** *line up and face the audience.*

Skilling   Now, let's see Citigroup!

The **Citigroup Analyst**, *after a drum roll, reveals his/her verdict*

Citigroup Analyst   Strong buy!

The stock goes up.

Skilling   And JP Morgan!

JP Morgan Analyst   Strong buy!

The stock goes up.

Skilling   And finally … Deutsche Bank!

Deutsche Bank (*in German*)   … Strong buy!

The stock goes up.

It's reached half of its full height. **Skilling** *looks genuinely touched by this.*

The **Analysts** *become a barber shop quartet and sing:*

Analysts (*singing*)

ENRON, ENRON, ENRON, ENRON.
If your company bank accounts need filling!
He's available, and willing.
To see to it that you make a killing!
Skilling, Skilling, Skilling, Skilling, Skilling,
Be boo doo wop wop ba doo!

Skilling   Thank you for recognizing our work and I'm happy –

Skilling *notices the stock price rise.*

Skilling   I'm so excited –

He sees it rise again.

Skilling   I'm a little sad?

It drops very slightly.

Skilling   Ha! I'm Enron.

He's delighted by his power and effect. Grinning at the recognition and level of belief.

Lay *comes down and approaches his protege.*

Lay   I got something for you, golden boy.

Lay *hands him a fifty-dollar bill.*

Skilling   What, are you tipping me, Ken?

Lay   I'm handing out fifty-dollar bills to every employee I see today. My own money. This is the first time we've hit a fifty-dollar share price!

Skilling   Is it right you're taking the jet later?

Lay   Yeah. Going to visit the kids.

Skilling   The *company* jet?

Lay   Time with the family. That's important.

Skilling   Just thought we were getting you out to Washington?

Lay   I'm stopping off in Washington. Bill and I are playing a little golf. I'll pretend I don't see him switching the balls in the rough.

Skilling   But deregulation's on that agenda?

Lay   Relax, will ya? These things take time.

Skilling   Okay, well, enjoy your kids.

Scene Six – Time is Money

A memory.

Daughter (*V.O.*)   One, two, three, four, five, six … seven, six …

Skilling   You can do this. Seven …

Skilling*'s* **Daughter**   *appears somewhere high up, not close to him.*

Daughter   Show me the money!

Skilling (*amused*)   God, I can't believe your mother let you watch that.

Daughter   Show me the money!

Skilling   Okay, once more, but you count with me this time.

Skilling *gets a stack of one-dollar bills out of his pocket and begins counting them out ostentatiously, as a familiar game.*

Skilling   One, two, three, four, five, six, seven … come on! / Seven …

Daughter   / Seven, eight, nine, ten!

Skilling   Good girl. Eleven, twelve … How long you think before I've counted out a million dollars?

Daughter   Um.

She doesn't know, she fidgets.

Skilling   One dollar bill a second. No stopping, how long before I counted out a million dollars? – Guess.

She makes a noise, enjoying the attention of her dad but not comprehending.

Skilling   It would take daddy at one dollar a second, eleven days to count out a million dollars. Eleven days! No sleeping.

Daughter   Again!

Skilling   What d'you mean again? Okay, one, two, three, four … how long would it take for daddy to count out a *billion* dollars!

Daughter   No!

Skilling   Yeah there's such a thing, a *billion* dollars! One, two, three, four – I'm gonna do it now –

Daughter   No!

Skilling   Okay. I'll work it out instead.

He calculates in his head.

Skilling   Counting a billion dollars would take me … thirty-two years?!

He scowls, checks.

Skilling   Yeah, around thirty-two years.

*His **Daughter** fades into the dark.*

Daughter (*V.O.*)   One, two, three, four, five, six, seven …

The counting continues into:

Skilling   Okay people! Come on! Time is money!

Physical sequence:

The company at work. The **Traders** *dance. As they do they create a round table.* **Skilling** *holds meetings around it. People come and go. Meetings end and begin. Fast, ordered, fluidity. Numbers fly through the air. The stock price throbs, but never altering much, gradually edging up in comforting, rhythmic pulses. Time passes.*

Eventually, **Claudia Roe** *makes her way through the building to* **Skilling***'s office.*

Scene Seven – Skilling's Office

Skilling *is watching the financial news.*

Roe   I've been trying to avoid you.

Skilling   Well. This is my office.

Roe   Yeah. Maybe it was the wrong place to come.

Skilling *turns the sound down on the television.*

Skilling   You probably want Ken's office. It's just down the hall.

Roe   Come on.

Skilling   Have you seen the stock price today?

Roe   I see it every day. I see in the elevator, I see it on the walls. I see it on my desk.

He nods.

Roe   I said to people, wait, just wait, the shine'll wear off, get ready for the dip folks. And … . a year goes by, two. But I keep saying it because, if I stop, it's bound to happen and the worst thing would be to not being able to say I told you so.

Skilling   Well. I'm sure you've got more class than that.

Roe   I don't. I don't think you do either. Go on, you can say it.

Skilling   It's not about that.

Roe   Oh come on! I know what you guys call my division on your biking weekends in Mexico.

Skilling   That's traders. I don't call it that.

Roe   Tits Industries. It's not even clever. At least it used to be … what did it used to be?

Skilling   I don't know.

Roe   You know.

Skilling   Skank of America.

She nods. Beat.

Roe   I came by to say an old college friend of mine emailed. He's a Professor at Harvard now. He used to drink his own urine for a dare by the way. Now he's a professor. Anyways. He asked if I could put him in touch with you. They want to use Enron as one of the business models they teach.

Skilling   At Harvard?

Roe   Yeah.

Skilling   Give him my number.

Roe   I did. Just don't ask him for the stories about *me*.

Skilling   I heard about your party for the opening of the plant at Dabhol.

Roe   It was a great party.

Skilling   You hired an elephant.

Roe   Shame you couldn't make it.

Skilling   I don't have time to jet off to your consolation prize in India. I'm running a company here.

Roe   Ouch.

Beat.

Skilling   You know the whole thing was a coward's way of getting things done.

Roe   I had to go to Ken. You wouldn't have – Every time I look at my assets there's less of 'em. You're selling everything I have!

Skilling   That's not true.

Roe   It is! I'm running a division which isn't expanding, it's not even contracting, it's having its *balls* cut off.

Skilling   That's business!

Roe   It's *your* business.

Skilling   Damn right it is!

Roe   I'm fighting to survive here!

Skilling   Either I'm running this company or Ken is.

Roe   You should tell *him* that.

Skilling   I do! He just … nods and … gives me a cigar!

Roe   It's his company.

Skilling   It's the shareholders' company.

Beat.

Roe   You need smart people around. To disagree with you.

Skilling   I don't know if Ken is the smartest guy ever to run a company or the dumbest motherfucker in the world.

Roe   I meant me. You look good, by the way.

Skilling   I … you mean I lost weight.

Roe   Sure, but. You know three guys in my division got Lasex on their eyes after you. Can't find a soul in the building with glasses now. Everyone's copying Daddy.

Skilling   It works.

Roe   It's not dangerous?

Skilling   Well, I don't know, Claud, I guess. It's lasers in your eyes.

She uses this as an excuse to look into his eyes.

She's deliberately close to his face. She puts her hands on his face.

Roe   Have you ever failed at anything, Jeffrey Skilling?

Beat.

Skilling   Don't. I don't think that's / (a very good idea)

Roe   / I'm not.

Beat. **Skilling** *closes his eyes. He leans in.*

Just then, over her shoulder, **Skilling** *spots a massive graphic flash up on the screem showing the financial news – 'ENRON!'*

Skilling *spins around. Once he sees what she's referring to, he's just as excited as* **Roe**.

They both scrabble for the volume control. One gets there first and turns it up.

Business Anchor – Gayle   Welcome back, I'm Gayle Davenport.

Analyst – Elise   And I am Elise Deluka.

Business Anchor – Gayle   (By close of market today, energy darling Enron's stock rose 26 per cent in a single day to a new high of $67.25. That's staggering isn't it, Elise?)

Analyst – Elise   (It sure is, Gayle. That's why we're naming them our Must Buy of the Week!)

Business Anchor – Gayle   (It's astounding their ambition and creativity –)

Analyst – Elise   (Yeah, yeah – they're unstoppable. They're the light of the new economy. I mean, I'd rate them, right now, at being worth sixty billion dollars.)

Business Anchor – Gayle   So Jeffrey Skilling over / at Enron's certainly doing something right! /

Analyst – Elise   / He sure is!

Skilling *reacts to his name.*

Business Anchor – Gayle   (Now let's go over to Francine for a tale of two very different cities …)

Roe   Sixty billion dollars! How can we be worth sixty billion dollars?!

Skilling   If someone's prepared to pay that much then that's what we're worth –

Roe   But that's huge! That's fantastic!

Skilling   Sixty billion dollars. That's nearly two thousand years.

Beat.

Roe   What?

Skilling   Forget it.

Fuck. How is that possible?!

Roe   Hey, we're announcing profits all the time. Everyone's behind you! And I'm just saying that includes me.

Skilling   Yeah.

She makes to leave.

Roe   Oh, and I don't know if you heard. You know your guy in finance, with the suit and the hair?

Skilling   Andy Fastow?

Roe   He's had a baby. Little boy. Named him Jeffrey.

Scene Eight – An Unholy Partnership

Below, darkly, **Fastow***'s lair; a dingy place at the bottom of Enron.* **Fastow** *flits happily between complex piles of paperwork, records and maybe screens.*

Fastow (*to us*)   I don't know if you're big fans of hedging. I can't see how you wouldn't be. A hedge is just a way of protecting yourself from risk. You literally hedge your bets. If you got a lot of money in airlines, for example. You might think, hey this is all going really well, lots of people fly – my investment is safe and going up. But what happens if there's a huge airplane crash, maybe people die, oh no, folks get scared of flying and your stocks plunge. Well, the smart guy hedges his airline investment with – maybe – an investment in a car rental company. When air travel frightens people, they want to feel in control, they'll drive interstate. So when your airline shares go (*noise and motion of plane crashing*), your car rental shares go (*noise and motion of car brooming upwards*). So you never lose money. With enough imagination you don't ever have to lose anything. When I write down everything that can possibly go wrong, as a formula. A formula I control. Nothing seems scary anymore.

Fastow *goes back to his calculations.*

Skilling *enters.*

Skilling   Andy. Andy, you had a baby.

Fastow (*delighted*)   Yeah.

Skilling   Congratulations, fella. You got a picture?

Fastow   In my wallet.

Skilling   Okay.

Fastow *starts looking for his wallet.*

Fastow   Oh man, it's down the hall. Shall I –? You really wanna –

Skilling   I don't (mind). Do it next time.

Beat.

Fastow   He's called Jeffrey.

Skilling   Wow. Great name(!)

Fastow   Hey, who's done more for me in this world, you know?

Beat.

Skilling   You know what I was doing when my daughter was born?

Fastow   What?

Skilling   I was on the phone from the hospital negotiating my deal. To come work here.

Pause.

Fastow   You get a good deal?

Skilling *makes a so-so gesture and sound.*

Fastow   You know when you have a baby and it gets handed to you for the first time? I had this incredible, indescribable feeling; this defining realization that in my life, from this point on – So. Many. Things could go. Wrong.

Skilling   I guess.

Fastow   And I say that as a man who knows how to manage risk. It's just the fear of losing something. Risk is life basically.

Beat.

Skilling   These. What are these?

Skilling *goes back to the piles of papers, he has found a few scraps of papers, covered in complex scrawlings. Maybe half-screwed up.*

Fastow (*proud*)   Oh, these are the Raptors.

Skilling   Raptors?

Fastow   Financial models I'm / working –

Skilling   / Are these hedges?

Fastow   Not as you'd normally understand them. But they're a way of managing risk. I'm playing with them. Just in my own time, just for …

Skilling   For fun?!

Fastow (*finds all three*)   Raptor one, raptor two, raptor three …

Skilling   Raptors.

Fastow   *Jurassic Park.*

Skilling   You're thirty-seven years old.

Fastow   It's actually really well done.

Skilling   So these are protecting you against losses in investments.

Fastow   Yeah. Like, you know, with hedging how – say you got a lot of money in airlines –

Skilling   I know about your planes and cars thing, Andy, I've heard you at parties.

Fastow   Okay, well, I've been seeing if there's a way of making a model that acts like the car rental company, without actually having to actually give my money to the car rental company.

Casually intrigued, **Skilling** *looks through them all.*

Skilling   A little theoretical.

Fastow   Well, that's the thing. A theoretical car rental company hedges your airline investment just as good as a real one does. On the books.

Skilling   Well sure, unless planes fall.

Fastow   Yeah but they almost certainly won't. It's crazy to have all this money flying out the door for things that probably won't happen. This model locks in the high value of your first investment. You own that, that's real.

Skilling   These are interesting.

Fastow   Yeah …?

Skilling   I could do with more guys like you.

Fastow *beams.*

Skilling *is having some pain.*

Fastow   You okay?

Skilling   These shoes … they're not broken in.

Fastow   What size are you? You want mine?

Skilling   No, Andy, I don't want your shoes. Thanks.

Fastow   You like 'em? They're Italian.

Skilling   Yeah I, jeez, I don't know. They're fucking shoes.

Pause.

Fastow   Great news about the stock price.

Nothing.

Skilling   You want to get a beer?

Fastow (*excited*)   I got a beer.

Fastow *opens up a tiny fridge that's been installed somewhere in his office/lair.*

Skilling   You got a refrigerator?

Fastow   Yeah, I just asked 'em. I called up and said. Came down same day. Put it in.

Skilling   Who did?

Fastow   We did.

Skilling   Wow.

Fastow   It's a long way up to the … thing.

They open and drink two beers.

Skilling   I got a problem, Andy. We got great stock price. We're declaring huge profits using mark to market. Correctly. But those *actual* profits aren't coming in yet. So.

Fastow   There's losses.

Skilling   That's right. We've got the best business plan, the highest share price, the smartest graduates. Trouble is. Right now. We're not making any money.

Long pause.

Fastow   How bad?

Skilling   You with me?

Fastow   Always.

Skilling   I can't find. Any area. Right now. Except trading. And there, day to day, we might lose as much as we make.

Pause.

Fastow   Wow(!)

Skilling   Yeah(!)

Fastow   You're not kidding?

Skilling   I am not kidding.

I don't know what I'm gonna do. I don't mind taking losses. But I can't *report* taking losses right now. The gap between the perception and the reality is ... (*he has one hand up at neck level indicating the high perception and the other he puts lower to indicate the reality.*)

Skilling *stares at him, holding his pose.*

Skilling   I don't know what I'm going to do.

His arms droop despondently. **Fastow** *dives in to hold the perception hand up.*

Fastow   Wait, you got a perception here, a reality here. You just need something for this to lean on while we bring this up.

Fastow *brings the lower hand up to meet the higher hand. Beat.* **Skilling** *shakes off the foolish physical intimacy.*

Skilling   If those Washington fucks would just deregulate electricity like Clinton promised, we'd *have* those profits!

Fastow   Hey. Fuck it. Two guys in a room.

You want my help?

Beat.

Skilling   What you got?

Fastow   How you doing with a Chief Financial Officer?

Skilling   I haven't found him yet.

Fastow   You considered everybody?

Skilling   Everybody / with experience (of) –

Fastow   / You considered me?

Skilling   For CFO …? One of the most powerful positions in / any corporation …?

Fastow   / Yeah.

Skilling   You're not a people person, Andy.

Fastow   You really care about that, Jeff?

Beat.

Skilling   Two guys in a room.

Fastow   You ever had an affair? When you were married.

Skilling   None of your fucking business.

Fastow   That's a yes.

Skilling   Is this something you've heard?

Fastow   No, okay, wait, that's wrong. You like porn?

Skilling   Do I –? I don't have time to take a *shit* –

Fastow   I think porn could save every marriage in this country. As internet porn goes up, divorce rates gonna go way down –

Fastow *makes gesture of one thing going up as the other goes down.*

Fastow   (That's the industry to get into, I'll say that …)

Skilling   Find the point.

Fastow   I want to give Enron a mistress.

Beat.

Skilling   That's why I like you, Andy. You're fucking nuts.

Fastow   Having something off the books, even if it's Jenna Jameson in an unmarked folder, your *virtual* mistress – she supports your marriage, strengthens it. We can do the same for a company.

Skilling   Explain.

Fastow   For those occasions we need to … 'offload'. We create a company that exists purely to fulfil Enron's needs.

Skilling   Example.

Fastow   We could push debt, we could push those losses into this other entity, *sell it* to this entity. So we make money *and* move a loss off the books, wait for it to turn to profit –

Skilling   Then move it back.

Why doesn't everyone do this?

Fastow   How would we know if they did?

Skilling   Andy.

Fastow   I mean it! This is an area where we're expected to be creative. The regulations *encourage* it.

Skilling   This isn't one of your theoretical models. A whole investment fund with money enough to buy bad assets off Enron? Who would do that? Who would invest?

Fastow   Maybe nobody has to invest. We could make the company ourselves. I could use these raptor models. To make a sort of shadow company. A virtual Enron.

Skilling   We can't do business with ourselves –

Fastow   Of course not. But. The rules state, if we're gonna do business with another entity, it has to be *independent from us*.

Skilling   Exactly.

Fastow   But. Here's the kicker. To qualify as independent it just means *three per cent* of its capital has to come from independent sources.

Skilling   Only three per cent?

Fastow   Yeah, so ninety-seven per cent of a whole shadow company could just be … Enron stock.

Skilling   So Enron can do business with a company that's ninety-seven per cent Enron?

Fastow   Sure.

Skilling   Still gotta find that three per cent.

Fastow *is excitedy scoping out the room they are standing in.*

Fastow Maybe. Look, say this entity, let's call it … LJM. If this room is LJM – it's filled with Enron stock, now we own that, we don't have to pay for and it's worth a great deal. *But* we need three per cent of it to be real. The equivalent of this file cabinet.

Fastow *walks around clearing the area to make the three per cent clear.*

Fastow   What if this three per cent is a smaller entity, designed the same way, which itself is made up of Enron stock –

Skilling   Except for three percent.

Fastow   Yes, wait.

Fastow *opens the cabinet/table/desk to take out the shoe box which formerly housed his new shoes.*

Fastow   Here. But what if this three per cent is an even smaller entity …

He opens the shoe box.

Skilling   Made up of Enron stock …

Fastow   Except for three per cent!

Fastow *produces a matchbox.*

Skilling   On and on.

Fastow   Until for all this to be real, for this huge shadow company to exist, all we actually need …

Fastow *opens the matchbox and takes out a tiny red, glowing box.*

He holds it up, the men are bathed in it like some totem from an Indiana Jones film.

Fastow   Is this ...

Skilling   And how much is that?

Fastow   Chump change. Few million.

Skilling   If that's a few million ...?

Fastow   Imagine what the whole structure is worth, what it could do for Enron.

Skilling   It's made entirely of Enron stock ...

Fastow (*brandishing tiny dot*)   Aaah, not entirely, this is what keeps it independent.

Skilling   But we can use it to *support* Enron stock, making sure it doesn't fall ...

Fastow   Yup –

Skilling   The same stock that it's made of ...?

Fastow   Yes.

Beat.

Skilling   That's fucking brilliant.

Fastow   It is, isn't it?

Skilling   So this shadow company, what did you call it –?

Fastow   LJM. After my wife and kids, Lea, Jeffrey and –

Skilling   This LJM can buy bad assets off Enron. And if anyone looks into it –

Fastow   It's just box after box after box. Russian dolls, until you get to ...

The tiny box glows red and throbs.

Fastow   And who's gonna notice something as small as this? How's something this *tiny* ever gonna cause any trouble?

Skilling   Andy, you fucker! This is a whole new thing!

Fastow   And this is just a few million, hell, *I* could put that in.

Skilling   No, I don't like that.

Fastow   Oh. Okay.

Skilling   Doesn't that feel a bit cheap? A special purpose entity financed by the CFO?

Fastow   The CFO?

Skilling   Why not? Come on, we'll get banks to put that in; Wall Street money.

Fastow (*slightly surprised*)   Yeah, but don't we gotta check with our accountants?

Skilling   Sure.

Hey! Get me Arthur Andersen!

Arthur Andersen *appears to one side. He has a ventriloquist's dummy,* **Little Arthur**.

Arthur Andersen   As your accountant, we think this idea is:

Little Arthur   Poor to very poor.

Arthur Andersen   This is due to:

Little Arthur   Conflict of interest.

Fastow (*to* **Skilling**)   Well, maybe we just need a more sympathetic accountant.

Beat.

Skilling (*to* **Arthur Andersen**)   We could always take our business elsewhere.

Arthur Andersen's *dummy's eyes flit wildly.*

Arthur Andersen   Arthur Andersen will

Little Arthur   Approve

Arthur Andersen   Approve the strategy.

Little Arthur   If the lawyers approve.

Fastow   That's what we pay a million dollars a month for?

Skilling   Yeah, that's *exactly* what we pay a million dollars a month for.

I need the lawyers!

The law firm of **Ramsay** *and* **Hewitt** *appears to their other side; one male, one female. They appear as 'justice' with one blindfolded with sword, the other carrying the scales of justice.*

Ramsay   This is not a legal issue.

Hewitt   This is an accounting issue.

Skilling   The accountants say it's a legal issue.

Ramsay   Well, it was ever thus.

Hewitt   It's against your own code of conduct –

Ramsay   It's *their* code of conduct

Hewitt   Oh yes. Quite right. Your board could waive it.

Ramsay   Ask your board.

Hewitt   It's really not our business.

Ramsay and Hewitt   We'll bill you later on today.

Skilling   I need the board.

And then, revealed on the level above **Skilling** *and* **Fastow**, *the board appear. The board is made up of shadowy, dark, imposing figures with the heads of mice and, in the centre,* **Ken Lay**.

Skilling   The accountants and lawyers are okay with it if you're okay with it, Ken.

Lay   Oh, well in that case … One moment.

The board briefly consult.

Lay   Who's gonna run this thing?

Fastow   I will. I mean. I want to.

Lay   And who are you?

Fastow (*to* **Skilling**)   You know you won't find anyone you can trust like you trust me.

Lay   Young Andy Fastow?

Skilling (*arm round his protégé*)   He's our new Chief Financial Officer.

Fastow *is delighted at this.*

Lay   Okay(!)

Arthur Andersen   Okay?

Hewitt and Ramsay   Okay?

Lay   Okay?

Skilling   Okay?

Little Arthur   Okay.

Hewitt and Ramsay   Okay.

Lay   Okay.

Fastow   Okay!

All   Okay!

Lay   Here's to LJM.

Lay *signs papers in front of him.*

The board, **Arthur Andersen** *and* **Hewitt** *and* **Ramsay** *disappear.* **Fastow** *and* **Skilling** *hug in the centre.*

Skilling   You've saved my fucking life.

Fastow   It's good, isn't it?

Skilling   All I have to do is keep the stock price up.

Fastow   Which makes LJM exist.

Skilling   Which makes Enron strong.

Fastow   Which keeps the stock price up.

Skilling   It's better than good. It's perfect.

Scene Nine – Party Like It's 1999

Flashes from cameras.

A media event becomes a party filled with employees, press and analysts. It's a financial love-in.

Skilling *is being photographed for yet another magazine cover as the dynamic CEO changing the world. The* **Photographer** *is beneath him to make him look impressive, god-like.*

A **Reporter** *interviews him.*

News Reporter – Gayle   World's Most Innovative Company, how does that feel?

Skilling   I'm just pleased we're giving shareholders value for money.

News Reporter – Gayle   I guess it's a work hard, play hard sort of environment?

Skilling   We're aggressive, we take risks and that's why we're successful. Way I see it, if your executives aren't waking up at four in the morning, their heart beating out of their chest, they're not doing their job.

The **News Reporter** *flirts a bit.*

News Reporter – Gayle   Sure. So, here we are at the end of a millennium! Can you let me know what the next big innovation's gonna be?

Skilling   Well, I was gonna wait to announce this later tonight, but I'll give you a sneak preview. Video On Demand. We've teamed up with Blockbuster and Enron's gonna be streaming movies directly into your home by this time next year.

News Reporter – Gayle   Oh my god!

The stock price goes up.

Skilling *is approached by* **Lay**.

Lay   (Jeff, you know the congresswoman?)

Skilling   (Hi, great to meet you.)

Congresswoman   Hi, how are you?

Lay   Anne's been very useful for us up on the hill.

Congresswoman   Such a creative atmosphere. I'm thrilled to meet you, you're the expert in energy trading, right?

Lay   That's like saying Alexander Graham Bell knew about telephones. You're meeting the guy who invented the *concept.*

Congresswoman   Well we're all just thrilled to be here. I don't know how you're doing it, but you keep on doing it.

Split scene.

Below:

Fastow*'s lair is revealed. He is finishing constructing LJM.*

LJM is a huge construct that has been designed to literally and metaphorically 'support' the level above it, Enron.

Fastow*, dressed in an even more dandy-ish fashion, is in his element.*

He takes calls on his phone. He's hugely in demand.

Fastow   Hi you're talking to Andy Fastow, Chief Financial Officer to the stars. Hey Rex you fuck, you know how many other divisions are begging for help with their numbers right now?! You're gonna have to hold. – Lou baby, now don't tell me bout your numbers – hey, I know those targets were unhittable, *I* know that. But you gonna take those losses? I didn't think so! No I'm not going up to the party. I leave my office the whole world falls apart, you know what

I mean? Don't worry. I'll make the numbers work. Everything's developing nicely down here.

Above:

Lay   Where's our Chief Financial Officer?

Skilling   Still working I guess.

Lay   No harm. He's hardly the life and soul –

Skilling   He's not a performer, he's got his own qualities.

Lay   Claudia thinks we should keep an eye on him.

Skilling   Oh for – seriously, Ken? You're listening to *her*!? She's jealous! Look around, all these ideas are mine!

Lay   It wasn't my intention –

Skilling   Broadband, electricity, energy trading, Video On Demand –

Concerned **Employees** *approach* **Skilling**.

Geek 1   Can we talk about Video On Demand?

Lay   Of course we can, sir, of course we can.

Who doesn't want movies streamed direct into their homes?

Geek 2   I don't think it's physically possible for next year.

Skilling   Video On Demand?

Geek 1   I can't see how it's possible at all.

Lay   I don't like that talk. That's unsupportive.

Skilling   We've got our best people working on it.

Geek 2   Sir, that's us.

Geek 1   We're the ones working on it.

Skilling   Tell me what you need and you'll get it.

Geek 1   It's not that –

Geek 2   It's about what's physically possible. There's not bandwidth capacity for it.

Skilling   Bandwidth?

Geek 2   It's the sort of … lines that internet information travels / along –

Skilling   / I know what the fuck bandwidth is. Buy as much as we need.

Geek 1   It doesn't work that way. There's a finite amount available.

Skilling   There's a finite amount?

Geek 1   Yeah.

Skilling   And people want it?

Both Geeks   Yeah(!)

Skilling *slaps the employees on the back. He turns back to the press interview.*

Skilling   Listen up, people, here's the next big thing: trading bandwidth.

Reporter   *Trading bandwidth?*

Skilling (*turns to everyone*)   Yeah, it's a hell of an Enron idea. If you're not using your bandwidth capacity, we can sell it on. It's tradeable. But people don't think in those terms because it's a virtual commodity. Well, Enron *gets* virtual. We're changing business, we're changing people's lives, we're changing the world.

Lay *applauds. The* **Employees** *are congratulated and sheepishly proud. The stock goes up hugely. Reaction is ecstatic, like a religious cult.* **Skilling** *is messiah-like.*

A huge party: absurd, luxurious, delusional; the peak of bull market excess. **Skilling** *shakes hands with everyone, treated like a movie star.*

Just then, **Roe** *makes a grand entrance to the party. Never one to be outshone, she is on a Harley motorbike, dressed entirely in leather.*

Skilling   You've got to be kidding me.

She shows off the back on which is stitched 'ENRON'. Whoops of celebration. She removes the helmet, revealing herself and shakes down her hair. Everyone loves it and all attention is lavished on her.

Skilling   This is what I'm talking about. Everything's the Claudia Roe show.

Lay   It's a very entertaining show!

Fireworks are starting to go off in the distance. The party reaches a peak of excitement as everyone goes upstairs to view them and celebratory opulence.

As everyone gets ushered out onto the balcony.

Below:

Fastow *hears/senses another presence in the lair of LJM.*

Fastow   Is someone down here? Hello?

Above:

Roe *marshals guests into place for the countdown she will be leading.*

Below, during:

Fastow *goes to seek out the source of the sound. Uncanny silence. He can sense someone … but where?*

Another movement from the opposite side … **Fastow** *swings around – what the …?*

And then, offstage, at the end of one of the streams of Raptor papers, he sees something hiding in the shadows.

Above:

Roe *begins a countdown to welcome in the new millennium. Others join in.*

Roe   Here we go!

Ten!

Nine!

Eight!

Seven!

Six!

Five!

Below, during:

Fastow *tensely, curiously approaches the shape. But, not wanting to get too close, he begins by reeling in the concertina-d string of papers it seems to be holding. Out of the shadows, a* **Raptor** *appears. It creeps forward, cocks its head and considers* **Fastow**. **Fastow** *stares back.*

Four!

Three!

Two!

One!

Above:

Roe *turns on the party's big event – the lighting up of a huge neon display welcoming in the new year: 2000.*

Below:

Fastow *turns slowly around to see the other two* **Raptors** *have taken corporeal form also and have crept into LJM.*

Fastow   Clever girls.

Blackout.

End of Act One

Interval

Act Two

Opening – Enron commercial with ethereal voices singing 'Why?'

Scene One – LJM

Fastow's *lair where LJM has been fully and complexly constructed.*

Among the shadows, there are strange movements going on. The **Raptors** *scuttle about. Not entirely human sounds. In the centre,* **Fastow**.

The tiny red box is safely put away, buried. We can see it throb. The **Raptors** *creep eerily around in the shadows.*

Skilling *enters. The* **Raptors** *hide.*

Skilling Andy? Is everything right down here?

Fastow Jeff! Everything's peachy.

Skilling This place has got big.

Fastow You won't believe the investment I got us. You wanted LJM to look official. Well? I've got fifteen million from JP Morgan, ten million Credit Suisse, five million from Merrill, everyone wants in with LJM –

Skilling … Everyone wants to invest in our shadow? … Why?!

Two more figures emerge from the shadows: it is the **Lehman Brothers**.

Lehman Brothers Hey, Mr Fastow!

Fastow Oh, wait a second – it's the fucking Lehman Brothers. What do you guys want?

Lehman Brothers We we were wondering …

Fastow I'm busy here, what the fuck d'you want?

Skilling That's one of the biggest investment banks in the world. You can't talk to them that way!

Fastow   No, but that's the thing, Jeff. I can! They're all so desperate to be seen alongside Enron. And who's Enron's CFO? Check it out.

Lehman Brothers   We were in talks about doing some *underwriting* work for Enron.

Fastow   For Enron?

Lehman Brothers   Yeah, we were hoping you'd consider giving us the contract –

Fastow   Way I see it, if I give you a contract worth tens of millions of dollars, least you can do is invest in a side project I got going on. Course Enron could take its business elsewhere –

Lehman Brothers   No, no, no, Andy, we heard. What you looking for?

Fastow   Let's start small, how 'bout ten million?

Lehman Brothers   Ten million! Everyone up at Enron okay with this, Jeff?

Skilling   What you asking me for?

Lehman Brothers   I mean, we assumed it was fine.

Skilling   You got a problem with LJM?

Lehman Brothers   Not at all.

Skilling   You got a problem with Andy?

Lehman Brothers   Well, he's got a certain –

Skilling   You do, you got a problem with me.

Lehman Brothers   No sir. Absolutely not. LJM's a real groundbreaking strategy.

The **Lehman Brothers** *give* **Fastow** *the money.*

Lehman Brothers   Nice doing business.

Fastow   Good job, fellas.

Skilling   Hey, Lehman Brothers!

The conjoined figures struggle to turn round in unison, both pulling in opposite directions. Eventually, they manage it.

Lehman Brothers   Yeeees?

Skilling   What's your analyst rating our stock at?

Lehman Brothers   Uh, Buy –

Skilling   Not Strong Buy?

Lehman Brothers   Not right … now.

Fastow   Let me.

Skilling *nods graciously.*

Fastow   If you rated us Strong Buy, more people would invest in Enron, right?

Lehman Brothers   I guess …

Fastow   And if more people invest in Enron, we can finance more projects, which makes Enron stronger and therefore …

Lehman Brothers   *Making* it / a strong buy …

Fastow   / A strong buy! See how it makes sense now?

Now, get the fuck out before I change my mind.

*The **Lehman Brothers** slink out.*

Skilling   I can't believe it. Everything upstairs is bullshit compared to this.

Fastow   I know! I think we've found the future of business … by accident.

Skilling   But where does all the debt go?

Sounds from the shadows.

Skilling   What's that?

Fastow   Nothing.

Skilling   What is it?

Fastow   Don't worry about it.

Skilling   What the fuck is this?

Skilling *goes to explore. One of the* **Raptors** *approaches* **Skilling** *to check him out. It smells him cautiously.*

Fastow   The raptors. You like 'em? They like you.

Skilling   That's where the debt goes …?

Skilling   These sort of entities, we could never have them publicly at Enron, but LJM doesn't need to show its books. We can … experiment here.

He feeds one of them a dollar bill.

Skilling   They're consuming our debt.

Fastow   Yes! Debt's just money. All money is debt.

Skilling   In … what … sense?

Fastow   If the bank gives you money, you owe *them*. You put money in the bank, they owe *you.*

All money is debt. It's just how you present it.

The **Raptors** *gain confidence at this and play with* **Skilling** *a little.*

Skilling   Go on.

Fastow   Okay. Well this one here, is dealing with Broadband. This one's taking care of Video On Demand while we set it up. And that one … that one's consuming all the fucking debt coming out of that rusting hulk of a power plant in Dabhol.

Skilling   That plant has no power coming out of it. It's surrounded by *protesters*. When Claudia makes a deal it doesn't just lose money, *people march against it.*

Fastow   You gotta put a stop to all that.

Skilling   She thinks her balls are cut off, what about my balls?!

Fastow   A man's got a right to his balls.

Skilling   *This* is the future. Not Claudia and her gift from grampa.

Beat.

Skilling   You think her numbers are right?

Fastow   Her division's numbers?

Skilling   Yeah. You think she's doing anything … untoward?

Fastow   I'd be surprised if there was *nothing* untoward. I mean, everybody … you know.

Beat.

Fastow   You want me to take a look?

Skilling   If you have cause for concern.

Fastow   Well sure, I mean. I can tell clever numbers. I'm the king of 'em(!)

Skilling *strokes a* **Raptor.**

Scene Two – The Purge

Roe *catches sight of a* **Raptor** *intimidating her.*

Roe (*to us*)   Something is happening to business. At the beginning of this century. Things have started to get divorced from the underlying realities. The best metaphor is this. Say we hold a competition here to determine who is the most beautiful woman in this room. Everyone gets a vote, the woman would be the one with the most votes and you'd win if you bet on her. Now the smart player wouldn't look at all the women in the room and choose the one he finds most beautiful. No, the smart player would try and imagine what *average opinion* would state is the most beautiful woman, and vote for her. But there's a level above that, where the really smart person would assume that most other people are doing the same thing and so they would try and choose the woman that *most other people* would think was *most other people's* idea of the most beautiful woman and vote for her. And there's even a level above that, and above that. And those are the values that determine prices, commodities and everybody's future. And who actually is the most beautiful woman in the room … is irrelevant.

One of the **Raptors** *runs towards* **Roe** *and chases her out of the building.*

After a moment, **Lay** *enters* **Skilling***'s office, looking pained.*

Skilling   Did you do it?

Lay   Still feel raw about that.

Skilling   I felt she had to hear it from you.

Lay   Can't recall what our thinking was there now.

Skilling   She wouldn't have taken it seriously from me.

Lay   I never did like letting people go.

You want to have a cigar?

Skilling   I'm good, thanks.

Lay *gives him one anyway.*

Lay   I was very disappointed in the things Claudia said in there. Didn't show a lot of class.

Skilling   Regarding what?

Lay   I don't believe she had to go so far in trying to save her own skin.

Skilling   I didn't want to have to bring those figures to your attention – I know they didn't look like much –

Lay   Any deceit is deceit. If something's brought before me I have to act on it. Doesn't *have* to be brought to me of course.

Skilling   Sure.

Lay   Now you made that decision and you brought it before me and a chain of events was put in place. Difficult to break that chain. You wanna pray with me, Jeffrey?

Pause.

Skilling   Sure.

Lay *bows his head in prayer, his hands together. He closes his eyes.* **Skilling** *copies him.*

After a few moments, **Lay** *has not spoken.* **Skilling** *opens his eyes. He watches* **Lay**, *not sure what to do.*

He watches **Lay**, *fascinated.*

After a little while, **Lay** *stops his silent prayers and raises his head.* **Skilling** *immediately tries to bow his to make it look like he hadn't stopped.*

Lay   Amen.

Skilling   It's a privilege.

Lay   Don't you worry, son.

You know how you tell the scout on a pioneer wagon?

Beat.

Lay   He's the one with all the arrows sticking out of him.

Beat. **Lay** *touches* **Skilling** *on the shoulder. It's a paternal, almost saintly action but takes* **Skilling** *by surprise.*

Lay   Listen, I know it's not been easy, having an old man on your back. You want to ride out, get the bit in your teeth and I'm all for that. I'm gonna take a step back. Place you can use me is on the board, on the Washington golf courses, charity luncheons. That's what I'm good at. You just carry on making us millions.

Skilling   We really gotta get deregulation moving. That's how we're gonna make our money.

Lay   I'm gonna have more talk with Junior. I got hope for him yet.

Skilling   We're financing that whole campaign. If he doesn't come through –

Lay   These things take time. Government! Can't even smoke these indoors anymore.

Skilling   You can do what you want, Ken.

Lay   Can't even smoke indoors.

Lay *drifts off. Pause.* **Skilling** *picks up the cigar he left him.*

Scene Three – Rooftop

Roe *is having a last cigarette outside on the rooftop / terrace of the Enron building.*

Skilling *comes out.*

Roe *has been crying. She hastily attempts to cover any sign of her tears.*

Skilling   You're not gonna jump are you, Claud? /

Roe   / Fuck you.

Skilling   I'll leave you alone.

Roe   Don't move. Don't you dare go anywhere.

Skilling   You can go and get any number of jobs –

Roe   I WANT TO WORK HERE!

This is where I work!

Skilling   Not anymore.

Roe   That man had faith in me for fifteen years. I've given my life to this company. You had him come in and talk to me like I'm some thieving kid in his store.

Skilling   I asked Ken because I thought it would be worse for me to fire you –

Roe   I was not fired! I resigned. You show me one part of my numbers done differently from anyone else here – you lied to get me out.

Skilling   I didn't have to lie. You're an amateur.

Roe   We'll see about that.

Skilling   Did you tell Ken something I should know about …?

Roe   There's rumours. Is it true Broadband and Electricity aren't bringing in any money? That Video On Demand doesn't even have the technology developed?

Skilling   Why do people talk that way? We'll make those profits. It's like playing poker with these guys who get mad when you win on the last card, 'Why did you stay in? You're not playing properly!' It's *poker,* you idiot. Doesn't matter how you win – as long as you win! When electricity gets deregulated, the cash flow –

Roe   Oh, grow the fuck up. Electricity won't be deregulated! Ken's not gonna get that kid in the White House!

Skilling   We will.

Roe   I could have made India work! All your deals getting done all the time, bad deals. Sign it, book it, throw it over the fence. Doesn't matter if it's a bad deal, just get the deal done.

Skilling   You don't know anything.

Roe   I know you.

You know when you went to that college in Pennsylvania.

Skilling   I went to Harvard.

Roe (*shakes head*)   When your father showed you round his old college in Bethlehem, Pennsylvania. You told me about it our first night. You looked out that window saw all those abandoned steel mills, for miles. All that dead industry. That grey sky.

Skilling   I left all that behind.

Roe   No. That's what you're creating now.

Skilling   Get out of my building.

Roe   You know what I'm gonna do? I'm gonna go home, to my beautiful children. And I'm gonna sell every single one of my shares.

She stubs her cigarette out. She leaves him.

His **Daughter** *blows bubbles somewhere on stage.*

Daughter   One, two, three, four, five –

Skilling   I have to check the stock price.

Daughter   Why?

Skilling   Because that's how Daddy knows how much he's worth.

Daughter   Why?

Skilling   Well, the market knows how many people believe in Daddy. And that's important.

Daughter   Why?

Skilling   It's important because I want people to like me. I don't want them to go round saying bad things.

Daughter   Why?

Skilling   Because in business these things matter.

Daughter   Why?

Skilling   Because it's important to look strong. That's the first thing.

Daughter   Why?

Skilling   That's how we make money.

Daughter   Why?

Skilling   Because I want to provide for you.

Daughter   Why?

Beat.

Skilling   Because I love you. Now let Daddy go to work.

Skilling *turns to his daughter but she has disappeared, leaving only bubbles in her wake.*

Scene Four – The American Spirit

Skilling *gives a speech to* **Employees**.

Skilling   Our stock is so strong. So strong that I think all employees should have the opportunity to benefit. I want to extend the stock option to everybody. From the mail room all the way up.

Employee   Why be paid in stock and not cash?

Skilling   Because if you're invested in the company you work for you are literally investing in yourself – it is an act of belief in yourself. Which you should all have. Because, I believe in you. So, grab that opportunity. Now, tonight's a big night for us. I hope you've all voted. I don't know if you know, but we got a local boy in the race(!)

Laughter. They are now looking up concentrating on an image of America on screens.

Election coverage:

The screen goes red.

INDIANA CALLED FOR BUSH

+ 12

They cheer.

Screen turns blue

VERMONT CALLED FOR GORE

+3

They boo.

FLORIDA

They inhale.

TOO CLOSE TO CALL.

Scene Five – Andy's Lair of LJM

Skilling *enters.* **Fastow** *is with the* **Raptors** *watching the election results roll in.*

Skilling   You got it on down here?

Fastow   Sure. We're having a party.

Fastow *has a bottle of champagne he's swigging from. He's surrounded by his* **Raptors**. *They all stare at the screen.*

An electoral map of the United States on screen.

ALABAMA: TOO CLOSE TO CALL (GAYLE)

Skilling   *Alabama* too close to call?! You gotta be fucking kidding me.

Fastow   Hey, it's early.

Skilling   I'm going crazy with this.

Fastow   Hey, they're calling my baby –!

It's blue.

NEW JERSEY: CALLED FOR GORE (GAYLE)

+ 15

Fastow   Goddamn you, New Jersey. I love you but you break my fucking heart.

Beat.

Skilling   Now we got the big boys –

Fastow   Lone star!

It's red.

TEXAS: CALLED FOR BUSH (GAYLE)

+ 32

Fastow   Come on!

Skilling   Yeah but here goes the other side.

It's blue.

CALIFORNIA: CALLED FOR GORE (GAYLE)

+ 54

Fastow   (Surprise!)

Skilling   It's all about Florida.

Beat.

FLORIDA: CALLED FOR GORE (GAYLE)

+ 25

Fastow   No.

Beat.

Skilling   (Fuck fuck fuck.)

Fastow   What about Colorado, we might get Colorado.

Skilling   What the fuck we want with Colorado, eight fucking votes. This is chicken shit. Game's over.

Fastow   Hey, we've had eight years of this shit, we'll have eight more –

Skilling   No, Andy, you don't know. Clinton's been real good to us. This guy … this guy scares me.

Fastow   Scares you!? Come on, man –

Skilling   That's it. We're done.

Fastow   Have a little faith.

Skilling   Faith?! Andy, you gotta understand. I don't have any cash. I can't operate. I have no money.

Fastow (*shock*)   You, personally?

I got money – I can –

Skilling   Not me *personally*, Andy, you prick. What, you think I'm some drinking, gambling it away prick can't find cash on my salary? What is it you think?!

Fastow   No, no, I …

We'll get through this.

Skilling   Without someone friendly to us right now, we're dead.

Skilling *seems to be in pain; his stomach.*

Skilling   I haven't been sleeping. People need to get paid.

Fastow   Pay them in stock, with our stock price –

Skilling   Everyone *is* paid in stock. Already, *that's why it can't go down* –

Fastow   No, it can't. This whole set up is / founded on the stock price –

Skilling   / I know!

Fastow   Are you saying it's going down?

Skilling   I'm saying it *can't* go / down.

Fastow   / That's what I'm saying.

Skilling   Well, stop telling me what I already / know!

Fastow   / I'm trying to make it work here!

Skilling   Well that's your fucking job, ain't it?

Beat.

Skilling   (Sorry.)

Fastow   You need capital. You need the cash. One, two, three?

Skilling   More like four –

Fastow   Four million I can find …

Skilling *stares at him.*

Skilling   Million?! No.

Beat.

Fastow   You need four *billion* dollars? Cash?

Beat.

Skilling   We're the world's most innovative company. How can we not find four / billion dollars?!

Fastow   / That's not what I do. This is all … this is *structured finance*. This is how it *looks* … I can't make real money just *appear*.

Skilling (*losing control*)   Then what good are you …? What fucking good is any of this to me?! Then we're going down, Andy / and it's your –

Fastow   / Wait, –

Screens go red.

(GAYLE)

RECOUNT: FLORIDA CALLED FOR BUSH

Skilling   What does that mean?

Fastow   If you need actual capital …

Skilling   But they called it for Gore.

Fastow   If you need cash coming in the door, actual cash then you need to sell something real …

Skilling   I've sold everything!

So what, have we won?!

Fastow   Fox says yes!

Skilling   CNN says no.

Screens go blue.

FLORIDA RETRACTED FROM BUSH (GAYLE)

Fastow   No!

Skilling   What the fuck are they doing?

Fastow   Well they gotta decide.

Skilling   What's going on out there?!

Fastow   Someone has to call this.

Skilling   What dumbass is running this thing?

Fastow   They can't do this. If there's one thing this country won't stand for it's ambiguity.

Flicking through channels.

Fastow   Who's won? Who's / won?!

Skilling   / Who's won!?

*Just then, **Lay** enters, hanging up on a phone call. He is deliberately oblivious to the strange, exaggerated world of LJM. The **Raptors** scuttle away.*

Lay   Gentlemen. Guess who's just got off a call with the next President of the United States?

Skilling   Say we got a Texan in the White House.

Skilling *is clutching his stomach.*

Lay   Like father like son.

Skilling *falls to his knees with the relief.*

Lay   *And* we got ourselves a deregulated state to play with.

Fastow   *There's* your cash!

Skilling   A small state, or ...?

News Report   The state of California has announced it's going to be the first state to implement a deregulated electricity market.

Video footage of George W. Bush being sworn in as President of the United States.

Scene Six – Texas vs California

The floor is flooded with **Traders**.

During the following, **Traders** *are manipulating California's electricity market by moving energy around. It should be tremendous fun, extremely fast, physical and overlap is encouraged.*

Skilling (*addressed to the* **Traders**)   Gentlemen. We've finally got our chance to move out all across the country. This is about freedom. This is about competition. A deregulated system means one thing and one thing only controls electricity. *The market.* I'm setting you free in California, fellas, bring it on home.

Trader 8   Okay traders! We're going to get a little ... 'creative'. We're free to move power around. Take it out of the state. Move it out so the price goes *up*! Then, who they gonna run to?

Trader 3   California! Yes, people, an electricity market of such complexity, designed by people of such simplicity. Loopholes so big you could fuck a fat chick through 'em and neither of you touch the sides. Let's find arbitrage opportunities. Let's. Fucking. Play.

All right man, this is Clem up at Enron. We're buying as much electricity as we can and taking it out of the state.

Trader 4   Ricochet! Fat Boy! Burn Out! Death Star!

Trader 2   Hollywood wants their power back? Fucking *pay*!

Trader 6   There's a party in the desert, man, and we need it for the lights!

Trader 7   Wheeling electricity out of the state, push the prices up, get 'em high –

Trader 4   Sell it back when they're desperate!

Trader 5   The most beautiful thing about electricity –?

All Traders   It cannot be stored!

Trader 4   Holy shit, price is up through a hundred!

They all look.

Trader 1   I've never seen prices like these –

Trader 5   Welcome to the beautiful state of Californ-I-A!

Trader 6   We're making billions of dollars!

All Traders   For Enron!

Laughter.

News Report   (California's power supply came up short today, and the lights went out. Rolling blackouts have hit the sixth largest economy in the world. For the first time in 65 years, the electric power market is in chaos. Electricity rates are climbing and California has gone into meltdown.)

Trader 5   There's a fire on the core line!

Trader 2   More fires we have, more prices go up!

All Traders   Burn baby burn!

News Reporters (Gayle, Elise)   (Another day another death in the story of California's blackouts. The driver of a station wagon was killed early Friday when she collided with a transit bus at an Oakland intersection where the traffic lights were down. This after surgeons were left without operating lights in San Pablo forcing patients to be air-lifted out of state –)

Laughter.

Skilling   We are doing the right thing in California. I mean, people are saying we shouldn't trade electricity – do you really believe that? Let's, let's stop trading wheat. Let's stop trading – you know, we need automobiles to maintain the logistics system, so does that mean we can't trade steel? We are the *good guys* in California. We are on the side of angels.

Physical sequence.

News Reporters   (Today the governor of California, Gray Davis, declared a *state of emergency* after being forced to cut power for hundreds of thousands of people throughout the state.)

Lay (*on phone*)   Kenneth Lay here for the governor of California. Governor! I understand you're considering running for president. You think it's gonna help you any to have the sixth largest economy in the world go dark on your watch? Voters remember that sort of thing. So how 'bout paying the prices we're asking?

Well I'm sorry to hear you say that, Governor.

Lay *hangs up the phone.*

Lay (*to* **Traders**)   Boys, step it up.

Trader 5   Come on!!

Physical sequence.

A crescendo of sound and activity is being reached. It builds and builds.

Trader 1   This is the largest single transfer of wealth I've ever seen!

Trader 7   We're like the Roman empire! We're going fucking down!

Trader 4   Let's rape this muthafucker!

Trader 5   Push it through the fucking roof.

Trader 1   Okay, okay!

Trader 8   / Do it, do it!

Everyone and everything is at fever pitch, yelling and encouraging.

A climax.

Skilling   You know the difference between the state of California and the Titanic? At least when the Titanic went down the lights were on.

Every light in the world seems to go out.

Utter darkness everywhere. For a shade longer than is comfortable.

And then …

Nothing but the light from a small doorway.

In front of the light of the doorway, a man comes into view. It is the figure of **Ken Lay**. *A suited man comes on stage and goes through the door, first shaking* **Lay***'s hand.*

Lay   Hi, Mr Mayor, I'm sure we can get this blackout business under control.

Another suited man approaches the door. **Lay** *shakes hands with him.*

Lay   Thanks for coming out.

Another suited man right behind him, shakes **Lay***'s hand and goes in.*

Lay   Don't worry, I got just the guy to fix this.

And then, another suited man approaches. He is huge and square and muscular in his suit. **Lay** *looks up at him, His face breaking into a grin. They shake hands. The man's broad back fills the doorway.*

Lay   Mr. Schwarzenegger! I'm so glad you could make it. Now, let's go inside and talk about the future of California.

Arnold Schwarzennegger *steps in to the meeting, followed by* **Lay**.

The door closes.

Scene Seven – Skilling's Office

Skilling   I hate those guys. I hate those legislators and politicians – not because they restrict business and fuck up the markets, even though they do and it does. I hate government because I know those guys. I went to school with them. And let me tell you, the weakest, most ignorant, most drunken fucking incompetents went to work for the US government. Because they weren't smart enough for the private sector. And that's the truth. I got head hunted. And those bottom of the fucking barrel, frat party know-nothing fucks who never got the call *design* the regulations for an energy market they know nothing about. It's my *job* to find ways round that. Why should we respect ineptitude? Why should we look at the lazy fucking regulations they've put in place by committee and go, 'yeah, you suck at your jobs, fine, we'll ignore that and just suck at ours too.' Who do you think is gonna win in the end?! The greedy or the inept?! We're not perfect, but wait til you see the other guys.

Skilling *is in a meeting with the* **Lawyer**.

Lawyer   Understood.

Skilling   So why the fuck are people picketing my house!?

Lawyer   There were deaths in California. If I'm gonna represent you I need to know your level of involvement.

Skilling   I want to you represent me, not the company. I didn't kill anyone.

Lawyer   There may be civil suits against *you.*

Skilling   This is crazy.

Lawyer   I can find other companies that were out there doing this. But you're getting the bad press cos your guys gave it a name.

Skilling   What do you mean?

Lawyer (*consults his papers*)   Ricochet. Fat Boy. Burn Out. Death Star. All on record as your traders' names for their strategies in California.

Skilling   Death Star?!

Lawyer   What I'm saying. 'Death Star' – makes it sound like kids on a video game.

Skilling   That's a perception problem.

Lawyer   Jeff, sending a state into *chaos* is, you know, that's more than just a perception problem.

Skilling   Will this affect the stock price?

Lawyer   I'm a lawyer, not a stock analyst.

Skilling   Cos that cannot happen.

Lawyer   Maybe you should have thought of that before.

Skilling   But we didn't do anything illegal in California.

Lawyer   That's a matter of opinion.

Skilling   I got a group of the smartest people in the world here who can tell you why what they did was *not* illegal.

Lawyer   If it wasn't illegal, it was stupid.

Skilling   I don't think you understand how markets work.

Lawyer   I'm not interested in the economics.

Skilling   So what are you interested in?

Lawyer   Protecting you.

They're going to imply that your traders caused huge blackouts in California for months, maybe years. That you gamed the state –

Skilling   The state's regulations were a mess.

Lawyer   And you took advantage of that?

Beat.

Skilling   Took advantage of that. Are you kidding me(?) Took advantage of … (!) That's what we *do*. In business, you buy something at one price, you sell it at a higher one and what's in between, that's your advantage. Which you *take*. That's how the world *works*. If you want an objective morality present in every contract you're living in a dream. You know how difficult it is to get five people in a room to agree *anything*? The only way I can be sure I can *trust* a contract is cos every party's in it for themselves. So when you ask, 'did we take *advantage* of that'(!) … You know what I hear? I hear, do you make a living, do you breathe in and out, are you a man? So yes, we took advantage of that. And I know that the only difference between me and the people judging me is they weren't smart enough to do what we did. Now are you going judge me or are you going to help me?

Lawyer   There'll be a couple of guys in trading will take a fall, they'll get a little wire fraud. There'll only be a bigger problem if there's anything else, any underlying …

Skilling   Okay. Okay.

A large Enron **Security Officer** *appears in* **Skilling**'s *doorway.*

Skilling *shakes the* **Lawyer**'s *hand.*

Security Officer   You wanted me to take a look at something?

Skilling   Yes, please. Yeah.

Lawyer   I'll take care of it.

Skilling   Thanks.

The **Lawyer** *leaves.*

Security Officer   Sir.

Skilling   Hey.

Sorry, this is a little – can you, can you sweep this office for …
equipment or recording …

Security Officer   You think you're being bugged, sir?

Skilling   Maybe, something –

Security Officer   That might be a matter for the FBI –

Skilling   No, no, just take a look –

Security Officer   You think it's the government, sir?

Skilling   No –

Security Officer   A rival company –

Skilling   I don't know. I just got a feeling.

The **Security Officer** *checks around the office surfaces.*

Skilling   How's things in maintenance?

Security Officer   I'm in security, sir.

Skilling   Sure.

Security Officer   It's good.

Skilling   You all got your 401Ks? You're all okay?

Security Officer   Absolutely, sir. I got a daughter and I'd like her to go to college, do something real … Well, things become a lot easier with the stock options you've given us, that becomes a possibility.

Skilling   Yeah. Good.

Listen, can you hear, like a hiss like, you can tell something's on? … . Wait, maybe under …

Skilling *gets down on the floor. He eventually puts his ear near the floor.*

Skilling   Here.

The **Security Officer** *gets down on the floor too. He copies* **Skilling** *who puts his ear to floor. They listen, lying on the floor together.*

Skilling   There's a sort of, ticking sound.

They listen …

Security Officer   Might that be your watch, sir?

Skilling's *head is leaning on his wrist with his watch on. He gets up, embarrassed.*

Skilling   It was earlier.

Security Officer   Could be something just needs rewiring, sometimes a static charge / – (can build up)

Skilling   / Yeah.

Security Officer   Well, you let me know if you hear anything.

Skilling   Sure.

It's hot out, don't you think?

Security Officer   Real dry. The trees are bribing the dogs.

They laugh.

Skilling   Hey. You'll be straight. I've been thinking about our next venture. I've been thinking about taking Enron into weather.

Security Officer   Weather?

Skilling   Yeah, for investors or companies whose worth can be damaged by bad weather. We could carve out a market in protecting against that. Have people buy up shares in weather.

Security Officer   Like insurance?

Skilling   Sort of, yeah. We break up the risk, sell it off in parts like credit derivatives.

Security Officer   You're losing me, sir.

Skilling (*keen, looking for paper and pen*)   Sit down. I can explain it to you in minutes.

Security Officer   Sounds a little out of my –

Skilling   It makes total sense –

Security Officer   I just want to do my job.

Skilling   You don't want to hear what's next for the company?

Security Officer   You're telling me to –

Skilling   Sit down! You want to be a doorman the rest of your life? Sit down and listen!

Beat.

Security Officer   I'm a security officer, sir.

Skilling   Sure, I know.

Security Officer   I just got a shift I gotta do is all.

Skilling   I just wanted you to understand …

Beat.

Security Officer   Nothing to it. We trust you all up here, sir …

Skilling   Very Enron though. Dealing in weather?

Security Officer   Sure. It's your company, sir. You run it how you want it run.

Skilling *nods.*

Security Officer *leaves.*

Skilling*'s intercom beeps.*

Skilling   Yes?

Secretary (*V.O.*)   Mr Skilling, there's a reporter on the line from *Fortune* magazine –

The stock price sinks. **Skilling***'s face falls.*

Skilling (*down phone*)   Jeff Skilling.

I can't answer those questions right now. I am not an accountant. Look, I don't think you understand the complexity of the way we operate here. If you print an article now without our side, I person-ally think that's unethical. Sure, I'll send someone out, at Enron's expense. He'll fly out and help you understand the questions you're asking. Okay.

He hangs up.

Skilling   Goddamn.

Scene Eight – Andy's Lair

Skilling *enters* **Fastow***'s shady lair, all anxiety.*

The **Raptors** *stay out. Two have grown very bold now – fast and aggressive. One of them is weak and sickly, the other two flank it to protect it.*

Skilling *approaches to pet them and one of the strong raptors is aggressive. He backs off, it follows him and pins him.*

Skilling *is deeply unnerved by them.*

Skilling   Andy?!

No reply.

Skilling   Andy!

Fastow *enters.*

Fastow   Hey.

Skilling *swings around. There is something eerie about* **Fastow**.

Fastow *tazers a* **Raptor** *to protect* **Skilling**. *It falls down, ultimately unharmed. The others back off.*

Skilling   What the fuck was that …?

Fastow   Something's spooked 'em.

Skilling   What's wrong with that one?

Fastow   It's sick. I don't know. Maybe I gave it too much.

Skilling   Too much what?

Fastow   Hmm? Oh, of the debt, Jeff.

Skilling   Will it spread?

Fastow   No. I don't know.

Fastow *tries to look at and comfort the injured* **Raptor**.

Skilling   Well. That's a good reason. That's a good excuse, we're getting rid of them.

They seem to hear him and snap around, maybe moving towards **Fastow** *for support.*

Fastow   Jeff?!

Skilling   You heard me.

Fastow   We can't. They're consuming a billion dollars' worth of debt.

Skilling   Get rid of them.

Beat.

Skilling   I need you to fly out to New York.

Fastow   What's in New York?

Skilling   A reporter. *Fortune* magazine. They're running an article on us.

Fastow   A reporter wants to talk to me!

Skilling   It's not a positive article.

Fastow   What do you mean it's not a positive article?!

Skilling   They have *questions*.

Fastow   Fuck them! We don't have to –

Skilling   You got to go out there and explain how it works. How money flows through the business. That we're not a black box.

Fastow   But we *are* a black box, Jeff.

Skilling   We are not! We're a logistics company! With a ton of great ideas –

Fastow   I don't want to leave LJM.

Skilling   You're going and you're / (gonna) –

Fastow   / Please don't make me go.

Skilling   You're Chief Financial Officer –

Fastow   Jeff, I'm at my best here.

Skilling (*violent*)   Be a fucking man! You're going to have to choose between LJM and Enron.

Fastow   I created LJM.

Skilling   I created *you*!

Andy, I love you. And I would do anything for you. But you're gonna have to choose.

Beat.

Fastow   What am I gonna say?!

Skilling   Look, if we disclose everything, there'll be panic, right?

Fastow   Right.

Skilling   So for everyone's good, they don't want trouble, we don't want trouble –

Fastow   What if they *do* want trouble, Jeff? I mean, they're a *magazine*. What if they take a look, what if they take a *really close look* and they come to the conclusion that everything's just *hedged* against our *own stock* –

Skilling   Don't you dare say that in my (presence) –

Fastow   What if they look and they see that underneath there's *nothing actually there* / –

Skilling   / Nothing?! Twenty thousand employees taking home paychecks nothing? World's most innovative company? – We *run* Texas, is that nothing? Then the whole fucking thing's nothing. Then the world's nothing.

As **Skilling** *is at his most manic and the* **Raptors** *are circling,* **Ken Lay** *enters.*

Lay   Hey, Jeff! Here you are. Listen, I need your opinion. I don't know which of these for the cabin of the new jet.

He holds the choices up. Both men stare at him.

Skilling (*slowly*)   Andy has to fly out to New York.

Fastow   There's a loss of confidence. I think. Going on.

Lay   So I'm hearing. I'll talk to Dick.

Skilling   That won't do it. Ken, this has all been across your desk, you know what's / going on.

Lay   / Listen, if you boys are talking business –

Fastow   I mean, I was only doing what I was asked to do.

Skilling   And if the stock falls –

Lay   The stock is not going to fall. That is not going to happen. You're running this show, Jeff.

Skilling   We need to have a conversation / –

Lay (*threatening*)   I don't want to have a conversation! Once you bury a dead dog, you don't dig it up to smell it!

Now, which goddamn pattern?

Lay *doesn't look at the* **Raptors** *or anything except the material swatches and sometimes* **Skilling**.

Skilling, *desperately buying into the charade, points at one.* **Lay** *nods, satisfied and lowers the swatches.*

Lay   Okay. Okay, listen up. This is a confidence thing. You're gonna have to make a call with the stock analysts to reassure the market. This is just a confidence thing.

Beat.

Lay   Now!

Skilling, *dead-eyed, gets ushered off.*

Fastow   Okay, okay! I'll go! I'll just take all the paperwork. Throw information at them. Bury them / in it!

Lay *turns back, eyes the minion.*

Lay   You don't belong to me, boy.

Lay *leaves.*

Left alone with his creations, **Fastow** *rallies himself to do his master's bidding. He eyes the* **Raptors**.

Fastow   I'm sorry girls. I gotta take you off the books.

Fastow *approaches the wary* **Raptors**.

Fastow   I don't care what they say about the company. As long as they don't make me look bad.

Fastow *destroys the* **Raptors** *and torches LJM.*

Scene Nine – The Asshole

Skilling *climbs stairs like a man on his way to the gallows, unkempt and addled.*

He eyes the stock price.

Lay   Everyone just needs a bit of faith restored. Stand straight, Jeffrey. You couldn't shave?

Skilling   I know. I'm fine. I'm Jeff Skilling. Okay.

Lay   Here we go.

As they go up, analysts and journalists emerge from everywhere to listen to the conference call.

Skilling   Just an outstanding quarter, another outstanding quarter. We're growing real quick in earnings and revenue and we have the strongest position in every market we're in ... You know, so I have no idea why our stock's as low as it is, fifty-four dollars, that's crazy! People are saying we're opaque, we're a black box, we're not. That's like calling Michael Jordan a black box just cos you don't know what he's gonna score each quarter! We are very optimistic ...

Silence. **Skilling** *exhales.*

Lay   You'll take questions now.

Skilling   I'll take questions now.

Analyst (Grubman)   Hi, Richard Grubman here, hello.

Skilling   Mr Grubman.

Analyst (Grubman)   Hello. I don't really care about the earnings at this point. What I want to see is a balance sheet.

Skilling   We will have that done shortly. But until we put all that together, we just cannot give you that.

Analyst (Grubman)   I am trying to understand why that would be an unreasonable request.

Skilling   I'm not saying we can't tell you what the balances are. But we'll wait – at this point – to disclose those until all … the right accounting is put together.

Analyst (Grubman)   You're the only financial institution that cannot produce a balance sheet or a cash flow statement with their earnings.

Skilling   Well, you're … you – well, uh, thank you very much. We appreciate it.

Analyst (Grubman)   *Appreciate* it?

Skilling   Asshole.

There is utter silence as everyone realizes what he just said to an important stock analyst.

Everyone looks at each other. The silent shock of a tumbleweed moment.

As the call is cut, **Skilling** *looks over the edge of the upper level, looking for all the world like he's either about to be sick or throw himself off.*

Pause.

Business Anchor (Gayle)   Shockwaves were sent through the market today as Chief Executive of Enron, Jeffrey Skilling referred to a senior stock analyst with a common but offensive term.

The analysts all get on their phones and blackberries to their banks and brokerage firms

Analysts (*together, overlapping, merging into one*)   You're never gonna guess what the fuck just happened – I think the big JS is losing it here – You got share price on Enron? – Something's going on down there – Called a Wall Street analyst an 'a-hole' during a conference call – CEO's gone sorta postal – I'm gonna recommend we hold – I don't know for now – I'm hearin stuff here I don't like – Enron, the energy company – I want to ask for the books – Rumours they're a black box. You wanna sell? – I wanna sell – Are people selling? – Okay, we're outta there – Hold on

Enron – Sell – Hold – Sell – Somebody selling – Enron – Sell – Hold – Okay – Selling – What's the market doing? – Hold – Selling – Enron – Sell – Sell – Selling Enron, Enron – 'Asshole, asshole, asshole.'

*The **Analysts** have taken themselves off, hurrying back to their marketplace hubs, a sea change in the offing.*

But their effects are already painfully clear on the stockprice, which is freefalling.

*A spotlight on **Skilling** alone, unsupported. Just him and his representation of his self-worth, the stock price.*

Skilling *approaches it desperately, trying to regain former glories.*

Skilling   No! Come on. I'm happy, I'm … excited …

The stock price does not respond.

Skilling   Come on, this is crazy.

Nothing.

Skilling   IT'S ME! Everything will be fine, don't be idiotic!

*The stock price drops slightly. **Skilling** recoils with shock.*

Skilling   No, no, no, sorry –

It drops further. He's terrified.

Skilling   Jesus, no, stop. Oh god.

He goes to his phone. He calls a number. A moment.

Skilling   Hi, sweetheart. It's your dad. Are you okay? Yeah, I'm sorry, I know, it's four in the morning. Is your mom there?

Beat.

Skilling   Okay, well, this is important. I need you to tell her something. Are you awake? Okay. Tell her to sell her shares. Sell her shares. All of them. Okay. I love you.

He turns to the stock price.

Skilling   What do you want? You want me? Is that it? Is that what you want?!

He ends, his arms outstretched, crucifying himself before the market.

*The blocks beneath where **Skilling** was standing are removed by analysts and brokers as shares continue to be sold and the company weakens.*

A sour, tuneless version of the Enron barbershop quartet jingle plays.

Scene Ten – Private Meeting

Sheryl Sloman *and* **Ken Lay** *are in a meeting with* **Skilling**.

Sloman (*to* **Skilling**)   You're resigning?

Lay   We wanted to tell you first.

Sloman   When are you going public with this?

Lay   Later on today. We don't want the market getting the wrong idea. You've always been a great cheerleader for us.

Sloman   I'm a professional stock analyst. Let's not pretend, Jeff. This is highly unusual. There should be a *year* leading up to this, a structured handover. Jeff, *why* are you resigning?

Skilling (*teary*)   The company's in great shape it couldn't be less to do with that. I … A company like this, it consumes your life. I've neglected my daughter. This is personal.

Lay   It's not cos of the stock.

Skilling   I'm doing this for the company. It'll go up when I announce. The market's decided. It wants me out.

Sloman   But that's not true. People say all over, I'm not long Enron, but I'm long Jeff Skilling.

This seems to affect him deeply.

Skilling   You pour your life into something and, if it doesn't reflect back at you … I'm so tired.

I can't sleep.

Sloman   Are you worried about recent performance? Are there accounting issues /?

Lay   / There are no accounting / issues –

Sloman (*to* **Skilling**)   / Is that why you can't sleep?

Skilling   I haven't slept since I was fourteen.

Lay   I can honestly say the company's in the best shape it's ever been.

Jeff?

Skilling thinks he sees a **Raptor** *still at large in the bowels of Enron.*

Skilling   I should go.

Lay   Yeah, you go, get ready to announce.

Skilling *leaves.*

Sloman   Whoo. This is a blow for you.

Lay (*understating*)   I would have preferred he stay.

Sloman   That *Fortune* article raised a lot of questions. I've always been a supporter of Enron Corporation. But you know the CEO leaving like this? That doesn't spin.

You're gonna have to hold this thing together.

Lay   Don't you worry about anything here. I'm a safe pair of hands.

With a reassuring squeeze of her arm, **Lay** *stalks off, leaving* **Sloman** *thoughtful.*

News Reporters   In breaking news, Enron's CEO has resigned. Now the market's left asking the question the company is famous for: Why?

Act Three

Scene One – The Earthquake Hits

Sloman (*to us*) There's a strange thing goes on inside a bubble. It's hard to describe. People who are in it can't see outside of it, don't believe there is an outside. You get glazed over. I believed in Enron. Everybody did. I told people again and again to keep buying that stock and I kept rating it and supporting it and championing it like it was my own child. And people say how could you. If you didn't understand how it worked. Well. You get on a plane, you don't understand exactly how it works, but you believe it'll fly. You know – and everyone else boarding that plane knows – it'll fly up into the air and take you to your destination, crazy as that may seem. And if you got out your seat, said I'm not flying, I don't understand how it works, you'd look crazy. Well it's like that. Except. Imagine if the *belief* that the plane could fly was all that was keeping it in the air. It'd be fine. If everybody believed. If nobody got scared. As long as people didn't ask stupid questions. About what it is keeps planes in the air.

September 11th 2001.

Eventually ...

Ken Lay *comes out to give a speech.*

As the speech goes on, **Lay** *becomes surrounded by tiny piece of shredded paper being blown all over him, all over the stage. He keeps trying to carry on regardless. The shredding represents the huge destruction of documents going on at Enron and Arthur Andersen.*

Lay Well, I'm delighted to be back in charge. In more normal circumstances, I'd have a few words to say about September the 11th. Just like America's under attack by terrorism, I think we're under attack, at Enron.

News Report (Gayle) The terror attacks on New York and Washington have seen stock exchanges all over the world evacuated and all trading has ceased. Market confidence has dissolved today as Tokyo, London and then New York fell to record lows –

Lay I'm sorry Jeff did resign. Despite the rumours, the company is doing well both financially and operationally. When our very way of life is being threatened, we remain proud of who we are and what we do. This is not the time for doubt, not the time for our confidence to be shaken –

News Report (Elise) (With the world's markets still reeling from the recent tragic events, a formal investigation has been opened into energy trading giant Enron, deepening its share price crisis. The company has lost 60 per cent of its value since peaking last fall …)

Lay Truth is the great rock. Whether it will continue to be submerged by a wave – a wave of terror by those attacking us – will be determined by Enron employees. We will testify to the truth. We will let the light shine in. We won't let this cloud of lies cover all our good works and deeds.

Collapse.

News Report (Gayle) Today saw the largest corporate bankruptcy in the history of the world as energy giant Enron fell. The company has collapsed after it was found to have disguised billions of dollars of debt, leading an outraged Senate to call for an immediate investigation.

Scene Two/Three – Circle of Blame

The detritus of an unexpected fall litters the stage. Order must be restored.

Trials/hearings.

Senator These hearings are an attempt to investigate America's largest corporate bankruptcy. What happened, why did it happen and who is responsible for it happening?

Those responsible are present around the outskirts of the stage, maybe some sort of a circle: **Lay**, **Fastow**, **Ramsay** *and* **Hewitt**, **Arthur Andersen***, the* **Board***. But not* **Skilling***.*

A light moves from player to player as they speak.

Member of the Board (*as a statement*)   The Board is shocked and dismayed by events. We are not lawyers and had no idea Mr. Fastow was doing anything illegal.

Ramsay   As a law firm, we had a responsibility to the law.

Hewitt   If illegal practises went on –

Ramsay   *After* we signed off on LJM

Hewitt   That's entirely another matter –

Ramsay   Another matter entirely.

Ramsay and Hewitt   We explicitly avoided the illegal.

Hewitt   We are not accountants.

Arthur Andersen   I am an accountant. For my sins(!)

These procedures were unusual.

Little Arthur   They were *not* illegal.

Arthur Andersen   Arthur Andersen are happy to provide all Enron-related documents.

Little Arthur   Except for all the ones we shredded.

Arthur Andersen *wrestles his dummy into acquiescence.*

Fastow   Mr. Chairman, on the advice of my counsel, I respectfully decline to answer the questions put to me based on the protection afforded me under the United States Constitution.

Lay   I have been instructed by my counsel not to testify based on my fifth amendment constitutional rights.

Skilling   I will testify. I'll answer any question you got. I'll take a lie detector test right here, right now. This whole situations's been terrible for a lot of people, and I'm here to explain what happened. And how I can help.

Senator   With due respect, Mr Skilling, I'm not going to ask you to help. Let me put something to you: Is it a matter of coincidence that a few months after you left Enron the company collapsed?

Skilling   When I left Enron corporation, on August 14th of the year 2001, I believed that the company was in – was in great shape.

Senator   Do you have personal worth of more than a hundred million dollars?

Skilling   I don't have the records with me.

Senator   Would it be surprising to you to learn that you had that?

Skilling   No, that would – that would not be a surprise.

Senator   And how do you feel about the employees whose families have lost their life savings?

Skilling   Well, I guess –

Senator   You donated any of that money to employees?

Skilling   At this point I have … thirty-six separate law suits against me. It is my expectation that I will spend the next five to ten years of my life battling those lawsuits.

Senator   And you don't believe you've done anything wrong?

Skilling   The markets were … destroyed after September 11th. There were allegations of accounting problems, of accounting irregularities. In business terms, that's tantamount to yelling fire in a crowded theatre. It becomes a run on the bank.

Senator Judge (*to us*)   Thank you, Mr Skilling.

A few bad apples have shamed American corporate culture here today and I find it scandalous that he could turn up here hoping to make it the Jeff Skilling show. Well today is *our* day … Day for the US senate, the courts. And the people. And we will see that those millionaires with their private jets and luxury lifestyles are forced to explain to those of us with normal lives on the ground what misdeeds have been done. The American Government will not stand for corporate crime on this scale. I mean, on any scale.

Skilling   That was a show! Democrats trying to win votes from poor people they've never fucking met.

Lawyer   It's irrelevant now. It's about the trial.

Skilling   Well fuck them, fuck the trial and fuck America!

Lawyer   I take it we're pleading not guilty?

Skilling   I'm gonna fight this thing till the day I die.

Lawyer   What about your CFO?

Skilling   Andy's blood runs Enron, he's gonna be as mad as me.

Lawyer   Jeff, if Andy's got a lawyer half as good as me, hell, if Andy's got a lawyer who can read, he's gonna be telling him one thing – he's gonna be telling him to blame it on you.

Gavel bang three times. Trial.

Lawyer   Mr Fastow, you've spent a great deal of time today describing your actions as a 'hero of Enron'. Do you really view your behaviour as heroic?

Fastow   I think I said I was a hero and I believed I was a hero in the context of Enron's culture.

Lawyer   You must be consumed by an insatiable greed, is that fair to say?

Fastow   I believe I was extremely greedy and lost my moral compass. I've done terrible things that I very much regret.

Lawyer   That sounded awfully rehearsed, Mr Fastow.

Fastow   With respect, your questions sound pretty rehearsed too.

Lawyer 2   Are you smart, Mr Skilling?

Skilling   Yes.

Lawyer 2   Sure you are. So you knew and understood what Mr Fastow was doing at your company?

Fastow   We knew and understood that it was wrong.

Skilling   I knew and understood that it was legal.

Lawyer   Did you steal?

Fastow   We stole. We all benefitted financially.

Skilling   I would never steal from Enron.

Lawyer   Did you profit personally, illegally from LJM?

Fastow   Yes, I did.

Skilling   I did not know that.

Lawyer 2   You did not *want* to know.

Lawyer   How much?

Fastow   It's difficult to say.

Lawyer   Try.

Fastow   Around forty-five million dollars /.

Lawyer   / Forty-five million(!)

And how much did Mr Skilling profit personally?

Skilling   None.

Fastow   None. *Directly.*

Lawyer   None! So doesn't it make sense that you'd protect yourself today? Say anything to get your boss convicted, maybe make arrangements with the federal government!

Lawyer 2   Objection!

Lawyer   He promoted you, supported you and trusted you, did not profit at all yet was betrayed by you!

Lawyer 2   Mr Skilling, During the period of February '99 through June 2001 did you convert your stock worth sixty-six million dollars?

Skilling   That sounds –

Lawyer 2   All the time telling employees to invest?

Fastow   When you misrepresent the nature of your company –

Skilling   I believed in Enron.

Fastow   Then cash in your stock options, that is stealing –

Lawyer   We all know you know 'bout stealing, Mr Fastow –

Fastow   He committed crimes at Enron.

Lawyer   No, you committed crimes at Enron!

Lawyer 2   You thought the company was fine, everything was fine, with things in such great shape, why did you resign?

Skilling   I resigned because the market demanded it.

Lawyer 2   You left a sinking ship! Women and children first, right after Jeff!

Skilling   The company was worth what it was worth *because* of me.

Lawyer 2   Does that include the nothing it's worth now?

Beat.

Lawyer   When the history books are written about what happened at Enron you know your name is going to be on that page. You want to make sure Mr Skilling's name is on that page also.

Fastow   You know what I'd like written on that page? That I had the courage to admit I did something wrong.

Judge   Andrew Fastow, you are found guilty on two counts of criminal conspiracy.

Kenneth Lay, you are found guilty on six counts of conspiracy and securities fraud.

Lay *and* **Fastow** *are cuffed.* **Skilling** *is cuffed.*

Judge   Jeffrey Skilling, you have been found guilty of nineteen separate counts of securities fraud, wire fraud and insider trading.

Fastow *and* **Skilling** *share a look before* **Fastow** *abandons his former boss, leaving Skilling alone.*

Skilling   *You – you* failed *me.* You didn't believe enough. Don't you see? This is my life!

A funeral cortege of former employees engulfs him.

Scene Four – The Funeral

Black umbrellas go up. We're outside. Before a funeral.

Guests in mourning black gather. **Claudia Roe** *enters in mourning black;* **Skilling** *sees her.*

Skilling   Claudia.

Skilling *is escorted by a* **Police Officer** *in a suit and dark glasses.*

Skilling   Can you just give me a minute?

Police Officer   I can stand over there.

Skilling   Then could you do that please?

He does.

Roe   I didn't think they'd let you come.

Skilling   Dispensation. For an hour.

Roe   Did they tell you what happened?

Skilling   To Ken? Heart failure.

Roe   Yeah, that's the official verdict anyway. I heard you're gonna appeal.

Skilling   I told my daughter I was innocent. I believe I'm innocent.

Roe   Neither of those things make you innocent. Is it true, when it fell – the only part of the business with any worth at all was my division? The things you could hold?

Skilling   You got out!

Roe   Not by choice.

Skilling   Well, aren't you gonna thank me!?

Irene Gant, *a more mature woman, approaches* **Skilling**.

Irene Gant   Mr Skilling? My name is Irene Gant. I worked for Enron for twenty-five years. I did everything you asked. I took all my savings and I invested them in the company I worked for. I've lost a hundred and fifty thousand dollars. I have no money to retire on. And I'm living at my sister's. I wanted you to know because I swore, if I ever saw you in person, well, I don't wanna say.

Skilling   What do you expect me to say to that?

Irene Gant   I want an answer from you –

Skilling   I don't have any answers.

Irene Gant   I have lost everything!

Roe   This is not the place –

Irene Gant   Oh, am I embarrassing you? I'm sorry, am I embarrassing you?! /

Security Guard *from earlier scene approaches the hubbub.*

Security Officer   There trouble here?

Skilling   No.

The **Security Officer** *glares at* **Skilling**. **Skilling** *recognises him.*

Security Officer   There you are.

Skilling   I should go wait in the car.

Security Officer   Do you know who I am?

Skilling   Yes. You're a security officer.

Security Officer (*shakes head*)   I was.

You know what you are? You an ordinary crook. Doesn't matter how you dress it up. Nothing special about it. Took a lot of people down is all.

Skilling   It's called equity for a reason. Everyone shares what's left.

Security Officer   Everything's gone. A future of a certain kind is gone.

Skilling   I understand you're angry. And you're looking for somebody to blame.

Irene Gant   Won't even apologize.

Irene *spits at him. The* **Security Officer** *ushers* **Irene Gant** *back into the funeral throng.*

Roe   That guy's not here to stop you running. He's here to stop you getting hurt.

Skilling   Can I walk in with you?

Roe   I got to take care of myself here.

Beat.

Baptist church bells. **Roe** *leaves to enter the church alone.*

Skilling *is left alone watching the employees enter the church. He eventually turns to leave.*

Epilogue

During this chorus section, **Skilling** *changes into prison garb and hands in his possessions.*

You may wish to intersperse **Skilling's** *speech with the chorus comments, rather than playing them one after the other.*

Board   When Enron was declared bankrupt, they were over thirty billion dollars in debt.

Security Officer   Days before employees were told to leave, the latest round of bonus cheques was handed out to Enron executives, more than fifty-five million dollars.

Employee   That week alone, twenty thousand employees lost their jobs.

Senator   The financial practises pioneered at Enron are now widespread throughout the business world.

Business Analyst (Elise)   Over the last two years, the US Government has pumped over ten trillion dollars into the financial system to try and keep it from collapse.

Sloman   Counting that amount at a dollar a second would take more than 320,000 years.

Employee   Kenneth Lay was found dead in his Aspen ski-home prior to being sentenced for his crimes.

News Reporter (Gayle)   Andy Fastow received a reduced sentence of six years in minimum security in exchange for testifying against his former boss.

Lawyer   Jeffrey Skilling was sentenced to twenty-four years and four months in prison. His case is going to the Supreme Court.

Skilling (*to us*)   I'm not a bad man. I'm not an unusual man. I just wanted to change the world. And I think there'll come a time when everyone understands that. They'll realize they were banishing something of themselves along with me. I believe that.

I know it's hard to understand. How can something be worth a million dollars in the morning and nothing by the afternoon? Same way a man goes from captain of all industry to a fraud sitting in jail. You want to look at something and know it has. . a worth, a fundamental value? Bullshit. You wanna hold a mirror up to nature?

The huge crack along the wall of the building glows from behind and becomes the jagged line graph of the Dow Jones Index over the last century.

The line on the graph/the crack glows.

Skilling (*to us*)   There's your mirror. Every dip, every crash, every bubble that's burst, that's you. Your brilliant stupidity. This one gave us the railroads. This one the internet. This one the slave trade. And if you wanna do anything about saving the environment or reaching other worlds, you'll need a bubble for that too. Everything I've ever done in my life worth anything has been done in a bubble; in a state of extreme hope and trust and stupidity. Would you have had kids if you'd known the true pain of them arriving, and then of them leaving? Would you have gotten married if you could see her face twenty years on turn to you through tears and say, 'You never knew me at all'?

Skilling *points to spikes and dips on the graph.*

Skilling   All humanity is here. There's Greed, there's Fear, Joy, Faith … Hope …

And the greatest of these … is Money.

The sound of prison doors slamming.

The End.

The Effect

A play for four people, in love and sorrow

The Effect opened at the National Theatre, directed by Rupert Goold, and co-produced with Headlong on 13 November 2012, with the following cast and creative team:

Doctors

Dr Lorna James	Anastasia Hille
Dr Toby Sealey	Tom Goodman-Hill

Trialists

Connie Hall	Billie Piper
Tristan Frey	Jonjo O'Neill

Director	Rupert Goold
Designer	Miriam Buether
Lighting Designer	Jon Clark
Composer	Sarah Angliss
Sound Designer	Christopher Shutt
Projection Designer	Jon Driscoll

Author's Note

The parts were written with specific actors in mind and when it comes to matters of nationality, physical references or the 'tricks' the volunteers perform for each other, the performers should feel free to mould the text around themselves.

/ Slashes indicate overlapping dialogue.

Dialogue in brackets indicates that the audience doesn't necessarily have to hear the detail but the actor may wish to say it.

Characters

Dr Lorna James, *47 years, 59.5 kg, 169cm*
Dr Toby Sealey, *45 years, 91 kg, 188 cm*
Connie Hall, *26 years, 55kg, 163 cm*
Tristan Frey, *30 years, 80 kg, 173 cm*

Experiment begins.

Dr James   Have you ever suffered from depression?

Connie, *one arm across herself, leaning back slightly.*

Connie   No. I've felt depressed. But.

Dr James   In what way?

Connie   What I mean is, I've been sad.

Dr James   But not depressed.

Connie   No.

Dr James   There's a difference (?)

Connie   Yeah. I –, it's an illness, isn't it.

Dr James   Mmhm.

Connie   Well, you tell me. I just mean I haven't got an abnormal amount of chemical – in the brain or anything.

Dr James   And that's depression?

Connie   Yeah. Sorry, I –

Dr James   No, I'm interested.

Connie   Just. I'd never say, oh I'm depressed. Well I would, but just meaning sad. You know cos. That's. I'm not. So.

Dr James   You're just sad?

Connie   When I am. I'm sad.

Dr James   K. And there's no chance you could be pregnant?

Connie   No.

Dr James   What contraception are you using?

Connie   None.

Dr James   Are you in a relationship?

Connie   Yup.

Dr James   Are you sexually active in that relationship?

Connie   I have had sex. Um, I hope to have sex again.

Dr James   But you're not having sex at the moment?

Connie   No, not … Right at the moment (!)

Dr James   And what was the date of your last period?

Connie   I always feel like I should know that. A couple of weeks ago? Maybe?

Dr James   Are you asking me or telling me?

Connie   I am … pretending to know.

Dr James   K. I need your help, Connie. It's mostly men here. This is why. Drug trials are safe but you consent for yourself. You can't consent for someone else. So I need to know for sure you're not pregnant.

Connie   Well give me something to wee on and I'll wee on it.

Dr James   Right. Do you smoke?

Tristan *is sat. He leans forward, one foot dancing.*

Tristan   No.

Dr James   Have you drunk alcohol in the last twenty-four hours?

Tristan   No.

Dr James   Have you taken drugs, medicinal or … otherwise in the last six to eight weeks?

Tristan (*thinks*)   Hmm, pretty su – No (!)

Dr James   Have you had any poppy seeds in the last forty-eight hours?

Tristan   Poppy seeds? … No.

Dr James   So if our test for opiates comes back positive I'll assume that's the heroin? Not a bagel?

Tristan   Fine by me (!)

Dr James   Do you or have you ever suffered from irritable bowel syndrome?

Tristan   No.

Dr James   Cancer of the bowel?

Tristan   No.

Dr James   Cancer of the throat, lungs or skin?

Tristan   No.

Dr James   Arthritis?

Tristan   No.

Dr James   Dementia?

Tristan   No.

Dr James   Type 2 diabetes?

Tristan   No.

Dr James   Type 1 diabetes?

Tristan   No.

Dr James   Have you ever been diagnosed with a mental health problem or been in hospital for a period of more than 24 hours?

Tristan   No.

Dr James   K.

Tristan   Done well there then. Full marks for me.

Dr James   I'm not sure avoiding senile dementia is something you can take full credit for.

Tristan   My body can.

Dr James   So you know and accept you must remain within the facility for the four-week period and hand over all electronic devices during that time?

He hands her a phone.

Tristan   One mobile phone. There's no passcode on it so don't go looking through the photos!

Dr James   You've done this before, I see?

Tristan   A few times I have.

Dr James   Then you know what happens now. Can you fill this?

Tristan   What, from here?

(No!) I'll take myself off and empty myself out.

Dr James   K.

Tristan   You've got a nice smile, Dr James.

Dr James   Thank you, Tristan.

Connie *and* **Tristan** *both clutch specimens of their urine. Hers is paler.*

Tristan   Would you like me to take that for you?

Connie   Pardon? No. Sorry.

Tristan   That's alright.

Connie   Do you work here?

Tristan   No I was just going that way with – So. I'm the same as you. Here.

Connie   Oh I don't, are you allowed to take other people's –?

Tristan   Probably not. You've got to sign all that shit. I could do anything to it! I won't (!) You don't have to hide it.

Connie   I'm not particularly.

Tristan   Can I see, then?

Connie   No.

Tristan   It's warm, that's the thing isn't it? But you're warm. If it was cold you'd be dead.

Connie   You need to drink more water.

Tristan   I do! I will. Don't usually get many girls here.

Connie   You a lot of these then?

Tristan   A bit.

Connie   They're alright, are they?

Tristan   Yeah! Used to be better. Now everyone comes in with headphones and laptops, it's a bit more (*gesture*) … used to be like a social experiment. The hard thing's living in a small space with a bunch of strangers.

Connie   This is a long one.

Tristan   It is it is. Don't worry though.

Connie   I'm not.

Tristan   You might not even be on it, but you can tell. People say they wouldn't do this, people who'd take a pill off a stranger or do a line at a party, bollocks do they know what *that* is. You from the university?

Connie   Yeah.

Tristan   I think they pay you more, you know.

/ Connie   What (!)?

Tristan   Yeah. Trials like this they don't want the immigrants they usually get. They need English, so you can, you know, talking isn't, you know, – no trouble how to, uh … –

Connie   Articulate?

Tristan (*smiles*)   There you go (!) Fuck. Sure you don't want me to carry that for you. Like a gentleman would.

He reaches out for her specimen.

She scowls. She is holding it by the top, uncomfortable.

Connie   No.

Tristan   Let me see it, then.

Connie   No!

Tristan   Don't be precious.

Connie   I'm not!

Tristan   Why you holding it like that then, it was part of you a minute ago ...

Connie I'm just. Nothing (!)

Tristan   I'm teasing.

Connie   I know. I'm not ashamed of it (!)

Connie   *goes over and touches his specimen.*

She lets go.

Tristan   Well, you're gonna have to be my friend now.

Admissions procedure. **Tristan** *and* **Connie** *(all volunteers) are changed into clinic outfits. Their blood pressures are taken, alcohol levels checked, weight, height are monitored*

Dr James *looks to her electronic tablet, the modern equivalent of a clipboard, and begins typing on it. When she does this, her words appear on a screen.*

Text, gradually appearing, reads:

First 25 mg dose of agent RLU37 given at timed intervals as of 13th November 2012, 19.11 (or whatever date and time it is).

Dr James, *armed with a timing device to measure the dosing intervals, gives* **Tristan** *a pill that has been emptied into a plastic cup and then a plastic cup of water to wash it down with.*

Dr James   5, 4, 3, 2, 1.

He swallows it. His mouth is checked. **Connie** *is next.* **Dr James** *indicated she should wait. She does.*

Dr James   5, 4, 3, 2, 1.

Connie *takes hers. Her mouth is checked. It continues, theoretically, with other volunteers.*

Medical tests are carried out; temperature, weight, height, pupil dilation, reaction and electrodermal response.

Connie *and* **Tristan** *both eat the same amount of the same food from the same sort of trays. They drink the same amount of water from the same plastic cups.*

(Maybe they both have a cannula fitted to their arms.)

Connie *and* **Tristan** *are put into beds, sitting up, and an ECG monitors their hearts.*

Tristan *has blood drawn. He watches the process.*

Blood is drawn from **Connie** *who looks away from it, slightly squeamish. Her heart rate goes wild.*

Connie *looks away, grimacing.*

It ends. She uncrumples. Both have been provided with a juicebox and a biscuit.

Connie   D'you want my biscuit?

Tristan   Thanks but I can't. If I'm one biscuit up and you're one biscuit down that could throw out all of medical science.

She starts to eat her biscuit.

Dr James   Wait here, please.

Dr James *has been administering the tests. She leaves the room at this point but comes and goes throughout.*

Tristan   Where d'you sleep?

Connie   Oh, down the corridor, they showed me.

Tristan   I'm with ten sweaty blokes. You're biologically blessed.

She is biting her nails.

Tristan   You bite your nails?

She nods, guilty.

He holds his hand out to her to show he does too, badly.

Tristan   Me too.

She takes it, looks, smiles.

Connie (*warm*)   God (!) They're really bad!

Tristan *sees her wristband.*

Tristan   No shit!

Connie   What?

Tristan   We have the same birthday.

Connie   The 29th?

Tristan   Yeah!

She looks at his DOB on his band.

Connie   Oh yeah!

Tristan   How weird is that? The exact same – birthday (!)

Dr James   Could you lie down please.

Tristan   What are the chances of that!

Connie   Actually, I don't think it's that unusual, I mean it's not as unlikely as you'd think.

Tristan   How d'you know what I think?

Connie   Sorry, than most people would think. I mean in a group of people, the group doesn't actually have to be that big for you to maybe share a birthday. Cos probability-wise you're not saying how likely is it this person was born on a particular date – one in 365 obviously. You're just saying, of *all* the dates, how likely is it that two people in a group have the same?

Tristan   Oh. Well I think it's a sign.

Connie   Right.

Tristan   I think we're twins. Identical twins. They decided to raise us in very different environments to see what effect it had long term. Me a quaint little shithole on the coast near Coleraine. And you?

Connie   Basingstoke.

Tristan   Basingstoke. Turned out it had a massive effect.

Dr James   Can you sit down please?

Connie   What are you doing for your birthday?

Tristan   Leaving and never coming back. This is for spending money. I'm going travelling.

Connie   Oh cool!

Tristan   Does your man not mind you doing this then?

Connie   My man? No. I – No, I do what I … like (!)

Tristan   Course you do, it's like that. I got a man but I don't need a man. Beyonce and shit.

Connie   He's away so –

Tristan   Away for work, is he?

Connie   No.

Tristan   Stag do?

Connie   No.

Tristan   Is he in prison?

Connie   What? No! He's visiting family.

Tristan   Oh right. Not with you though.

Connie   No, with a friend.

Tristan   Oh.

Connie   With his son. He's got a little boy. From before.

Tristan   Nice. So you're happy?

Connie   Don't do that.

Tristan   What?

Connie   That. Are you happy thing. That thing guys say when / they're –

Tristan   / I'm sure you are –!

Connie Cos who ever actually says, yeah I'm perfectly completely –

Tristan Some people do.

Connie Okay, yeah, well.

Tristan What?

Connie I am.

Tristan What?

Connie (*unhappily*) Happy!

Tristan Where would you go? India I'm thinking.

Connie I don't know. I wouldn't go anywhere exotic actually. Somewhere American. Not the cities, I mean. The real, the dust, those states. Somewhere it's horizon on both sides.

Tristan The plains.

Connie I'd like to see a wild horse.

Tristan Oh yeah?

Connie And hold a gun.

Tristan Right.

Connie I wouldn't shoot the horse (!)

Tristan Why don't you go then?

Connie Why don't I *go*?

Tristan Yeah.

Connie Money, time, life. There's just so much to do.

Tristan Yeah. It's great.

She laughs, looks at him, intrigued.

We hear their ECGs gradually slow and settle into a calmer rhythm and eventually they beep/beat together.

'DEATH'

The word appears on a screen in a blue font.

Connie and Tristan   Blue.

Dr James *types and text reads:*

The Stroop Test.

(It is useful to have the following explanation of the test either appearing in text onstage or spoken out loud for the audience.) Volunteers view trigger words but name only the colour in which the word appears. Subject takes longer to distinguish the colour of words that are psychologically relevant or troubling to them.

Various words have appeared on the screen in colour. **Tristan** *and* **Connie** *(separately in theory) have been naming the colours they appear in.*

During above, as needed. (BEAUTY. CHAIR. TEST.)

GUILTY

Connie *names the colour after* **Tristan**.

BABY

Together.

FATHER

Tristan after.

JOY

Together.

DIET

Connie after.

LONELY

Together.

BREASTS

Tristan after. He's amused.

MEMORY

Together.

BLUE (but in another colour)

Connie   Blue. Shit. Sorry.

She corrects herself. **Tristan** *gets it right.*

Connie   Dr James.

It is now just **Connie** *and* **Dr James**.

Dr James   Yes.

Connie   Sorry, I don't know if it matters. But I thought I should say. I know about the Stroop Effect. I know it's about how long you take to say the colour, that the more meaningful the word, the longer it takes. I don't know if it matters. If you know.

Dr James   No.

Connie   Really? I thought knowing might make me try to *beat it.*

Dr James   In most cases being aware of your own bias doesn't actually mean you can affect that bias.

Connie   Really?

Dr James   Yes. It's one of life's tragedies. Do you want to hear this story again? You can hear it a total of two times.

Connie   Okay.

Dr James   You open up a dry cleaners. On the border between two towns. Your shop is the only one of its kind in the surrounding area. Your business prospers and reactions from your customers indicate the cleaning is of good quality.

Connie   Okay.

Dr James   You hire more staff which is an outlay but improves customer service, and you wonder about applying to the bank for a loan to open up a chain of such shops. As you had expected the bank approves the loan.

Connie   Go me!

Dr James   Now a quick memory test, can you tell me the nature of your business? Was it A) greengrocers or B) dry cleaners?

Connie   B.

Dr James   And where was the shop set up was it A –

Connie   On the border / between two towns.

Dr James   / In the centre of town or B on the border between – yes. And the reason for your business success, was it A) lack of competition or B) A good business plan?

Connie (*thinks*)   Sorry, what?

Dr James   The reason for your success –

Connie   You didn't say. So am I me? Am I now a dry cleaner?

Dr James   Remembering the story I told you, what was the reason for your success?

Connie   It's impossible to say. Is this a test of memory?

Dr James   This is the last question.

Connie   But the business and the town are fictional. Even the me is kind of fictional.

Dr James   Could I have an answer?

Connie   Afterwards will you tell me why?

Dr James   Why?

Connie   I'm a psychology student.

Dr James   Then you can work it out for yourself. What was the reason for your success? A, lack of competition, or B, a good business plan?

Connie (*shrugs*)   A) lack of competition. May as well. There'll be like a hundred factors in this fictional town's economy.

Dr James   Okay.

Connie   So if I'd said my business plan.

Dr James   Then what?

Connie   Then I'd be taking responsibility for the success –

Dr James   Right ...

Connie   So what's that got to do with the trial?

Dr James   People prone to depression, Connie, they tend to attribute success to external causes and failure to internal ones.

Connie   So if I do well it's because of something outside of me, but if I do badly it's because of my stupid self.

Dr James   Exactly.

Connie   What would a 'normal' mind do?

Dr James   Well a so-called 'healthy' mind, the healthiest mind would think if things go well it's down to me, I did that. And if it goes badly –

Connie   They've been unlucky.

Dr James   Victim of circumstance, yes. So you're studying psychology?

Connie (*nod*)   And social science.

Dr James   Gosh. Never too late to become a real doctor, you know (!) So is that why you're here, interested in trials?

Connie   Yes, and depression.

Dr James   Interesting. Is that ... personal experience or ... (a parent?) –

Beat.

Sorry. My background's in psychotherapy. How do you feel?

Connie   A bit awkward.

Dr James   I mean physically.

Connie   Oh. Fine. A bit tense you know 'up' like, something's going to happen. I keep thinking my hearing's really good, that's crazy isn't it?! But Tristan said the same.

Dr James   Well the agent's designed to increase levels of dopamine –

Connie   Right.

Dr James   And that's what's stimulated by new, exciting experiences generally so ... There's an old joke actually. How does it go. So. There's this medic at a conference and he's fallen for a girl there who hasn't looked twice at him. Now he knows dopamine is the initial trigger in falling in love but also that dopamine is stimulated by new, exciting experiences. So to try and get the girl he arranges for them to go *bungee jumping* together to sort of set up his own chemical reaction. So the instructor ties them together and they stand over this incredible valley and he's got his arms round her and they fall headlong into this incredible, adrenaline filled rush – and their dopamine levels go wild. And eventually, they get lifted back onto the bridge, they get their breath back and he looks into her eyes and says, 'Wasn't that amazing?!' And breathlessly she answers, 'Yes! And isn't the instructor handsome!'

Beat.

Dr James   It's sort of a science joke so ...

Connie   No, I like it. Cos it's the instructor ...

Dr James   Yes, that she's ... yes.

Toby *enters, perusing medical records* **Dr James** *has given him.*

Toby   This is very good isn't it.

Dr James   I'm not sure it's good or bad it's just the case.

Toby   Well done. Different from what you're used to I bet.

Dr James   Different.

Toby   Easier.

Dr James   Different.

Toby   Elevated mood.

Dr James   Yes.

Toby   Increased energy levels.

Dr James   Yes.

Toby   Weight loss (!)

Dr James   Mm-hm.

Toby   And increased height?!

Dr James   Average 2 cm.

Toby   Height?

She nods.

Toby   Doesn't seem likely.

Dr James   Well I'm not raising the floors.

Toby   I didn't think we were even monitoring height.

Dr James   I monitor everything.

Toby   I see that. Why are you doing psychological tests? Of this quantity. It's a phase 1, physical.

Dr James   Well everything's physical in the end isn't it.

Toby   An anti-depressant effect in healthy volunteers. That'd be extraordinary.

Dr James   Barely a week in, they know they're being given an anti-depressant, it'll be mostly their own expectation, surely?

Toby   Could be. But the new design is fast acting so ...

Dr James   Sorry, I just assume it's psychological.

Toby   Robust objectivity. Quite right. It's good to see you Lorn. I mean I know I saw you at the – but I mean alone. You look really well.

Dr James   –

Toby   I bet you think I'm looking old.

Dr James   What? No, don't say that, you make me think you're thinking that about me.

Toby   No!

Dr James   I should say thank you for all this. I know I wouldn't – it's very um, good of you.

Toby   Oh don't (even) – it's just great to see you and for you to be here. Let's just make sure this is done really well.

Dr James   What does that mean?

Toby   With lack of bias and precision.

Dr James   Well I wasn't just going to circle random numbers, Tobe (!)

Toby   No no no, I'm honestly trying to help. You know how things are. We could do with fresh eyes. It's a touchy area.

Dr James   Rightly so.

Toby   Believe me *I* don't want to spend five weeks on a trial that gets discredited. Why we're developing new gens in the first place.

Dr James   Because the old ones have been discredited.

Toby   They haven't been discredited, the studies that discredited our original trials have themselves been discredited now.

Dr James   In new studies by you.

Toby   Yes. Well us. Don't worry, I'm the one always persuading them not to relocate the trials out to West Africa. Anti-depressant trials!

Dr James   I'm sure they get depressed in Gambia.

Toby   I'm sure they get fucking depressed in the Gambia, doesn't mean we should use them as guinea pigs then disappear off with our drugs.

Mini-beat.

Dr James   I read you were advising the government on psychopharmaceuticals at the moment?

Toby   No, I'm on a panel. I'm not –

Dr James   I keep expecting to see you on a TED talk or something.

Toby   Ah! No I. They have asked actually, but no I'm saving that for the day I write that book (!)

Dr James   And how are you? How are the kids?

Toby   Great, thank you, yeah. I got engaged!

Dr James   Oh! Congratulations! Wow (!)

Toby   Yes and divorced obviously, I should probably say those the other way round.

Dr James   Ah, okay. Well, congratulations again.

Toby   I realize that should probably have happened a while ago ...

Dr James   Well. That must have been hard.

Toby   No. For the best. It's all good.

Dr James   No, I think I heard actually, is she a lab assistant at MB?

Toby   Yes, where did you hear that?

Dr James   I ran into Bill Fitzgrove at customs ages ago and he said –

Toby   God Bill, did you, yes, he worked with her –

Dr James   Yeah.

Toby   How is he? Is he still at Brown?

Dr James   Yes. He's Alzheimer's now.

Toby   Great! You mean he's –

Dr James   Oh yeah, researching, he's not ... (!)

Toby   Good (!) huh. Yeah. Did we – Did I meet him with you?

Dr James   Yes at that conference.

Toby   My god, yes, and he came over at the bar –

Dr James   That's right. It was after your talk and you / dropped –

Toby   / That's right. I still do that talk –

Dr James   I know.

Toby   Well a variation of it, for Raushen.

Dr James   With the uh?

She mimes an action, carrying a bucket. He mimes it back.

Toby   Yes.

Dr James   (*remembering*) Yes, I remember. He came over after and you dropped your cigarette, and I was hopping about cos it burnt my leg –

Toby   What?

Dr James You remember.   He was introducing himself –

Toby   No, I do, but you dropped it, and – I don't smoke.

Dr James   Of course you don't, nobody smokes *now,* you did then.

Toby   Did I? No I didn't – very ...

Dr James   I have a scar!

Toby   Well to be fair we can't say what caused that (!)

Dr James   No.

Toby   But I'm sorry if that's true.

Dr James   I wasn't being serious. When you could smoke indoors (!)

Beat.

Toby   Really glad to see you looking so well, though, Lorna. /

Dr James   / And you.

Toby I've got to do one of these trial development seminars tonight, but I'll be back for the scans. I'll sign off first dosage escalation now if you're happy?

Slowly and slightly **Dr James** *nods.*

DOSAGE INCREASE: 50mg

Dosages are administered. (5, 4, 3, 2, 1)

Connie I've been having the most extraordinary dreams.

Tristan Yes! Me too.

Connie Vivid.

Tristan Yeah! And so fucking ...

Connie Mundane!

Tristan Bizarre!

Tristan Mundane?

Connie Yeah, last night I dreamt my whole weekly shop I do. Round the whole supermarket, near where I live. My brain must have designed every label, every detail. In real time, for hours. And when I woke up I was like, what a boring dream! And then I thought, god no, what a boring *life!*

Tristan I had a dream about you, I think.

Connie Did you?

Tristan Yeah. Not like that!

Connie Oh yeah.

Tristan One week in, this is where it hits you.

Connie Yeah I'm feeling that.

Tristan I'm climbing the fucking walls.

Connie I'd kill for a cigarette.

Tristan I snuck out once for a fag.

Connie   Did you?!

Tristan   You know round the back of here's an old asylum?

Connie   What?!

Tristan   You know, a mental hospital.

Connie   No (!) What's it like?

Tristan   You want to see?

Connie   We're not allowed out.

Tristan   I might know a way.

A man enters with a bucket. It is **Toby**.

Toby (*to audience, at an industry event*)   Hello. This couldn't be more glamorous, could it, a man coming on with a bucket? But fear not, the money's gone on what's inside. Welcome to Raushen. Don't worry, I'm not going to ask anyone to volunteer but I would love to talk to you about why it's so important that people do. I'm Toby, I'm a psychiatrist, I'm afraid. My father was a heart surgeon and when I told him I wanted to specialize in psychiatry he said, 'Oh *really?* The *Cinderella* of medicine?' Which um, (*he gestures to a knife in his heart, casually*) because dad thought psychiatry was all nonsense about Freud and how we're all obsessed with our parents. So I devoted my life to proving him wrong (!) But seriously, I do think I've vanquished my father in a way because, I didn't want to be a heart surgeon. I didn't want to be a *plumber* of the body. I wanted to be an explorer.

He removes something from liquid in the container, holds it aloft and looks at it. It is a human brain.

Toby   So I became a psychiatrist and of course, like all doctors, my chosen speciality is defined by what goes *wrong*. When the brain goes wrong, there are symptoms and causes, as with anything else. But because we *think* with our brain we struggle to frame it as a piece of biological machinery. We're happy to have heart transplants and liver transplants but we can't imagine a brain transplant. Because nowadays we think our soul is in here. But that sense of 'us' is only a tiny part of what's going on at any moment. As you sit listening to me your brain is taking care of a lot of things so you don't have to, consciously – your temperature, forcing food through your gut, positioning your spinal column in your seat, which doesn't look terribly comfortable, I'm sorry about that. Swallowing so you don't choke on your saliva. Now if we suffered a neurological oddity that meant we couldn't swallow we'd see nothing wrong with addressing and repairing that in the brain. It's the same with mental health issues. There are diseases of the brain. That doesn't make people crazy or incapable or dangerous in soul. They're ill. We are many of us going to experience a mental health condition in our lifetime. We're past the the notion of the sane and the insane! Why not call ourselves the insane and the 'not insane at the moment'? Managing our mental hygiene is a life's work. The psycho-pharmacological revolution is the defining occurrence in medicine in my lifetime. I'm *proud* to have been a part of that. My father lived just long enough to see it. He ran three miles a day into his seventies, he didn't touch red meat, what got him in the end was up here. But in one of his more lucid moments, he decided to donate his brain to science for teaching and research into this field. (*He talks to the brain.*) So thank you dad. Thanks to people like you, the Cinderella of medicine got to go to the ball.

Moonlight.

Connie *and* **Tristan** *enter a very large room. It is an unused dilapidated recreation area, once something grander.*

Connie   Oh my word.

She instinctively gets closer to him.

Tristan   Fuuuck.

They laugh. They make noises that echo.

Tristan   Why do they keep it? It's falling to bits.

Connie   It'll be a listed building. It'd probably cost more to do it up than to close off like this.

Tristan   You're such a grown up.

Connie   It's amazing to be somewhere with space.

She enjoys the space. She does something gymnastic.

They share a cigarette.

Tristan   Imagine them all in here, rocking.

Connie (*re. her gymnastics*)   Can you do any tricks?

Tristan   I'll show you on one condition.

Connie   What?

Tristan   Come travelling with me after this.

Connie (*sound*)   !

Tristan   Why not? Doesn't have to be for long. We like each other, don't we?

Connie   I get the feeling you like everyone.'

Tristan   Where do you want to go? We'll go anywhere you like.

Connie   I'm not going travelling with you. I barely know you.

Tristan   What do you want to know?

Connie   Tris, I'm not doing that, my course, my relationship, my work.

Tristan   Don't be so practical!

Connie   You're the one being practical! For me it's insane!

Tristan   Do you think your parents would like me?

Connie   !

Tristan   Do they like him?

Connie   Piss off.

Tristan   I bet they don't. He must be older, right? Is he older?

Connie   He's in his forties.

Tristan   Oh, nice and vague. Just tell me he's not your teacher or something.

Connie   He's not – stop it.

Tristan   Just tell me it's not that.

Connie   It's not. He never taught *me*.

Tristan   Oh fuck.

Connie   The reason I'm not at all bothered about what you think is I know what you think and I know it's not true.

Tristan   Boring anyway. Let's get back to what do you want to know about me?

Connie   Nothing, Tris, seriously.

Tristan   Nothing?!

Connie   No I do, course I do. You're very interesting. I just feel weird. I don't feel what I'd feel like in real life.

Tristan   This *is* real life. When is it real?

Connie   No I mean. The anti-depressant, the doctor said, they're designed to stimulate certain, like dopamine. Which is the rush you get if something exciting happens or, when you – well it's fake, it's a chemical that feels like. Like falling for someone.

Beat.

Tristan   So?

Connie   So forgive me if I take everything with a big pinch of, you know ...

Tristan   What you think I don't like you properly because of the –?

Connie   I think it's a strong possibility.

Tristan   Bullshit. I can tell the difference between who I am and a side effect.

Connie   With respect Tristan, no you definitely can't.

Tristan   You're saying any attraction is a result of the trial.

Connie   Part of it could be.

Tristan (*quietly pleased*)   You must be basing that on feeling a sort of attraction then?

Connie   I didn't say that ...! It's a chemical reaction, is what I'm saying

Tristan   But I'm still me.

Connie   No, yes, you're you, but under the influence of something. If you were really pissed and going 'I love you, you're my best mate' I wouldn't believe it either.

Tristan   Why not? Men mean it when they say that, they just can't say it when they're sober.

Connie   Yeah but they'll have known that person (ages) – and I don't know, I'm just telling you what the doctor said.

Tristan   Ah, what does she know? They don't know anything, Knowledge is a myth.

Connie (*unimpressed*)   Okay ...

Tristan   They wouldn't be trialling if they knew. One time I had chronic diarrhoea for six days straight, nobody predicted *that*. They say all sorts of shit, they say you have to give in your phone because it *interferes with the equipment*.

Connie   You *do* have to give in your phone because it interferes with the equipment.

Tristan   Jesus, do you want a phone? I'll give you a phone. I gave in a dummy.

He roots around in his bag and tosses her a phone.

Tristan   Say you have to make a call, get your phone, go to the loo, swap sims. 'Interferes with the equipment', it's like they say that on planes. It's just it's really hard to control a bunch of people if they've all got phones. Anytime anyone says turn off your phone you should worry that's a situation where you might die, not worry about the fucking equipment.

Connie   Can I actually have this?

Tristan   Yeah I normally sell them but that's a shit one.

Connie   I like it, it's like the Nineties.

Tristan   You don't really think that? That I only like you, cos I'm high or something.

Connie   Why not? Everything we do is just about what's pumping round us, isn't it?

Tristan   Well that's a cold way of looking at a person.

Connie   Why?! We *are* our bodies, our bodies are us, ... there's not something *more* ... And that's fine. That's enough. It's like, the world is incredible and beautiful, even though we know there's no god behind it. It's even *more* amazing for that.

Tristan   Hang on, we *know* there's no God behind it?

Connie   Yeah, I mean, Sorry. Oh, Really?

Tristan   What?

Connie   You believe in God?

Tristan   What? It's alright, you look disappointed (!)

Connie   No, it's terrible isn't it, you just assume – when you meet someone and you ...

Tristan   When you meet someone ...

Connie   And you get on, you assume ...

Tristan   I knew it! You're disappointed I believe in God because you like me! (Thank you Lord).

Connie   Sorry that's awful.

Tristan   No no no. Let's say you're right, let's say we're attracted to each other, (because we are you just admitted it and you can't take it back) let's say we're attracted to each other and that's been kicked off by these ...

Connie   The dopamine.

Tristan   Drugs or whatever. So what?

Connie   What d'you mean?

Tristan   What difference does it make?

Connie   Well clearly then it's something to be wary of.

Tristan   It is what it is. Doesn't matter why.

Connie   It matters massi – ... It's all that matters.

Tristan   Why?

Connie   Because, it's the *reason!*

Tristan   So?

Connie   I can't work out if I understand something you don't or you understand something I don't.

Tristan   People meet each other and fall in love all sorts of ways, doesn't matter what starts it. I'm sure there's a rush of something chemical if you meet on holiday or on a bus with a bomb on it, doesn't mean Keanu Reeves and Sandra Bullock aren't really in love.

Connie   Are you talking about the movie *Speed*?

Tristan   Yeah, it was on in the rec room last night. But you think it's fake? So what you think a few years on, Sandra and Keanu are just sat in a restaurant in silence thinking why did I marry this loser, all we had in common was a bus!

Connie (*laughing*)   Yeah I do actually, I do!

Tristan   I like your laugh.

Connie   D'you know why?

Tristan   It's sexy.

Connie   No actually why. It's a show of submission.

Tristan   What?!

Connie   Laughing is a way of showing submission, so men like it when women laugh. It shows they're dominant.

Tristan   In my fuck! You laugh when something's funny.

Connie   No. You don't laugh out loud alone watching a sitcom.

Tristan   Yes you do.

Connie   You don't. It's a social thing … It says 'I get the joke, I'm clever', or you use it to show you're attracted to someone. The head thrown back, the throat exposed.

Tristan   That's not why you laugh. You laugh at something. I've taken drugs before, right? There's not a drug in the world can really make you look at someone find them attractive or listen to 'em and find them interesting or –

Connie   Yes there is!

Tristan   Not smell them and … know.

He's advanced closer and closer until now they can just about smell the other.

Connie   That's pheromones isn't it?

Tristan   Is there no mystery for you?

Connie   There is, but it's more than smelling isn't it? It takes work.

Tristan   That is *such* a lie. You don't believe that.

Beat.

Connie (*defences down*)   I just think it comes and goes. There's a period of time, maybe enough to raise a child and then …. You know, the few times I've ever loved anyone they've always, at some point they've written I Love You in the snow or the sand – on holiday – to me. And it's wonderful, but the next time someone … it happens, or the next even … you think, Oh okay. Again. And you think of the last time. And what that meant. And, just for it to get washed away or melt or ....

Tristan Some people never get loved like that.

Connie I know.

Tristan If I did that, for you, I'd be holding back the sea from ever coming in.

Connie (*touched*) You're sunshine, you know that. I bet you thought the dry cleaning business was a success cos of your great business plan, didn't you?

Tristan Of course. It was!

Connie So you take drugs then, proper ones?

Tristan / Sometimes. You?

Connie No. I just think of drugs as like fags or cheese or something, if you get to a point and you're not into them, don't get into them you'll only have to give them up down the line cos they're bad for you.

Tristan It's about trying something new.

Connie Sure but it's only new once. Then it's the same as everything else.

Tristan But everything has to be new once!

Connie Sure but it's essentially a way of distracting yourself.

Tristan From what?

Connie From the fact that you and everyone you love is definitely gonna die.

Mini-beat.

Tristan Good! I'm glad I'm distracting myself from that! Good!

Connie That thing of oh this thing will make me happy, no this thing, no it must be that next thing. Like why are you going travelling?

Tristan   To see things, meet people. Have my mind … expanded.

Connie   Cool man.

Tristan   What's wrong with that?!

Connie   Nothing.

Connie   Just. Like look at this square metre. (*She's talking about the floor.*)

Tristan   What?

Connie   There's a whole world here. It's just what you notice. Look at the floor.

Tristan   Tiles.

Connie   Yeah, used to be. Different colours.

Tristan   Tiny tiles.

Connie   Mosaic. That seems weird.

Tristan   Why would people put a mosaic on the floor of a mental asylum?

Connie   Maybe it wasn't a mental asylum when it was built.

Tristan   Or maybe they thought mental patients spend a lot of time looking down.

She smiles at him.

Connie   See all of this, you can get all of this from one square yard. You don't need to change continent every day.

Tristan   That would work, that would work except for one thing.

Connie   What?

Tristan   You wouldn't have seen any of this if it wasn't for me.

Beat.

Tristan   Come travelling with me.

Connie   Oh come on – I don't know you, I can't trust you –

Tristan   You've come into a mental asylum with me at night! You trust me. I'm going to see a lunar rainbow. In Zambia, three days a year, the full moon hits this waterfall and it refracts the moonlight. You got that in your square yard?

Connie   Do your trick.

Beat.

Tristan   I could actually.

Connie   I really want to see it.

Tristan   Do you?

Connie   Yeah.

Tristan   (I might go outside your square yard is that okay/)

Connie   (/That's fine)

He cycles through tracks on his phone. He plays one.

He gets drawing pins from an old notice board and stabs them into his soles.

Tristan *performs a tap-dance to the music. It is surprisingly good. (The talent displayed here should be whatever the actor feels he can do. It should have the quality of something romantic, as well as being a traditional 'male display'. Change lines accordingly.)*

Tristan   Regional junior Ulster tap champion 1994!

Towards the end he puts his arms around **Connie** *to half-dance with her and leading to a kiss. During,* **Dr James** *enters*

Dr James   Oh thank god, where have you been?! I was about to call the police!

Connie   Sorry.

Dr James   Are you okay?

Connie   Fine.

Dr James   What's going on?

Connie   Nothing sorry.

Dr James   Did you climb out of a window?!

Tristan   No, fire / escape.

Connie   / Fire escape. Sorry.

Dr James   Was there a fire?

Beat as they work out whether this is rhetorical.

Tristan   We were going a bit mad in there and wanted to check out / outside –

Dr James   / Sorry I didn't realize I was in charge of a bunch of school kids –

Connie   Sorry.

Tristan   Sorry.

Dr James   You signed a protocol.

Tristan   We haven't done anything to mess / with the –

Dr James   / You have no idea what you've done. Have you been smoking?

Dr James   It stinks of it.

Tristan   Alright, but yeah we're not at school, so you don't need to be a bitch/ about it

Connie   / Tris –

Dr James (*furious*)   / Nicotine will inflate your dopamine levels for hours which are already elevated from the agent, that affects my results. I'm sorry if my experiment that you're being paid to do is getting in the way of your moves.

Dr James   Connie?

Connie   Mm?

Dr James   You came here willingly, I assume?

Connie   Yes!

Tristan   Steady (!)

Dr James   Just to be clear, you have signed a consent form committing to refraining from sexual activity.

Connie   Yeah, I know (!)

Dr James   You can't disappear with psychiatric medication coursing through you, I'm responsible for your safety –

Connie   Sorry.

Dr James   Bed please. We have fMRIs tomorrow, go and rest your brains.

Dr James   *lights a cigarette and smokes it and hears herself over the speaker. As she hears her own voice she tries to control a swelling sobbing growing in her from anxiety.*

Dr James   (V/O) Okay. Just relax. Everything's fine. Exhale. There's no need for anxiety. Just keep your head in one place. Okay. Now I want you to think of something positive. They think of one another.

Connie   Tristan.

Tristan   Connie.

During above, their beds become MRI machines and the loud, otherworldly, claustrophobic darkness of MRI envelopes each lover in their own minds.

Scans of two brains, theirs, on screen.

Importantly, which scan belongs to which volunteer is unknown.

Observing the two brains cans are **Toby** *and* **Dr James**.

Toby   What do you think?

Dr James   What do *I* think?

Toby   Yeah, what do you think?

Dr James   I think it's too early to say.

Toby   What?!

Dr James   I think it's too early to say.

Toby   Dampened amygdala activity.

She nods.

Toby   Strong activity in the dopaminergic pathways and the reward centres of the brain in general. An anti-depressant effect if ever I've seen one!

Dr James   If you say so.

Toby   It's on a scan, Lorna, right in front of you!

Dr James   I don't doubt there's an 'anti-depressant effect' going on. But I don't think it's got anything to do with your drug.

Toby   Well that seems rather a coincidence.

Dr James   You're seeing what you want to see, Toby. It's what you do.

Toby   Professionally speaking, why don't you think it's the drug?

Dr James   *Professionally* speaking, two very good reasons. You asked to see the scans of the volunteers showing the greatest effect. Are you interested in who they are?

Toby   Of course.

Dr James   K. Two very different clinical histories, backgrounds, genders even. But they have one thing in common. They are both involved in an intense and protracted flirtation, with each other.

Toby   Really? Right … So you think *that's* what I'm looking at?

Dr James   I think their physical symptoms and this neural activity is a result of that … attraction and frankly it's obscuring any sense of what the drug itself is doing.

Toby   Unless it is what the drug itself is doing. If the agent is causing all these symptoms, why on earth *wouldn't* they assume they were infatuated?

Dr James   You think because they feel all the things one would associate with infatuation they are just … assuming that's what they are.

Toby   Assuming, exactly. The body responds a certain way to what it's being given, they can't sleep, they can't eat, they're in a constant state of neural excitement ever since they met, what's the brain going to conclude?

Dr James   You think it mistakes that for love?

Toby   Not even mistakes it, creates it. To make sense of the response.

Depression's deadness of emotion, right? Insularity, lack of engagement with the world and those around you –

Dr James   Is it?

Toby   So the other end of the spectrum, where the agent could be taking them, is *extreme* emotion, excess engagement, overwhelming purpose and feeling. What does that sound like –?

Dr James   Bollocks?

Toby   What does it sound like?

Dr James   I'm pretty sure it's not drug effect, Toby (!)

Toby   How? Don't forget it was just a blood pressure trial where they discovered Viagra.

Dr James   So what? You're thinking you've discovered a Viagra for the heart?

Toby   Don't be simplistic. It's just not impossible. Cannabis we know increases susceptibility to schizophrenia. Likewise I'm sure you can create a chemical vulnerability, to something more positive –

Dr James   Sounds a bit Rohypnol to me.

Toby   I mean it rather romantically! Medical science has extended everyone's lives without taking any responsibility for us having to be married longer. We could do with a bit of help!

Dr James   Instead of giving up and starting over?

Mini-beat.

Toby   Yeah. And you'd try anything in the worst of it.

Beat.

Dr James   It seems to me you're trying to stress the chemical nature of things, for *my* benefit.

Beat.

Toby   No. But okay, yes, equally, if you have a chemical imbalance that makes you sleep all the time, feel lethargic, have trouble focusing, of course you're going to eventually feel *depressed.*

Dr James   Oh for god's sake Toby, you ask someone about their history of depression they don't say I felt tired one day. They say, I lost my job, I lost my wife, there are external events they / respond to –

Toby   / Everybody loses their job, everybody loses their wife!

Dr James   No they don't, Toby! It's about an interaction with the world. It doesn't just appear. I know this depression as disease thing is good for business but –

Toby   Don't. Don't say that in front of me.

Dr James   Don't say that in front of *me!* I was a clinical psychiatrist at Barts for ten years while you were greasing your way up the ladder, don't tell / me what ...

Toby   / Why would you grease a ladder?!

Dr James   You know what I mean.

Toby   You weren't there a lot of those ten years.

Dr James   You don't know that at all!

Beat.

Toby   I'm sorry that's not the point.

Dr James   You don't!

Toby   And it's irrelevant.

Dr James   Are you interested in *why* I don't think it's a drug effect, Toby?

Toby   Of course, what do you *think* I'm interested in?!

Dr James   I think you're interested in whatever's most interesting.

Toby   Come on then, what makes you *so* sure this isn't our drug?

Dr James   Thank you doctor, I'm glad you asked. Because number seven here is on a placebo! All the physical symptoms *and* apparent anti-depressant effect!

Toby   Ah.

Dr James   Yes ah.

Toby   Placebo.

Dr James   Yes. So with one of them the effect's entirely natural.

A sound to indicate scan's end, resumption of trial protocol and attendance for dosing.

DOSAGE INCREASE. Text reads: Increase in dosage: 100mg

Connie *takes her dosage but goes for the wrong one.* **Dr James** *corrects her.*

Dr James   No, that's not yours.

Connie   Sorry, does it matter –?

Dr James   That one, please.

In another space **Tristan** *receives his dosage.*

Tristan   Can I go to the rec room now?

Dr James   No, you're on your own now.

Tristan   Why?

Dr James   Both of you. I'm here to monitor physiological effects, I can do without you going off creating your own.

The two lovers are kept apart. This distresses them and heightens responses.

The following in overlapped once separate spaces, as **Dr James** *records stated symptoms:*

Dr James   Anxiety? Is that what you're saying? Anxious.

Connie   Sort of. Yeah. But there's some / thing else.

Tristan   Anxiety, yeah, but anxiety if it's good. Is there a word for that?

Connie   I do feel – yeah, I can't think of another word. But yeah.

Tristan   Alive. Really alive.

Dr James   More 'alive' than usual?

Connie   Yeah, my thoughts are racing, the speed of thought, the repetition.

Tristan   Alert, you know? Like everything's more vivid?

Connie   Can I ask you something?

Tristan   / Can I ask you something?

Dr James   Sure.

Tristan   How's Connie?

Connie   Tristan. When you do these trials, someone has to *not* be on the drug right?

Tristan   Connie said the same, thoughts racing.

Dr James   What do you mean by that?

Tristan   Connie.

Connie   Tristan. Gosh, my heart.

Tristan   My heart.

Connie   Feels like it's going –

Dr James   Going –?

Tristan   Going –

Connie   Going, you know?

Tristan   I don't know, faster.

Connie   Can you see that?

Dr James   See what?

Connie   If someone isn't on the drug, right? Sorry, I can hear my heartbeat in my ears. But you can't tell them, right?

Tristan   I just feel, vivid. Everything is vivid.

Dr James   It's not for you to worry about, much better you just tune in to what you feel.

Tristan   My mouth tastes like metal when I swallow.

Connie   Can I have some water? Sorry, oh, I'm feeling sick.

Tristan   My stomach.

Dr James   Are you going to the loo okay?

Connie   It's just a bit upset, that's all, at least I'm losing weight (!)

Tristan   I could shit through the eye of a fucking needle!

Dr James   Well we can try that later.

Connie   Oh look, God, I'm shaking.

Dr James   When did the shaking start?

Tristan   Today, right, I'm not sleeping, really, look it's stopped.

He's holding out his hand. **Connie** *is holding hers out, it's trembling.*

Connie   Is this bad?

Dr James   You're probably dehydrated.

Connie   Cos I feel –

Tristan   I feel –

Connie   I feel –

Tristan   I feel –

Connie   I feel –

Tristan   I feel like I've lost weight.

Connie   My skin looks better. But I don't know if that's, you know –

Tristan   And I don't know if this   **Connie**   And I don't know if
is the kind of thing you're after –   this is the sort of thing you want –

Connie   And I don't know if this is the sort of thing you want –

Connie   But I think there's an effect on um ...

Tristan   Sex drive's mental!

Connie   'Libido.'

Dr James   Right.

Tristan   I feel ... more awake.

Connie   I've never felt this alert before.

Dr James   Just try and breathe, relax, it's lights out soon. If you
can get some sleep, that would be better.

Connie   Sleep?!

Tristan   Sleep? Sleep's for the weak.

Connie   I feel like I might never sleep again (!)

Dr James   Alright. Straight back to your room now, please. Make
sure you've got your box on, yeah? Someone comes to collect it in
the morning.

Tristan *and* **Connie** *inhabit bodies racked with expectant, alert
physicality, aroused and nervy in separate rooms. They begin texting
each other on the phones that Tristan provided. Every glowing
vibrating missive is a jolt of dopamine; a high, punctuated by a
stressful low awaiting the response. They become faster. It has the
quality of shared, separate electroshock therapy or cardiac paddles
that shock. It builds, the separation fuelling it.*

Eventually **Tristan** *has snuck into her room and he watches her
comittedly typing out a message to him with affection. He receives
it silently, and, unseen, sends her another. She leaps to the phone.*

Slowly, she turns round to see him.

Connie   You shouldn't be here.

Tristan   I know.

Connie   How are you feeling?

Tristan   I feel. Full. I feel almost ... holy. Like life is paying attention to me. I don't want to tell you anything about what I feel about you and what's just hit me about how I feel about you ... because it's not fair when you're ... I want to be good for you.

Connie   You're sweating.

Tristan   It's hot.

Connie   I'm cold.

Tristan (*touching his sweat*)   God.

Beat.

Tristan   How do you feel?

Connie   Bursting. I can't stop it. Something's in me but it's like it's come from outside of me. Like having the weather inside.

Tristan   I do too.

Connie   Do you? Really?

Tristan   Yeah, I'm just not fighting it.

Connie   Tristan?

Tristan   Yeah?

Connie   Do you feel different?

Tristan   Yeah. No. I just feel ... happy.

Tension. Sexual.

Tristan   I'm not going to take advantage of you.

Connie   I think I'm going to take advantage of you.

Tristan   I think I'm in love.

Connie   Are you?

Tristan   Maybe you are too.

Connie   Maybe. I'm not sure what it is.

Tristan   I feel it really though.

Connie   Do you?

Tristan   If you're in love there's nothing you can do about it.

Connie   But if it's something else, something else controlling me –

Tristan   Then you're not in control.

Connie   Yes.

Tristan   Yes.

Connie   There's nothing I can do about it.

Tristan   Yes.

Beat.

Connie   I'm in love.

Tristan   Yes.

Connie   That's such a relief.

They rip off the telemetry boxes they are wearing to measure their heart rate. They make love.

Darkness.

Light. **Connie** *and* **Tristan**.

Tristan   What are you thinking?

Connie   What?

Tristan   What are you thinking?

Connie   I don't know how to begin answering that.

Tristan   Just, tell me what you're thinking.

Darkness.

Light.

Connie *is hitting* **Tristan** *with his own hand.*

Connie   What are you hitting yourself for? What are you hitting yourself for?

Tristan   I want you to hit me.

Connie   Why?

Tristan   Cos then I can show how much I don't mind.

She hits him a bit too hard and then kisses and squeals in apology.

Darkness.

Light.

Connie   I'm really heavy though.

Connie *is climbing onto* **Tristan***'s legs who is lying on his back. He balances her thighs on his feet as she balances in the air, making herself 'fly'.*

Connie   Whoo!

Tristan   Shhh!

Darkness.

Light.

Tristan   Where will we live?

Connie   Paris, New York. A farm. Anywhere.

Tristan   I'm opening a dry cleaners.

Darkness.

Light.

They look directly at each other, look away, look back.

Darkness.

Light.

Tristan   I know they don't want to see me. You know I hear that from people. But you know I would have settled. I would have – I was okay being a disappointment. I was happy to be an acceptable failure.

Darkness.

Light.

Connie *and* **Tristan** *are making love face to face.*

Connie   Ask me who's in charge.

Tristan   What?

Connie   Ask me who's in charge.

Tristan   Who's in charge?

Connie   You are.

Darkness.

In the darkness.

Connie and Tristan   I / I love you.

Pause Experiment Here

Wait fifteen minutes.

Begin Again

A memory:

Toby   Are you okay?

Dr James   Yeah, you?

Toby   Yeah.

Dr James   I remember with mine, it took ages. You know, years. And this nurse said to me one day, everyone dies like this now. Unless it's a motorbike crash or someone really old in their sleep, occasionally, but everyone else it's like this. A long time and really really bad.

Toby   Sure. I mean we're all supposed to be dead by now. We're designed for what, thirty or forty at most? People have kids now when they should die. (*A laugh.*)

Dr James   Sometimes I think I am. I'm dead and my body just hasn't caught up.

Toby   What?

Dr James   Don't you get that?

Toby   No (!) How's your leg?

Dr James   Oh yeah, fine.

Toby   It's more than fine, it's beautiful.

Dr James   No.

Toby   Show me the scar.

Dr James   No Toby.

They part.

Back today.

Dr James *holding a variety of tampons in her hands.* **Connie** *is choosing between them, slightly shyly.*

Dr James   When did the bleeding start?

Connie   Just now. This morning.

Dr James   Before or after your dosage?

Connie   Before.

Dr James   I'm sorry I can't give you any painkillers.

Connie   I don't need any. It's just early, I think.

Dr James *pockets the surplus.*

Dr James   So. It seems your telemetry box must have come off last night while you were in bed.

Beat.

Connie   Oh, yeah, did it?

Dr James   But then you must have put it back on.

Connie   That's right.

Dr James   It's best to reattach it *before* you drift off, when you're comfortable.

Connie (*makes to go*)   Okay.

Dr James   The exact same time as Tristan's did too.

Connie   Oh.

Dr James   Looks like I'm missing eight hours of each of your hearts.

Pause. Breathing.

Dr James   / Connie.

Connie   / That's weird. Sorry.

Dr James   What is it you're sorry about?

Connie   Nothing, actually. I wanted to see if he was alright, he was ill, we've both been feeling pretty dodg–

Dr James   How do you know he was feeling ill?

Connie   How do I know?

Dr James   How did you know?

Connie   Text.

Dr James   He texted you on a phone?

Connie   Yes.

Dr James   You know phones are banned, they interfere with the equipment.

Connie   I know.

Beat.

Connie   How?

Dr James   Sorry?

Connie   How do they?

Dr James   The signal they give off.

Connie   What though?

Dr James   It … interferes with medical electronic devices.

Connie   It doesn't seem like that can be true though, people would just be dying everywhere wouldn't they?

Dr James   Have you had sex? I need you to be honest with me.

Beat.

Connie *makes a sound of discomfort.*

Dr James   Just answer the question, medically! Have you had sex in the last twenty-four hours?

Connie   Yes. But none of it went, where it would have to go.

Dr James   He didn't ejaculate inside you?

Connie   God (!) No! Don't write a sonnet about it.

Dr James   You know that's no protection against anything. There's still all sorts of risk.

Connie   Really? Or is that like the way phones interfere with the equipment?

Beat.

Dr James   You know you're going to have to leave.

Connie   Fine. Chuck us off. Least then I'll know.

Dr James   Not both of you. You.

Connie   Why?

Dr James   Because twinkle over there doesn't have a womb.

Connie   No! – Look, we didn't really. I'm sorry. We were just messing about. There isn't any risk of anything.

Dr James   I'm not your sex education teacher, Connie. I'm trying to run a trial, which you've put into jeopardy.

Connie   I understand there's a leasing of bodies involved here, but you can't expect to police how we feel.

Dr James   That is exactly my role. The drug is designed to stimulate transmitters that are linked to poor decision making and risk-taking –

Connie   You can't give us something that causes poor decisions and risks then have a go at us for … taking risks and making bad decisions!

Dr James   That's not a bad point but you don't know what you feel.

Connie (*deeply distressed*)   I know and it's horrible!

Dr James   This has to stop.

Connie (*ferocious*)   I think only one of us in on the drug, the way you give them out and the way I feel today I think he is and I'm not.

Dr James   During all trials someone has to be on placebo, to compare to, a control.

Connie   But if I'm on a placebo, he's on it, saying all this I can't believe him. It's driving me mad!

Dr James   That's exactly why you shouldn't be involved.

Connie   I think I might be in love with him! You have to tell me.

Dr James   I can't give you any information. It compromises the trial.

Connie   I'll just tell Tristan we both have to leave and then … then –

Beat.

Dr James   Is that what you want to do?

Beat.

Connie   At home in real life. I have a boyfriend.

Dr James   Right.

Connie   And I do love him I think. But if I did why would I –? I keep thinking is this real, or is that … real?

Dr James   I can't help you with that.

Connie   Why? Aren't you a psychiatrist?

Dr James   I'm a person (!)

Connie   Talk to me like a person then.

Dr James   Okay … (?)

Beat.

Dr James   I was having a rough time, quite a few years ago. I'd broken up from a long relationship I'd been in forever and that was a big decision and I'd lost a parent after a long … time. And I was supposed to be going away for work, a conference, but I didn't know if I could, I'm afraid of flying and I nearly didn't make it. But I did, and that week turned out to be one of the best weeks of my life. Professionally and just – I met lots of interesting people and got very – you know it was good. And I got on very well with one guy there who was great and funny and a force of real joy in the room. Even though I was a mess – and well he was married – but it was one of those chance encounters that give you hope, because you think god, there are great people out there and they seem to think I'm great and … So on the flight back I was sat next to another doctor, a woman, and she recognized me and we talked and she knew this guy and she said, oh you didn't sleep with him did you? And I say no why?! I did. So apparently he really puts it around, he's this notorious shagabout on the conference circuit and younger, less astute girls would, you know. And it was strange because it wasn't til then – … As we flew back I sort of felt something dissolve, in the jet stream, like something got eroded down. And by the time I got back it was dark.

Connie   I'm sorry.

Dr James   No (!) I'm saying it should have ended there, that's all. But it went on.

Connie   Tristan's not like that.

Dr James   OK.

Connie   Please. Just tell me what this is.

Beat.

Dr James   Tristan's not on the drug. Connie. He's on a placebo.

Connie   Oh.

Dr James   You see?

Connie   Right.

Dr James   So he's vulnerable in a different way.

Connie   But – he says he feels like he's on it –

Dr James   That's what happens. It's normal.

Connie   Is that okay? To lie to him like that …?

Dr James   It's essential. You know, the history of medicine is mostly just the history of placebo since we know now almost none of it worked.

Connie   Gosh. My head. It has to stop, doesn't it.

Dr James   It has to stop. We're scheduled to increase dosage again today. If you can keep this … you can stay.

INCREASE IN DOSAGE: 150mg

Connie *and* **Tristan** *take their pills. A moment of* **Connie** *blanking or rejecting* **Tristan**.

Tristan   Something's wrong, I can feel it.

Dr James   Wrong in what way?

Tristan   Why's Connie pissed off with me?

Dr James   I don't know that she is. I want to focus on the physical.

Tristan   I'm shaking like a leaf, I feel on the edge of a heart attack –

Dr James   Really.

Tristan   Yeah are you not interested?

Dr James   Of course I'm interested.

Tristan   Can I say anything?

Dr James   You can. You're completely safe.

Tristan   Quite intense thoughts. You know. Bit much.

Dr James   Intrusive –

Tristan   Yup. A lot of. Sexual. You know.

Dr James   Okay. Well. I wonder why that might be.

Tristan   Normally it's graphic, but this is … quite angry.

Dr James   Right.

Tristan   Do you not give a shit? Sorry (!) No actually screw it, this is your drug I'm living. I'm supposed to tell you. I feel giddy and I feel dizzy. And I feel tense.

Dr James   Okay.

Tristan   (*aggressively jokey*)   I feel giddy. I feel giddy. (*Sung.*) I feel giddy and dizzy and tense!

Dr James   Okay –

Tristan   'Okay'.

Dr James   Is it not okay?

Tristan   No, just, I tell you that and you're like, 'Okay'. Feels like, I don't know, like that joke, what's that joke, that guy in a doctor's office and he's showing him those ink blot things and he says, 'that's some people fucking' and he shows him the next one and he says, 'that's more fucking' then he shows him another one and he says, 'God that's extreme fucking fucking'. And the doctor says, 'Do you ever think you might have a sexual problem?' And your man goes, 'Hey, doc, you're the one with the dirty pictures'.

Beat.

Dr James   You know humour is a great way of disguising hostility.

Beat.

He makes a noise to scare her.

Tristan   That's it not disguised, is that better? I miss Connie. I miss her mouth.

Dr James   You know she's in a relationship.

He is wounded by this and made angry.

Tristan   Yeah I know what the fuck's it to you?!

Dr James   Do you want to take a break and do this later?

Tristan   Not particularly, not fucking particularly.

Dr James   Okay.

Tristan   Why are you looking at me like that?

Dr James   I'm just noting your agitation. Is there anything else to report?

Tristan   No. Yeah. Why I was – Look. Even if I have sexual thoughts, and I am, there's no reaction, downstairs. Nothing's happening.

Dr James   Right. Are you talking about temporary impotence?

Tristan   Well I hope it's fucking temporary. You don't want to get sued.

Dr James   For how long?

Tristan   Today and last night?

Dr James   Just today?

Tristan   That's not normal for me, okay? I know my body.

Dr James   I'm sure.

Tristan   Something's wrong.

Dr James   That must be worrying.

Tristan   Yeah.

Dr James   Are you worried something's damaged?

Tristan   But you can't look at that, can you?

Dr James   Because I'm a woman?

Tristan   No because you're not a doctor like that.

Dr James   Psychiatrists are doctors. We go to medical school and everything.

Tristan   Oh right.

Beat.

Dr James   Do you want me to –

Tristan   Are you going to have a look?

Dr James   Are you happy for me to?

Tristan   Yeah. Delighted. Fuck it. Yeah.

Dr James   Okay, do you want to just get yourself ready?

Dr James *exits, presumably to get gloves.* **Tristan** *begins to undo/ take down his trousers.*

Tristan *waits a beat, then doesn't see why he should, does up his trousers, and runs, free, to find* **Connie.** **Tristan** *has found* **Connie.** *He hugs her. They kiss passionately.*

A man in a doorway. His shoulders heave with breathing. It's **Toby.**

Dr James   I feel like something awful's going to happen.

Toby   … Okay.

Dr James   I think we should exclude one of the volunteers from the trial. A boy, a guy, the man who's on placebo in fact. He's not dealing with the environment. He's shown aggression and instability, now he's not eating. In any other environment I'd be worried for his mental health.

Toby   They've been in a sealed ward for weeks now, anyone would get frustrated –

Dr James   It may be linked to his relationship with the other volunteer.

Toby   There's only one dosage left, surely invalidating the trial –

Dr James   It's not going to invalidate the trial, removing one control subject –

Toby   We have a duty of care to him at this stage.

Dr James   No we don't, he's clean! We can just discharge him today –!

Toby   That's not appropriate.

Dr James   I'm used to helping people, you know, not putting them in a situation that distresses them. I don't think I can do this.

Toby   Yes you can.

Dr James   Is it me? I'm terrified it's me. Have I done something? It doesn't make any sense.

Toby   Okay, Lorna … Calm down. This isn't what you think. He is a test subject. His symptoms are relevant. And we need to monitor him as such.

Dr James   I give out the pills, Toby, /

Toby   / You don't know what you're giving out. They're active agent just packaged differently. Deliberately. He's on the drug. We're testing practitioner bias, alongside. As well. To see if there's a difference in what you report, according to what you think they're being given.

Dr James   You're testing *me*?!

Toby   It's not un/ usual –

Dr James   You're testing *me*!

Toby   I know how you feel about all this and I *still* got you the position here, because I know you're a good / doctor.

Dr James   / Oh god okay, I'm grateful. Thank you Mr Raushen, thank you for picking me up off the street in your limo on the way to the next expo –

Toby   All we're doing is monitoring you for practitioner bias which we often do with new recruits –

Dr James   Bullshit!

Toby   – in key areas, and I know you're feeling exposed –

Dr James   You lied.

Toby   – or confused and you know that's an irrational response.

Dr James   I thought I was losing it! That's why you're testing me isn't it? So our volunteer *is* being medicated with powerful psychiatric drugs and I'm telling you they cause aggressive behaviour and paranoia, it's dangerous to continue.

Toby   We don't know that's the drug! You just said, you said yourself it's about the relationship with this girl! I'm not closing down a whole trial because of a lovers' tiff!

Dr James   (This can't be pulled apart. We're crazy to think it can.)

Toby   This is why we do trials! We're here to record side effects and if aggression is a side effect, we'll note it.

Dr James   There's no such thing as side effects, Toby, they're just effects *you* can't sell.

Toby   God that's bitter, Lorna.

Dr James   I've seen you hold that brain and fleece them for money. But somehow *I'm* the one that's biased – (!)

Toby   You sound it, listen to yourself. You've spent this whole time refusing to accept the drugs have any effect, until you think there's something damaging!

Dr James   You literally only publish trials with the results you like!? But apparently you're unbiased and I'm … What?

Toby   You are a good doctor, who suffers from profound depressive episodes which she refuses to medicate. And you're desperate for any evidence that supports that position.

Beat.

Dr James   (They don't work.)

Toby   Pardon?

Dr James   They don't.

Toby   How would you know?

Dr James   There's no real evidence for the efficacy of anti-depressants, there never has been. / Everyone who knows, knows this has been the biggest disaster in the history of medicine!

Toby (*in frustration*)   / Mmmmmmmm. you can do what you like but you can't speak for most people. Most people improve on anti-depressants.

Dr James   In the short term!

Toby   If you're going to kill yourself tomorrow, what do you care if it's short term? Every time you have an episode, every time, the brain is altered and makes the next one longer and deeper. The sooner you start to medicate, the more you protect yourself. You could have done that –

Dr James   What, forever?

Toby   No! Or yes, depending how you are, it's very common –

Dr James   It's not an it, Toby, we're talking about me! What if it's a symptom, not a disease? What if it's a useful pain, throbbing, saying 'change your life, change your life' then you come with your pills and take all that away –

Toby   Well you never took them, Lorn, how'd your life go?

Dr James   Fuck you! You know us so called depressed people actually have a more accurate view of the world, a more realistic view of ourselves and others –

Toby   In mild and moderate depression, yes.

Dr James   Who are the vast majority being medicated! We're not deluded, you are.

Toby   This is why I get annoyed, Lorna. You cling to the mystery. You celebrate it, almost.

Dr James   I do what?!

Toby   You don't want it to be curable, you want to make it grand and tragic, it doesn't have to be.

Dr James   You think I *like* it! You think I like it!?

Toby   It doesn't make it less to accept it's chemical. It *helps* most people.

Dr James.   Say I'm mad if you like. But don't say I've got a disease.

Toby   Call it what you like –

Dr James   Oh thank you –

Toby   All I've ever wanted is to help you.

Dr James   I don't want your help!

Toby   I know and it's infuriating!

Tristan   I love you. I'm sick with missing you. (*He kisses her. She pulls away.*)

Connie   No.

Tristan   What?

Connie   I want it to be fair.

Tristan   Fair? What?! Is this about him? Have you talked to him?

Connie   I'm just trying to keep this safe.

Tristan   Safe? Are you frightened of me now?

Connie   No. Should I be?

Tristan   Yeah I'm a fucking monster. Just say what you mean.

Connie   I am. I'm saying no.

Tristan   To what?

Connie   I'm in a relationship and you're clearly not a relationship kind of guy –

Tristan   Where did that come from?!

Connie   You're a flirty, you know, bit of a player type –

Tristan   No I'm not!

Connie   I've seen you flirt with the doctor for god's sake.

Tristan   Are you joking? Christ Connie, she's nearly fifty!

Connie   Yeah, are you saying women can't be attractive in their forties?!

Tristan   What, I'm the one that's been flirting with her apparently! … Has she been saying things about me?

Connie   It's none of your business.

Tristan   You're not telling me something.

Connie   You're being weird.

Tristan   You're lying.

Connie   I haven't said anything, how can I be lying?!

Tristan   By not telling me stuff.

Connie   There's loads of stuff I'm not telling you all the time, otherwise it would be unbearable!

Tristan   That's exactly the sort of thing people say when they're lying.

She runs her hands through her hair in stress. Her hair comes out in her hands.

Connie   My hair's coming out.

Tristan   Mine's coming out too.

Connie   Yeah but not because of the drug.

Tristan   Fuck you.

Connie   I didn't mean that!

Tristan   Just don't rewrite what's happened. Don't make out / I'm –

Connie   / I'm not! What do you care anyway? That's in the past. I thought you wanted to live *now?*

Tristan   I want *you* to live *now.* You're always talking about what happens afterwards or how we got here, tell me what you feel *now?*

Connie   It doesn't matter what I feel, what does it matter –

Tristan   / Because I'm asking you!

Connie   I don't know!

Tristan   You're so scared. Why are you so scared all the time?! It's like being with an old woman. What might go wrong though?

Connie   This is my life!

Tristan   Exactly!

Connie   You don't care do you?

Tristan   Course I do.

Connie   Because you just want it now. You know maybe you *should* start thinking about the future a bit.

Tristan   What?!

Connie   This isn't exactly a gap year, Tris. It's become a sort of gap life.

Tristan   That's a terrible thing to say to me.

Connie   Then don't say I'm boring just cos I'm not giving you what you want!

Tristan   Are you saying I'm not good enough for you?

Connie   No I'm saying sort your*self* out / –

Tristan   / I'm punching above my weight?

Connie   – before you make out I'm a coward. I'm happy with my life.

Tristan   Ha! Yeah course you are, you look happy, you look fucking delighted!

Connie   You've got no idea how I feel.

Tristan   *Tell me*!

Connie   You're like a child.

Tristan   I'm fine for a quick fuck but secretly you want the older, duller man who's gonna *provide* and bring some cash to the fucking table?

Connie   Oh my god /

Tristan   That's basically what you said –

Connie   / what are we even talking about?!

Tristan   Gap life!

Connie   I'm the one that's sat there and watched you do your cheeky twinkly stuff with the doctor and you were a bit of a sleaze with me early on what am I supposed to think?!

Tristan   I don't – You're the one in a relationship, as you keep going on / about

Connie   *You* go on about it!

Tristan   – I'm allowed! I can do what I like!

Connie   Oh so I'm a slag now?

Tristan   No! Put away your paranoia, love.

Connie   Don't call me love. It's so tacky.

Beat.

Tristan   Connie. Con. Come on. Kiss and make up.

Connie   No, I feel sick.

Tristan   I make you sick (?)

Connie   I didn't say that. I'm not going to kiss you. I don't want to be sick on you.

Tristan   I don't care. Be sick in my mouth. I'll eat it up.

Connie   I *said* I feel sick!

Tristan   Am I a bit coarse for you? Is that it? Are you used to something more refined? Some wine-drinking chino-wearing cunt?

Connie   You don't get to talk about him, you understand?

Tristan   I wasn't! Is that what he's like! Came to mind pretty fast!

Connie   You keep shaking up my view of him and I think it's manipulative –

Tristan   Of course it's fucking manipulative!

Connie   You've never met him!

Tristan   That's why it's easy to slag him off! Come on, it's a joke!

Connie   It's a joke. Your way of getting out of everything. It's a joke. So now I'm a slag with no sense of humour.

Tristan   Oh my god, you're insane.

Connie   Everything I'm saying makes sense if there's a problem it's with you understanding!

She makes a gesture of his stupidity. He frustratedly roars at her.

Connie   What do you *want* to happen? I mean, really?

Tristan   I'll tell you what I want. I don't want to *reason* with you. I want to know right now, in this moment, what you *feel*.

Beat.

Connie   I … I feel. Oh god. I think I don't love you the way that you love me.

Ow. (*Pause.*)

Tristan   Right. Well you want me to look into the future. Fine. Go home. Suck on his old cock. Stay with him for two years longer than you should, out of guilt for him having left his wife and kid for you –

Connie   He didn't –

Tristan   Tell yourself you've invested so much now and it was nothing with me and you're getting rougher looking while he's staying the same and he's a good dad and before you know it you're forty-five, fucked and caring for some old cunt with cancer.

Connie *bends double with the pain of it.*

Connie   I hate you.

Tristan   Have you been calling / him?

Connie   / I physically hate you.

Tristan   – telling him everything's fine, you miss him. Have you used my fucking phone to do that?!

Connie   You gave it to me.

Tristan   Give it to me.

Connie   I don't have it.

Tristan   You're a liar.

Connie   You're scaring me.

During this, there's a tussle. He gets the phone and practisedly looks through it. He throws it on the floor and smashes it.

Beat.

Connie (*cold*) You just broke your own phone you stupid Irish cunt.

They physically fight. She ends up getting hurt and this becomes clear.

Connie   Stop. Tris.

He sees she is bleeding. She sees she is bleeding. To him it is a tragedy, to her it is a triumph. He backs away, in distress. Then to her, in sorrow.

Tristan   I'm sorry. Sorry. It's the drugs.

Connie   *Now* it is?!

Tristan (*crying*)   I can't handle it.

Connie   Stop it.

Tristan   I'm losing it.

Connie   Bullshit. You're not even on the / drug, Tristan.

Tristan   / I'm having a whitey.

He seems about to be sick.

Connie   You're not on it. She told me.

Tristan   What?

Connie   You're on a placebo. This is all just you.

His body tries to absorb the information.

The doctors, elsewhere.

Dr James   Why am I here?

Toby   What, *here?*

Dr James   Yes. Why would you offer me work? This isn't what I do. I sit with people, I talk to them, I –

Toby   I want to help.

Dr James   Yeah but why? You see, I wonder if you feel guilty.

Toby   About you?

Dr James   Yes.

Toby   Not particularly.

Dr James   Not particularly?

Toby   Is this what we should be talking about now?

Dr James   I don't know. What do you think?

Toby   Are you saying you think I caused it?

Dr James *is silent. A therapist's silence.*

Toby   I don't think I caused it, Lorna.

Dr James   Then why am I here?

Toby   You're a good doctor.

Dr James   Then why are you testing me?

Beat.

Toby   I didn't cause it and it's a cruel thing to say.

Dr James   I didn't say it. You did. You seem upset.

Toby   Just –

Dr James   It was years ago.

Toby   I know.

Dr James   And I've had what you'd call episodes since then.

Toby   I know.

Dr James   So why do you feel so bad? Look at me. It's not your fault, Toby. In the mountain of shit the world dumped on me that year, the dump you took was minor. It was barely a contributor. It could have been anything or anyone. So don't *you* make it into some big thing.

Beat.

Toby   I don't think I caused your depression, by ending things, Lorna. I don't think I contributed even. But maybe, maybe I think I ended it *because* of your depression.

Dr James   Right.

Toby   And maybe that's worse.

Dr James   No. Just sad. And are you happy now?

Toby   Well not right now, but yes.

Dr James   So. And how old is she, this new one?

Toby   What does that have to do with anything?

Dr James   Just wondering. Twenty-eight? Twenty-nine? You're so keen to make me a prisoner of my insides. What about you? Her clear skin to indicate lack of disease? Waist not yet travelled up to her tits? All the signs of the fertility that you don't actually want? We're all just walking examples of a biological fact, Toby.

Toby   You're ill, Lorn. Please.

Dr James   I'm not though.

Toby   My choices, or biology, or whatever, don't cause me suffering.

Dr James   No, only others. So you'll be fine. You'll do fine. (*Pause.*)

Toby   It's entirely within our rights to assess you. It was never an indication of any lack of faith. I want you to finish this trial. I think you can do it. Then we'll talk about the future.

Dr James   (Fine.)

Dr James *leaves.*

Connie   Tris … Tris?

Connie   I love you. You can feel that (?)

Tristan   I don't know what that is.

Connie (*desperate*)   Yes you do! You do.

Tristan (*untouched*)   This is horrible.

Connie   I can't bear it when you're sad in case I caused it. And I can't bear it when you're happy in case I didn't.

Tristan   Sometimes I think I'll only be happy when you're dead.

They look at each other, and away, appalled.

Dr James *enters and begins preparing doses.*

Text reads:

Final dosage, highest toleration: 250mg single dose

Toby *enters and observes.* **Dr James** *facilitates, resenting* **Toby***'s stare and the drugs themselves.*

The final dosages are administered with the usual countdowns **Tristan** *first.*

Dr James   5, 4, 3, 2, 1.

Tristan *tosses his dose back with contempt for its nothingness.*

Dr James   5, 4, 3, 2, 1.

Connie*, anxious, gets given hers.* **Dr James** *avoids checking her mouth afterwards as she is glaring at* **Toby***. In the moment,* **Connie** *rushes to* **Tristan** *and kisses him full on the mouth. She's kept her pill in to transfer to him, which the kiss does. She covers his mouth with her hand to encourage him to swallow.*

Connie   (I love you.)

He makes the decision to swallow her pill. They look into each other's eyes. **Dr James** *notices something.*

Dr James   What's going on, / what did you do?

Toby   / What's happened?

Dr James (*to* **Tristan**)   Show me the inside of your mouth.

She checks the inside if his mouth with a light, then his eyes as she sees his pupils are dilating.

Dr James   Is everything okay, Tris/tan?

Toby   / Did he take something else?

Toby *seeks to intervene,* **Dr James** *turns to* **Connie** *who is worried they are going to stop him swallowing. This all happens quickly.*

Connie   No, let him!

Dr James   Did you give / him something else?

Toby   / Is your name Tristan? I'm Toby. Have you taken anything else?

Tristan   I'm / fine.

Dr James   / How much have you given him?

Tristan   Connie?

Connie   I'm here.

Tristan   You've got a … halo ...

Dr James   Tristan?

Tristan *makes a strange sound, he staggers, loses consciousness, falls to the floor, stiffens. His limbs jerk and twitch. His mouth gurns. He is fitting. He bleeds from his mouth and wets himself. It is horrific.*

A scuffle.

Connie *withdraws at the close up and puts her hands over her ears briefly in shock then begins tearing at her skin.*

Connie   Get it out get it out of me!

An alarm and darkness.

Connie *is taken away.*

Dr James *is left to clean up.*

Dr James *has a bucket in which she finds a brain.*

Dr James   All we are is this three pound lump of jelly. But it's not necessarily me is it? I want to be happy. I want to work hard. I want to not shout out swear words on the street. I want to sleep. It must know this. It must want that too. If it's me. But. Here I am, where my father held me on a climbing frame and I can see my shoes on the bar. Here, how much I like meringue. Here's my respiration control. Here's my impulse to kill myself. Here is my controlling that impulse. 'You're disgusting. And you're only going to get more disgusting. It's too late. This all gets worse and you can't even cope with now'. Shhh. Let's not. 'You're like your mother'. It's too hard. Other people manage (!) And still. 'You can't do anything. You can't work, well you could but you're lazy. This is the best you're capable of looking now and it's shit and you're decaying. Look at your teeth. And everything everyone says about you is right. And you're weak and you're a coward and you've ruined people's lives. And you should have done it a long time ago and you never will now'. Just put some clothes on and then we'll go from there. It would be better'. Just put on some pants. Then we'll deal with the next bit. Just do that. 'It would be better just to stop'. But people love you. No they don't. Even the people who love you hate you because you're hurting the person they love. Why can't you stop?

Collapse.

Eventually ...

Now it is **Tristan** *in a bed on a drip.*

Connie *enters, looks at him. Eventually, he sees her.*

Tristan   I'm thirsty. Do you have water?

She sees there is water, or gets water from her bag.

Connie   Hello.

Tristan   What day is it? You look scared. What happened? Is it me? What happened? (*He touches his face.*)

Connie   It's Friday.

Tristan   I don't know anyone. Why am I here? You look frightened? What happened?

Connie   You've had a blood transfusion. They told me you have something called transient global amnesia.

Tristan   Yes. Have I? Yes. Why are you looking at me, am I still me?

Connie   Yeah. You just have new blood. It's okay.

He panics.

Tristan   Can I see?

Connie   See what?

Tristan   I need a mirror.

Connie   Oh.

She thinks, looks round, scrabbles in bag, opens up a bit of make up with a tiny one, hands it over.

Tristan stares at bits of his face, waving it around to get sections of face and so a fuller picture. She stares at him.

Tristan   What's happening? What day is it?

Connie   It's Friday. It's your birthday.

Tristan   How is that today? Show me a thing saying that's today.

Connie   The date?

Tristan   Yeah.

She hunts, comes up with only her phone and shows it to him.

Tristan   You could have changed that.

Connie   Why would I do that?

Tristan   Have I been asleep then?

Connie   You've got something called transient global amnesia.

Tristan   Yes, I – transient, does that mean –

Connie   It's going to pass. They don't know when or how long –

Tristan   What was I doing before you got here?

Connie   I don't know. I wasn't here.

Tristan   What day is it?

Connie   Friday. It's your birthday.

Tristan   No. Is it? Something else.

Connie   That it's my birthday too. You remember that?

Tristan   No. Oh god oh god oh god.

Connie   You don't know me, do you? You're not retaining any new memories it's me, you know me, do you know my name?

He does not reply.

Connie   How do you feel?

Tristan   I'm hungry.

Connie *finds a yoghurt and gives it to him.*

Connie   We were on a trial. Do you remember?

Tristan   I'm not being stupid, something awful's happened, I don't know where I am!

Connie   You're in the hospital. Do you know what day it is?

Tristan   Yes.

Connie   It's okay if you don't.

Tristan   What day is it?

Connie   Friday.

Tristan *looks at the yoghurt in his hand. Meaning drains from it. He offers it to* **Connie**.

Tristan   Is this yours?

Connie   I'm going to feed you this yoghurt right now.

Tristan   Okay.

Connie   And then we'll go from there.

A glimpse of **Dr James** *who has taken to bed with depression.*

Connie *enters, casual, busy.* **Tristan** *is in bed. He is alert but blank.*

Tristan   I don't know anybody here. Why am I here?

Connie   Shh, it's okay. I know. I was just here.

Tristan   No, you don't understand, I just woke up!

Connie   I know, you've got something called transient global amnesia –

Tristan   Transient, does that mean –

Connie   Yes it's going to pass.

Tristan   What day is it?

Connie   It's Tuesday.

Tristan   Is that right?! Show me something, with the date on.

Connie *gives him a newspaper, practisedly. She gets out a mirror, practisedly, he looks at himself.*

Tristan   I have to go! I – why am I here?

Connie   You're having trouble remembering, forming new memories.

Tristan   I'm trying to think the last thing I remember.

Connie   That's okay.

Tristan   But I know you.

Connie   That's right, Tris.

She begins giving him a bed bath.

Connie   That's right. Before the seizure. You and me were on a trial. Weeks ago.

Tristan   Do you work here?

Connie   No. That's new, do I work here (!) How do you feel?

Tristan   Awful. My balls ache.

Connie   I bet they do. You've got a stiffy all the time. God knows why.

Tristan   I'm scared.

Connie   I know.

Tristan   I'm hot.

Connie   I know.

Tristan   I feel sick.

Connie   Relax.

She looks around. She touches his erection under the sheets.

Connie   Always. Poor thing.

Tristan   Jesus.

She masturbates him.

He sighs, relaxes.

Tristan   I thought you were my sister, maybe. – You're not, are you? Actually no don't tell me.

Connie   No. I do this most days. I love how you're funny. I would have thought you needed memory to be funny.

Tristan   I thought you were here to give me a bath.

Connie   Well do you want this or do you want the bath, cos there's no point giving you the bath first.

Tristan   No. This.

She masturbates him. It's affectionate but practical. When he's ejaculated she finishes washing him, and her hand. She pecks him on the cheek.

Tristan   Am I your boyfriend?

Connie   I broke up with my boyfriend.

Tristan   I'm sorry. I'm trying to remember the last thing I remember. What day is it?

Connie   It's Sunday. Do you remember me, Tris?

Tristan   You're who I know.

Connie   Yes but who is that?

Tristan   I – wait –

Connie   How many times d'you think we've had this conversation?

Tristan   You don't understand I can't remember waking up! I wasn't there! Oh god this is terrible! Get someone, for god's sake!

Connie   We say this every day.

Tristan   No!

Tristan   What day is it?

Connie   It's Wednesday. How do you feel? Are you thirsty?

Tristan   I'm freaked out. I'm trying to think what the last thing I was doing was.

Connie   I had a haircut.

Tristan   I can't remember anything.

Connie   I know. I'm sorry I was joking.

Tristan   What's going on?

Tristan   Something's really wrong I can't, there's nothing going on before this?!

Connie   I know.

Tristan   What –?

Connie   It's Tuesday.

Tristan   What –?

Connie   You had a bad reaction on a trial.

Tristan   Where?

Connie   Hospital. You have a thing.

Tristan   –?

Connie   Here.

She gives him a mirror.

Connie   Here.

She gives him a paper. She gets out a nail file.

He looks baffled.

Connie   This is the day we do your nails.

She files his nails.

Tristan   Do I love you …?

Beat. This is new.

Connie   I don't know. Do you?

Tristan   I don't know.

Beat. She absorbs this.

Connie   If you're there. Help me. I don't care what it was I see that now. You were right. I just want one conversation like it used to be so you can help me. You won't believe this but I swear, I would rather get old and argue with you every day than ever love anyone else.

Tristan   Why are you sad?

Dr James *in a bed.*

Toby *enters. He has a cup with pills in it.*

Dr James *can't really respond properly socially. Eye contact and natural limbic response is all gone. It's like she's elderly and exhausted. All social response and interaction takes effort, which she does her best to provide, and they are received with a grateful understanding for that.*

Toby   Hey you. Still here I see. Thought you might have made a break for it.

It's crazy weather today. Can't decide anything.

They wanted me to bang on at you about the fluoxetine again but I know you hate it and it's not my favourite either to be honest.

Do you want to know about anything else?

Dr James   (What about the boy?)

Toby   Well obviously we don't know what the long-term effects will be yet. Turns out he had history of childhood seizures which was undisclosed so that's … Nothing will be published obviously.

She indicates she wants to know about **Toby**.

Dr James   (What about you?)

Toby   Oh I'm okay. Don't worry. The lecture circuit. Lining up round the –. And I think now I might finally write that book.

Dr James   I'm sorry.

Toby   Don't be sorry.

She doesn't accept this.

Beat.

Toby   Wait, I can tell you something about the boy, he's going home with her, the girl from the trial. He's in recovery but …

It still hurts her and she blames herself.

Toby   It's not your fault.

Dr James   I don't have enough skin.

She cries.

Dr James   I just want to go. I want to go.

Toby   No no no.

Dr James   I'm sorry.

Toby   This is a storm. It passes.

She doesn't believe this.

Toby   I love you, Lorn. And it's not romantic with … the lies of that, and it's not family, like, a genetic trick. I just. I've built a bit of my brain round you. And it's important to me. So. Please.

This is too much emotion.

Toby   Do you want me to go?

She's emotionally exhausted. She nods.

Toby   I'm coming back tomorrow. I am. I've got a thing in the morning but I'll do my best. Please will you think about things for me?

He leaves a cup with drugs in for her.

Around her, but in a different space, **Connie** *and* **Tristan** *have been getting his things together to leave his ward. He is okay, but vulnerable, his physicality is of a different man, without some former bounce. She is practical, tired, supportive.*

Connie   What else?

Tristan   That's the lot.

Connie   Your shoelace.

Tristan   It's alright. I don't have any change.

Connie   It's okay, I got a cab. I told you.

Tristan   A cab (!) I'd have got the bus.

Connie   I know you would. I want a cab. We'll get cash out on the way. Did I do the drawer?

He looks. He's not sure. She checks.

Connie   I'm really nervous about you seeing it. It's a shithole.

Tristan   What is?

Connie   Where we're going back to. Mine.

Tristan   Why?

Connie   Because that's what we're doing today.

They head towards the door.

Connie   Why don't you just do it up?

Tristan   What? It doesn't matter.

She bends down to do his shoelace up. He doesn't want this and goes to do it himself.

Tristan   Fine.

He does bend down and does the laces.

Tristan   I'm not doing it up cos I can't. I honestly couldn't be arsed.

Connie (*during*)   (That's worse)

Tristan (*joking*)   Oh, will you … (shut up woman)

It takes him longer to do than it should an adult, but eventually he does.

He finishes.

Tristan   Is it cold?

Connie   It's coldish.

He adjusts some clothing appropriately. They both look around the room.

Connie   Right. Okay? Oh.

She suddenly checks her bag/pockets, looks round the room.

Tristan   Y'alright?

Connie   Yeah just thought I'd lost my phone. No there it is. Okay. Happy?

Tristan   Yeah. You?

Connie   Yeah.

Tristan   Okay.

Connie   Let's go.

Connie *and* **Tristan**, *unsmiling, together, walk out into the real world.*

Dr James, *alone, looks at the cup/pills* **Toby** *left, decides, and after counting down from five in her head, takes them.*

Underneath this we hear the sound of an EEG: electrical activity in the brain produced by neurons firing. Underpinning this is the bass of a heart beat from an ECG. These are the sounds of human love.

End experiment.

A Very Expensive Poison

For Marina

A Very Expensive Poison premiered at London's Old Vic Theatre on 20 August 2019 with the following cast and creative team:

Thomas Arnold	Emmerson / Sergei / Mario / Tim / Brezhnev
Tom Brooke	Alexander Litvinenko
MyAnna Buring	Marina Litvinenko
Callum Coates	Martin / Dr Virchis / FSB Officer 2 / Onstage Swing
Marc Graham	DS Hoar / Nurse David / Youth 1 / FSB Officer 1 / Ruslan / Onstage Swing
Amanda Hadingue	Professor Dombey / Lluba / Dr Bhatt / Photographer
Yasmine Holness-Dove	Natalia / FSB Officer 3 / Youth 2 / Waitress 2 / Dr Dudhniwala / Onstage Swing
Lloyd Hutchinson	Dimitri Kovtun / Kamishnikov / Radiologist / Yeltsin
Robyn Moore	Galina / Receptionist / Technician / Marie Curie / Onstage Swing
Peter Polycarpou	Boris Bereszovsky / Walter / Dr Gunner
Sarah Seggari	Cabin Crew / Australian Cleaner / Nurse Rezan / Youth 3 / Nurse
Michael Shaeffer	Andrei Lugovoi / Dr Gent / Gorbachev
Reece Shearsmith	Vladimir Putin / Jon
Gavin Spokes	DI Hyatt / Man with Stick
Bea Svistunenko	Anatoly / Nurse Michena / Waitress / Lludmilla

Written by	Lucy Prebble
Based on the book by	Luke Harding
Director	John Crowley
Set & Costume	Tom Scutt
Lighting	Mimi Jordan Sherin
Sound	Paul Arditti
Choreographer	Aletta Collins
Composer	Paddy Cunneen
Video	Ewan Jones Morris
Casting	Jessica Ronane CDG
Voice	Charles Hughes-D'Aeth
Dialect	Penny Dyer

Act One

A massive clap of thunder shuts us up.

Scene One

London. 2013. Coffee-shop

It's raining. Really raining. We're in London. A winter 5pm.
Marina Litvinenko (*40s, Russian, proper, alert, striking*) *sits one side of a small square table in a Pret-type place waiting for someone. An utterly drenched* **Ben Emmerson** (*50, Brit, charismatic, learned*) *enters. Raincoat soaked, glasses steamed.*

Emmerson   Marina, huge apologies.

He puts his broken umbrella in the umbrella stand-type thing by the door.

Emmerson   This bloody thing's broken.

Marina   Come, come. Don't worry, I'm early.

Double kisses. **Emmerson** *sits with her.*

Emmerson   So what's going on? How are you getting on?

Marina   I'm OK. I'm tired.

Emmerson   I'll say you don't look tired.

Marina   Well I am! Do you want any/thing?

Emmerson   / No I'm perfectly alright if they're alright with that, let's see. Yes. I wish I was bringing you better news.

Marina   Oh.

Emmerson   There won't be an inquest. At least not a meaningful one. The foreign secretary, in his infinite wisdom, has submitted something called a PII. Public interest immunity. It's to limit the scope. It means that the inquest could not consider at all whether the Russian state was involved.

Marina   O . . . K?

Emmerson   Yah, which kind of renders the whole thing meaningless.

Marina   But why? Why would they forbid us from discovering if the Russian state is involved?

Emmerson   Well it's what we've been seeing for the last few years. It's inconvenient. Um, they don't want to annoy the Russians or be seen to provoke in any way.

Marina   They think *we* will be seen to provoke?

Emmerson   Yes, quite. And I'm afraid in an additionally miserly gesture, Chris Grayling is . . . withdrawing any legal aid from you, going forward.

Marina   Oh God.

Emmerson   He really is a colossal tit. I don't want you to worry about that on my account –

Marina   No, of course I do!

Emmerson   It's all part of the same strategy really which is to try and get you to shut up about it! Which I suggest you don't.

Marina   You have to be paid.

Emmerson   I don't really. Apart from that bloody umbrella, everything I own is quite nice already.

Marina   No, I won't accept you working for me for free. I'm sorry / I don't have any –

Emmerson   / It isn't chivalry, Marina. It's the law. And for better or worse I find it rather galling when it's ignored.

Marina   But there's nothing now to do?

Emmerson   Mm. Except . . .

Marina   Ah!

Emmerson   Ah indeed. What might get you something approaching justice . . . I suggest forgetting the inquest –

Marina   Which is what they want us to do.

Emmerson   Yes, but what I suspect they very much don't want us to do is suggest a public inquiry.

Marina   And this is different?

Emmerson   Yes, a public inquiry, as it sounds, is out in the open, very public. How they did it, why they did it, and who is responsible.

Marina   In public? In the news?

Emmerson   Yes.

Marina   But we know what happened!

Emmerson   We do. But to turn the truth into justice – which I'm sorry to say are not the same thing – one has to tell the story. Not just to a lawyer, not just to a judge. To the country.

Marina   And it will stop it happening again, yes?

Emmerson   Ha, I think the government view this as a rather unique occurrence. I can see you might not want to relive it all. Things might get hairy.

Marina   I know what could happen.

But I have no money to pay you.

Emmerson   I'll tell you what I'm going to do. I'm going to take someone else's umbrella. It's very naughty. But consider it a down payment. Alright? Why don't you take one and come?

Marina   I'm waiting for the rain to stop.

Emmerson   You shame me, Mrs Litvinenko.

Marina   I have no intention to shame anyone.

Emmerson   Come on, room for two. I'll walk you to the Tube.

She relents, gets up.

Emmerson   What do you think, Marina? Shall we bring it to the country? Don't think they bite.

Marina   Of course.

Emmerson *and* **Marina** *step out of the scene under his umbrella. They look out at us.*

Emmerson   I'll let you speak.

Emmerson *goes, leaving his umbrella with* **Marina**.

She speaks to us, out there, in the darkness. She is nervous.

Marina   Hello. How do you do. In November 2006, my husband and myself came into the Accident and Emergency department of the Barnet and Chase Hospital in North London. He was complaining of a lot of pain and, well, maybe you will see. My name is Marina. Litvinenko.

Around her, NHS hospital staff swarm and that's cos we are in –

Scene Two

A&E Department, Barnet Hospital, North London – late 2006

Alexander Litvinenko (*40s, I will now refer to him by his nick-name,* **Sasha**). *Though tall, strong and handsome, he is very reduced right now, clutching his stomach, ill. For a moment,* **Marina** *sees him again, her dead husband. And then she is back in the past.*

Marina   Sasha! Come on.

Marina *and* **Sasha** *approach reception.*

Marina   Hello. We need to see a doctor.

Receptionist   Right OK, hi, are you the patient?

Marina   My husband is very ill. He is very weak. And . . . being sick. And from behind – there's blood in that.

Receptionist   OK. Don't worry, you're here now. This is him, yeah?

Marina   I'm his wife.

Receptionist   Can he talk to me?

Marina   Yes, but I am better.

Receptionist   OK, he has to answer a few questions.

Sasha *shuffles to front.*

Receptionist   What's your name?

Beat.

Marina   His name is . . .

Receptionist   Tricky one.

Sasha   Mr Edwin Redwald Carter.

Receptionist   And what's your address?

Marina   140 Osier Crescent, Muswell Hill.

Receptionist   And when were you born?

Sasha   I was born 12th December, 1962, in Voronezh in Russia.

Receptionist   Twelve twelve six two. OK –

Sasha   I am a British citizen.

Receptionist   I don't mind what you are, darling. So, vomiting?

Marina   Yes, and sick many times. And blood and shit I am sorry.

Sasha   I cannot eat. Pain. Stomach.

Receptionist   OK, someone's going to see you as soon as possible. Take a seat. Do you need a bucket?

Marina   I – . . .

Receptionist   For vomit or – . . . Well, vomit mostly, really.

Marina   Thank you.

They go to sit down.

Man with Stick   No no no no no Fulham!

Sasha   We should not be too far from the bathroom.

Marina *tries to comfort* **Sasha**, *stroking his arm and back.*

Marina   Are you going to be sick?

Sasha *is trying to tell. Is he? Maybe.*

Sasha   It's OK.

Marina   Have more water.

Marina *takes a small plastic bottle of water out of her bag and gives it to him.*

Sasha   You don't have to stay.

Marina   Why are you being ridiculous?! What you being like that for?

She holds his hand, shakes it with affection and worry, looks around for possible help.

Sasha   Let's go through the times so we can tell them. It started night before last night. After dinner, very sudden.

Marina   And you were sick, and it was that strange colour.

Sasha   And then – I couldn't breathe. Maybe write down . . . I was sick seven to ten times, in one hour.

Marina *makes a few notes on a piece of scrap paper.* **Sasha** *looks queasy.*

Jon   Has he been drinking, has he?

Marina   No.

Jon   You'll go in before me as well, you wait.

Marina   He is very ill, sorry.

Jon   That's OK. You live here then?

Marina   We live in London six years.

Nod.

Jon   So is he your husband then?

This is too depressing to acknowledge.

Man with Stick (*half-sung*)   No heroin, no heroin, no no no can make you feel!

Nurse Rezan   Mr Edward Carter?

Nothing.

Nurse Rezan   Edward Carter? No Carter?

Just as the **Nurse** *gives up,* **Marina** *realises.*

Marina   Yes! He is – yes!

Nurse Rezan   OK, hi! We've actually not got an area right now. There's a vulnerable patient who is using the space. So . . . Are you happy to talk quickly here?

Sasha *nods.*

Nurse Rezan   So what's the problem?

Marina   After dinner, very suddenly, and he was sick and it was not the right colour, he said and he was breathing very like . . .

Nurse Rezan   OK, Edwin? Does it hurt when you touch your stomach, Edwin?

Sasha (*trying*)   I don't know. There is pain.

Nurse Rezan   How long has he been feeling unwell?

Marina   Two days he has been very sick. Vomit. And diarrhoea. Blood in that.

Nurse Rezan   Any pre-existing conditions? Medication? Drugs? Any alcohol?

Marina   No. He does not drink alcohol.

Nurse Rezan   We've had a lot of winter vomiting virus at the moment.

Marina   No no no – my son had that.

Nurse Rezan   And they live in the same house?

Marina   Yes before, no this is different.

Nurse Rezan   And anything eaten or drunk that might be a cause for concern in the last forty-eight hours? Anything raw or undercooked or . . . ?

Sasha   I had some sushi from a sushi restaurant. But that is normal.

Nurse Rezan   Ahhh. I cannot get my head round sushi. I know it's the thing but I'm always disappointed, can't look forward to something cold. OK. What I'm gonna do is, if there's a room free, we'll do basic checks, blood pressure, urine.

Mrs Carter you can wait here or come along.

Marina *talks to us.*

Marina   I go in with them, of course. I just want to say he is not one of these men who, he was not 'Oh I have a cold I am dying' sort of man, yes? This was not normal. He was very healthy, fit, you say. It was difficult to get him to go and see a doctor. So in that way, I suppose, yes, like a typical man. I am saying this is why we waited, to come.

In the centre of the stage, a **Nurse** *readies* **Sasha** *for his bed. Tests maybe, also changing into a hospital gown. We are in –*

Scene Three

Barnet Hospital, Sasha's Room, 2006

Marina *is able to move between the room and us, tracking the days with trips to the vending machine.*

Marina (*to us*)   The first day everything seems better. He has a thing you put in your arm, you know? It is not so frightening. With everyone around.

The roll and the thunk of a dispensing vending machine as **Marina** *gets a drink. She hurries back and gives it to* **Sasha**. *They have been waiting a while.*

Marina   Has nobody come yet?

Sasha   No.

Marina *sighs. It's been ages. But then, at last! A doctor!*

Dr Bhatt   OK. Gastro-enteritis with mild dehydration.

Marina   Hello. Someone said they are checking for typhoid.

Dr Bhatt   Goodness me, that's imaginative. No, I think we're past typhoid these days. You look a bit better, though?

Sasha   Yes.

Dr Bhatt   Good strong voice. We've prescribed ciprofloxacin, that's a broad-spectrum antibiotic so very little's going to be able to hide from it, OK?

Sasha   A month ago I was made a British citizen.

Marina   They know that, darling.

Dr Bhatt   Keep drinking it out. Should see improvement in the morning. Lots of fluids. OK? You're in charge.

And the doctor has to go. And so **Marina** *finds herself heading out to the vending machine. The roll and the thunk of the dispensing vending machine.*

Marina (*to us*)   The next day though he is not better, in fact, some things are worse.

The roll and the thunk of the dispensing vending machine.

Marina (*to us*)   And the next day, again.

She takes that day's drink back (probably bottled water) into the room.

Day Four

A **Nurse** *is taking his temperature/replacing an IV. Fussy, kind.*

Marina   Is someone coming?

Nurse Michena   The normal doctors aren't around on Saturdays.

She clears away a mug, and exits.

Marina   You should tell them who you are.

Sasha   I have! What do I say?

Marina   That you know bad people. That someone might have done something to hurt you! That might change something!

Sasha   They are checking for everything. What am I supposed to say?

Marina   Why are you being so secret?

Sasha   I'm not! I just do not think that it is likely I was a victim of that!

Marina   . . . You're embarrassed, aren't you?

Sasha   No I'm tired. They will find out what it is and then I will be OK. I am a big boy.

Marina *isn't sure.*

She goes to the vending machine again. The roll and thunk of another day.

Day Five

Marina   On the fifth day, I decide to say to them, I do, I –
She enters back into the scene. But it's a different doctor.

Dr Dudhniwala *with* **Nurse David**.

Marina   Oh. Are you a doctor?

Dr Dudhniwala (*checking notes*)   Yes . . . I am – I know you've been dealing with Dr Bhatt, but she is . . . yes. OK, what we're concerned about today is there are two issues. One is that your . . .

Marina   Husband.

Dr Dudhniwala   Edwin's white blood cell count is very low which we don't normally expect with gastro-enteritis.

Sasha   You can talk to me also.

Marina   Could somebody have given him something?

Dr Dudhniwala   We have and we're wondering if, yes, it's a side effect to the antibiotics. Have you ever ta/ken antibiotics in the UK before?

Marina   / No no, someone put something in his food, before. My husband knows some bad people. He has been made ill by on purpose. He has – tell them, tell them –

Sasha   They will check for that.

Marina   He is embarrassed! He is embarrassed because he thinks he has been tricked by someone and he thinks that is impossible. That is what you think!

Dr Dudhniwala   Well that seems unlikely.

Nurse David (*to* **Marina**)   It's been a really long day today. Do you want a tea?

Dr Dudhniwala   But what I'm going to do is record that in his notes.

'Patient and wife concerned about intentional infection of patient, query, poison?'

Everyone feels a little silly. Except **Marina**.

Dr Dudhniwala   Your husband's right, that's very unlikely.

Nurse David   Don't be afraid to go home.

Marina *backs out to the vending machine. Another day, another drink. Another. The roll and thunk.*

Day Seven

Marina   This is the seventh day.

She returns to see two doctors already there. This is weird.

Marina   What is happening?

Sasha   The doctors are checking me for being made of metal now.

Dr Bhatt *and a new doctor,* **Dr Gunner**.

Marina   I am sorry but we will take him somewhere else I think. I do not know what you are doing with your . . . tests. Because every time is a different man, every time is a different woman.

Dr Gunner   You wouldn't want to move him to another hospital at this point.

Marina   I don't want to move him! It is not my position to move him! You do not know / what is happening –

Dr Bhatt   / It's nothing to worry about, in fact it's good news. Edwin does have slightly elevated thallium levels –

Dr Gunner   Which is a heavy metal.

Marina   I don't –

Dr Bhatt   But what we're saying is, he's not showing any of the other symptoms of thallium poisoning, no pins and needles, no numbness . . . I don't think that's our issue. That's good.

Marina   What is making his hair coming out?

The doctors check their notes. Nothing about this.

Dr Gunner   His hair?

Sasha   My hair is – . . .

Marina   When I was stroking his head. I put it in a cup.

She hands them the cup of his hair. They look at it.

Dr Gunner   Right.

Bit of a puzzle aren't we?

Another roll and thunk of the vending machine. Another.

Day Ten

Now worthy of more attention, **Sasha** *is being looked at by a collection of three – count 'em three – doctors.*

Dr Virchis   You know. It looks like. You know when someone's had very aggressive cancer.

Dr Bhatt   Has he ever had cancer or treatment for cancer?

Marina   No.

Sasha   I am still here, everybody.

Dr Virchis   Those patients with acute leukemia, the ones who have very intensive chemo. He looks . . . Have you ever seen anyone with acute radiation sickness?

The roll and thunk.

Marina (*to us*)   Day eleven. They actually put – what you call – a Geiger counter on him.

Three doctors, plus a radiologist, plus a technician who holds a Geiger-counter and wears a mask. No sound.

Technician   This is its normal sound. If there was anything it would go mad, clicking. Some of them make a whining sound. This, this is the one they use on building sites.

Dr Gunner   Do you ever work with dangerous materials? Building sites, that kind of thing?

Sasha   No.

They all look at each other.

Dr Virchis   Is there anything different, other than Beta and Gamma? That it could be?

Radiologist   Nothing we could test for. For Alpha rays you need to go to an actual weapons lab. Or maybe . . . we could try if we had enough urine?

Someone brings in a very big container for urine.

Marina (*to us*)   Day twelve.

Day Twelve

The roll and thunk. The roll and thunk. The roll and thunk.

Marina   This is all day twelve. They say he needs to fill a bottle.

Marina *has got lots of drinks from the vending machine.*

Sasha, *drinks as much as he can, drinks some more, pisses. Drinks some more.* **Marina** *watches, helps.*

Marina   I believe in you. Come on.

Sasha   Marina, listen, I need you to do something for me.

Marina   Of course.

Sasha (*almost clandestine*)   I need you to bring me something from home. In the boiler cupboard, there is a toolbox.

Marina   Yes?

Sasha   Bring me the toolbox.

Marina   OK. Can I ask why?

Sasha   The shower down the hall is broken. It is annoying. No one will fix it unless I do it.

Marina   No! You are an insane person.

A **Doctor** *and a* **Nurse**, *masked, gloved come in. The container is done up, taken.* **Sasha** *and* **Marina** *sleep. At 4am the door opens and light spills across the couple, waking them.*

DI Hyatt   Mr Carter, are you awake?

I'm sorry to call so late, Mr Carter, my name's Detective Inspector Hyatt of the Metropolitan Police's specialist crime unit. We're here investigating an allegation that you may have been poisoned in an attempt to kill you.

May I call you Edwin?

Sasha   Yes. But my name is Sasha.

Behind the policeman, doctors.

Dr Bhatt   This is Dr Gent from the atomic weapons facility. You'll remember we sent a litre of urine to Aldermaston to test the unlikely theory there was an internal source of radiation causing your illness.

Sasha   Yes.

Dr Gent   I'm Robert. I'm from Porton Down, the UK's military science facility.

The urine test has revealed the presence of a radioactive isotope called Polonium 210.

Sasha   Hello.

Dr Gent   Hello, Sasha. Polonium 210 emits Alpha particles which explains why it wasn't picked up by the tests done previously, which search for more common radiation types.

Sasha   And I guess I am not a superhero now.

Dr Gent   No. In sufficient quantities, quantities we believe you've ingested, death is inevitable, just not immediate.

Dr Bhatt   Your bone marrow is failing and you are neutropenic. Do you know what that is?

Sasha   It is why I have a fever.

Dr Bhatt   Yes. You don't have enough white blood cells. It is life-threatening, I'm afraid. Do you understand me, Edwin?

Sasha   So I will die?

Dr Gent   I'm sorry.

Marina *makes a sound.*

Sasha   When?

Dr Gent   We haven't encountered any example of this before. But I have to say, I am amazed I am talking to you now.

Pause.

Hyatt   Edwin, I am sorry to have to do this, but do you have any idea how this might have happened, or who might want to do this to you or why?

Sasha   Yes.

Marina   He knows who would do this.

Sasha (*to* **Hyatt**, *then himself*)   Detective. Detective.

Marina   He is saying he worked the same job as you. He knows.

Sasha   But they must be able to prove it.

OK. We have not much time. I need my notebooks. Take my email password and bank account number. You will find receipts for two Orange SIM cards bought from a shop on Bond Street in a black leather wallet on the table next to my bed.

Sasha *can speak to* **Marina** *or to* **Hyatt**. **Marina** *can speak to us.*

Marina (*to us*)   For you to understand, we have to go back to before London, back to Moscow. For him to understand also. He stayed up all night with them, the policemen. And he had to tell them everything about everything.

Hyatt   Why would anyone want to poison you?

Marina   There is a job he used to do in Russia.

Sasha   We have to go back, to when they asked me. When they said to do the murder.

Marina   We had just moved in together.

Sasha   Ten years ago.

Marina   Twelve. It was Spring.

Sasha   Yes. '94.

Marina   We were young, in love. We had both been married before so we knew a lot about who we were. Yes?

Sasha   I don't know what you want me to say.

Marina   We were happy, is all I am saying – ?

Sasha   Of course. It's just not relevant.

Marina (*to us*)   That is the best I'm going to get.

Hyatt   You were asked to commit a murder? By who?

Sasha (*to* **Hyatt**)   I was asked to do something, for work. It began everything and now I think it is coming back on me again.

Marina (*to us*)   It is Moscow. 1994. At this time everything is falling apart, in Russia it was chaos or some brave new world, depends who you talk to. Everything is upside down, inside out. But inside, you are just trying to be normal. Live.

Sasha, they're here.

Scene Four

The Moscow Flat, May 1994, 8.32pm

The young couple are joined by **Walter** *(***Sasha***'s father) and his partner,* **Lluba***. Greeting.*

Marina   Hello!

Sasha   Hello.

Lluba   Good evening. Nice to meet you.

Sasha   You know my father, you know Marina. Marina, this is Lluba, my father's . . . I dunno what do I say, girlfriend, not wife –

Lluba   Saviour.

Walter   Albatross.

Lluba   Just say concubine, nobody cares here.

Marina   Nice to meet you, Lluba. Oh thank you.

Some food has been given as a gift.

Walter   I told you she is beautiful.

Lluba   Yes!

Lluba *gestures, don't make out like we have been arguing about it . . .*

Walter (*about the apartment*)   Is this it, what I can see?

Sasha   Most of it, there is a bed. I don't think you want to see my bed.

Walter   No, I don't need to see your bed particularly.

Sasha   OK. Then yes, this is it.

Marina   We got it at a very good price.

Lluba   Is that because of the news we heard? Do they know? They know.

Marina   I know what you mean. It's fine. It wasn't here.

Walter   What are you talking about, so fast!? (*An impression of women talking fast.*)

Lluba   You know what we are talking about! You told me!

Sasha (*ever blunt*)   The guy who hung himself.

Walter   Ohhhhh.

Lluba   And we were saying, does that make the price better? It's ghoulish but I just asked.

Marina (*showing spread*)   Eat food.

Sasha   It probably did.

Marina   But it wasn't in here it was next door.

Walter   I bet they say that to next door too.

Sasha   Papa.

This hadn't occurred to **Marina**. *She turns on the radio.* **Walter** *and* **Lluba** *drink and smoke. Pop music plays.*

Walter   It doesn't matter, it's everywhere now. People either kill themselves or become millionaires, that is all there is now.

Sasha   Either way they move out of here, so. . .

Drinks have been served to **Lluba** *and* **Walter**.

Lluba (*toasts*)   Health!

Marina   Forgive us, it's bad luck with water.

Walter   You don't drink either, what a bore.

Marina   I do, I do, I do sometimes.

A new song begins. Russian but with Western influence. **Marina** *turns it up.*

Marina (*half-dancing, about song*)   I love this!

Walter   I'll dance with you in a minute, you see if I don't.

Sasha   Why do you say that like that? That's just a nice thing, that's a nice thing to say, why do you say it like it is dirt?

Walter   I am trying to be ribald. I am doing innuendo.

Sasha   That's not innuendo, that's just a fact that you will dance with her.

Walter   Marina teaches dancing.

Lluba   I thought she was an economist.

Marina   I trained in economics.

Lluba   I'd have thought there would be plenty of work for you now. Work out what the fuck is going on.

Walter   Ugh, you have a mouth like a sewer.

Marina (*about* **Sasha**)   Your son never dances with me.

Sasha   I dance constantly!

Marina   You liar!

Walter   I'd need another drink first. One or two. Then I'll polka. /

Lluba   / How long did that one last?!

Walter   So what? I am celebrating my son!

Sasha *has been somewhat ignored up till now.*

Sasha   I hadn't realised. Lovely.

Marina *pours* **Walter** *another drink.*

Lluba   What about your son are you celebrating?

Walter (*looking about for it*)   You know, he has a job. Look at that television. It's big. Is it American?

Sasha   Sony.

Marina   Look it has a controller.

She shows them the controller. They are impressed.

Lluba   You can do it from here . . . ?

Marina *dances a bit and sips water, watching them play with the controller. She swings her hips to the music.*

Sasha (*watching* **Marina**)   Hold on, she's dancing alone.

Sasha *gets up and goes to* **Marina**.

Marina   Very good. I trained him and said no woman can dance on her own –

Sasha (*private*)   Listen.

Marina   What?

Sasha   I think we tell them tonight.

He means about her pregnancy.

Marina   Oh you do?

Sasha   You told your mother.

Marina   My mother is who I want to know if something . . . goes wrong. If . . .

Sasha   Don't say that –

Marina   It's too early. They will buy presents and that will be a bad omen. When you can see it. When he is more there.

Sasha   But you're happy to say he?

She nods. Shrugs. Smiles. Dances away from him.

Marina   You want something else to talk about. That is what this is!

Sasha   No, I just think it might be ages till we see them again. Hopefully.

Marina   You do not use this child to make social situation less awkward. No thank you please.

Walter *is still impressed with the remote control. He points it at the audience.*

Lluba   I like this floor.

Sasha   Look, it's nine. That show we were talking about is on. Kukli.

Walter   I didn't understand what you were saying about it.

Sasha   I know, that's why I was saying you should watch it. Have you seen this, Lluba?

Sasha *takes charge of the controller. (Perhaps it is best if we don't see the TV and they face us to watch it).*

Sasha   Come. It's on NTV. Let's sit and watch it, it's funny.

Marina   I don't know how funny it is.

Sasha   You haven't seen this yet?

Marina   Oh, people have gone mad.

They gather to watch Kukli. Kukli *is a new puppet satire show with a slightly creepy tone. It is inspired by the British series* Spitting Image. *It mocks real politicians and famous figures.*

Marina *brings them all food without eating any herself.*

The olders are more confused.

Lluba   It's a cartoon?

Sasha   No, it's puppets, you know.

Lluba   But for children?

Marina   No no, it's puppets for adults. It's from Britain. A joke show. They are puppets in it but of real people in the world.

Walter   What puppets?

Lluba *scowls, leans in to see the puppets more clearly. As she makes out one of them, probably Yeltsin, her eyes widen and she physically recoils with shock, gasps.*

Marina *and* **Sasha** *laugh.*

Marina   She has seen!

Lluba *makes another sound.*

Walter   Who is it?

Lluba   The President! Look!

Walter *looks. Oh yes! They watch.* **Lluba** *laughs despite herself.*

Walter   Ah that is very stupid. It is childish.

Sasha   Papa.

Walter   It is mean-spirited. It is being personal to someone about how they look.

Marina   It isn't really, it's just a joke so you recognize him, everything's just bigger.

Walter   Turn it off.

Sasha   You're not even watching, you are talking over it! You can't hear it!

Lluba   Who is that one?

Marina   Who do you think?

Lluba   Shit, it's Gorbachev!

Walter   Why are people allowed to make fun of people this way?

Sasha   It's not very respectful.

Walter   I would be very upset if I was President Boris Yeltsin, say, with my family and I was sitting watching.

Lluba   Well he shouldn't be watching should he, he should be fixing the roads.

A knock at the door. **Sasha** *and* **Marina** *both go to get it.*

Marina   I got it.

Sasha   It's OK.

Sasha *gets there first, opens it to* **Sergei Ivanovich Orlov** (*FSB, 30s, dressed similar to Sasha but trendier, an edge of self-conscious style*).

Sergei   Forgive my intrusion, please, I am so sorry for it and my timing. I will go.

Marina   Please! You must not, I will be / so offended!

Sasha   / We're delighted to see you, Sergei Ivanovich. One moment.

Sasha *uses the opportunity to turn off the TV.* **Lluba** *is disappointed.*

Marina   Welcome! Come and have a drink.

Sasha   This is my father, Walter Litvinenko, and Lluba Litvinenko, his wife.

Lluba   Good evening.

Walter   Hey, I was watching that!

Sasha   You said it was terrible.

Walter   That doesn't mean I wasn't watching it. Good evening.

Marina   A drink? What will you have?

Sergei   Whatever Sasha's having.

Sasha   Oh no, that's water, I'm sorry, you forget how boring I am.

Sergei   Never, old friend! A tea man. Of course.

Walter   You'll take a vodka.

Sergei   I will. This is very nice.

Sasha *gets* **Sergei** *a drink.* **Sergei** *gives* **Marina** *some flowers he is carrying.*

Marina   You're very kind.

Sergei (*toasts*)   To your health and the occasion.

Sasha (*to* **Marina**)   Put the news on.

(*Back to* **Sergei**.) The bastards at work always say it's hard to trust a man who doesn't drink. And you know, I understand their / feeling –

Sergei   / Understand nothing except their need to cover up their own issues! I envy it, it's a sort of strength, you know. A person who will look at life as it is, continuously. I have to take breaks.

Sergei *swigs.*

Sasha   I have honestly thought of pretending, disguising water for vodka in my glass, to lie about it, just so people will trust me.

Marina, Walter *and* **Lluba** *watch the TV passively.*

Sergei   Beautiful family. I wanted to talk as a friend and tell you they're asking about you for a job and it occurs to me I should make sure you are interested before I recommend you.

Sasha   Oh! Of course. Thank you, Sergei.

Sergei   Otherwise you are in a position of . . . why did he, but you get it. You should do it. You're a good officer. And I don't mean to talk down to you as we are the same age but I say honestly, your detective works are excellent.

Sasha   Thank you, Sergei.

Sergei   No one would have had the courage to lead back where you have led back to.

Sasha   I simply followed the line of the case. You can't just stop when it's inconvenient. If you are smuggling . . . like that, someone is letting them in and then someone else is letting that go. Doesn't matter who, if it's our friends.

Sergei   They weren't *my* friends.

Sasha   No. Good.

Sergei   Took very large balls.

Walter *is trying to change the channel with the remote control but he doesn't know how to work it.*

Walter   Cannot see any of the – on the – stupid design!

Lluba   Give it.

Walter   I'll do it.

He can't do it. Frustrated, **Lluba** *goes to take it.*

Lluba   You haven't got your glasses.

Walter   Stop it woman!

He drops/throws it rather than give it to her.

Lluba   Why you always only angry or ashamed! It's like living with an ingrown hair. Just red and angry all the time. I have to (*mimes squeezing*) meh meh meh all the time to get anything out of you and when I do, it's horrible.

Sergei   You know Boris Berezovsky?

Sasha   Of course! Not personally.

Sergei   They are looking for somebody to help his security, look out for him. He was the victim of that terrible event, with the car –

Sasha   The car bomb, yes!

Sergei   And he is obviously an important man and a loved man, and don't get me a wrong, a somewhat eccentric man. The difficulty it seems with Boris, is to work out if anyone is trying to kill Boris or if Boris is trying to kill Boris. He's in the hospital now because he fell off his snowmobile while drunk. It's hard to know who to pin that on.

Sasha   This is not to take me from my duties. I'm a detective.

Sergei   Quite the opposite, You must still discharge your duties, we cannot lose you. It is because it is important. Anyway, I tell you because they will say so and you should have your answer prepared.

Sasha (*already on it*)   Yes, I see.

Sergei   And smile a little, Sasha. It's a very good job and, for everything about Boris, you know, it will be fun.

Marina   Will you stay for something to eat, Sergei Ivanovich?

Sergei   I have intruded enough.

Marina   Not at all, I insist.

Sergei (*gives in*)   Then you insist.

Marina *shoots a curious look to her husband. He gives her an affectionate squeeze, buoyed.*

Sasha   I'll tell you later.

Detective **Hyatt** *interrupts.*

Hyatt   Edwin. Maria.

He interrupts their intimacy.

Sasha   Detective.

Hyatt   So you were offered a job, to protect a man? I thought you were asked to kill someone?

Sasha   My job was to do what Russian government tell me. He was important man, very high up.

Hyatt   Are you saying the man you were asked to protect, he's in the Russian government?

Sasha   Boris is a businessman. But there is not the same divide in Russia.

Hyatt   But *you* were working for the Russian government?

Sasha   I work always in Russia for the FSB.

Hyatt   So I understand, Edwin, are you saying you worked for the FSB? Formerly known as the KGB?

Sasha   Yes.

Marina   No.

Sasha   Yes.

Marina   No, you say KGB. They think you mean spy. That is how they think . . .

Sasha   I worked for FSB in Russia but FSB is very big, many things, I work as a detective.

Marina   His work was against criminals.

Walter *has fallen asleep on the sofa with* **Lluba**.

Sasha   I work in the Anti-Terrorism and Corruption department of the FSB, my speciality, Organised Crime.

Marina   And he is very good.

Sasha   Yes.

Marina   Too good.

Sasha   Yes.

Hyatt   How are you too good?

Sasha   So, take typical man in FSB.

Alexander Kamishnikov (*older, heavier, tougher*) *comes in to the flat.*

Sasha   He comes in, he sees who can be of help to him. He see who could be threat to him.

Kamishnikov *gestures to* **Lluba** *and* **Walter** *sleeping: 'What's with these?'* **Marina** *shows them out.*

Sasha   He smokes, he drinks, he plays card. It's relationships that matter, loyalty is everything.

Kamishnikov *and* **Sergei** *sit with* **Sasha**. *The three FSB men are playing cards: drinks and cigarettes.*

Sasha   He never write anything down. You don't want records, you don't want evidence.

Marina   But this is the thing, Sasha breaks all of the rules. Just himself. He likes to do things, not to talk. And he is organized, he is careful, he writes everything down. It is very annoying!

Hyatt   So he has to work harder to be trusted?

Marina   Yes.

Hyatt   Because he is seen as too trustworthy?

Sasha *nods, now too in his own scene to risk speaking out loud.*

Marina   Exactly. Welcome to Russia. This is many months later.

Sasha, Sergei *and* **Kamishnikov** *are playing cards and drinking.*

Kamishnikov   Sasha, you can't go around turning things down. This is your job, not a woman's perfume shop, you look around, you try, no thank you.

Sasha   I was asked to do something illegal.

Sergei   He won't do wet jobs.

Kamishnikov   What, you think that's 'wrong', do you?

Sasha   Illegal. Yes and also wrong. If we're.

Kamishnikov   Christ.

Sergei   You know there is something about your . . . clarity, Sasha, which can be a bit much. It's like you've no flexibility of thought. Someone says something and you are black and white, it's child's logic.

Sasha   Just say I'm stupid, Sergei.

Sergei   Not stupid. But.

Kamishnikov   You're a Caucausus boy, aren't you?

Sasha   . . . ?

Sergei   Rude maybe.

Sasha   I was born in Vorozneh. My grandparents were in Nalchick and they raised me. I rather think you know all this.

Kamishnikov   Chechnya. Near enough.

Sasha   No, not near enough. You're either in Chechnya or you're not.

Sergei *and* **Kamishnikov** *exchange a glance.*

Sergei   You must discharge your duties properly. Otherwise it's embarrassing. You understand . . . ?

Sasha   Do I understand what?

They play cards.

Kamishnikov   Bereszovsky seems intent on pushing through a peace deal.

Sasha   Why are you – I just work for him. A peace deal with Chechen rebels is good for everyone surely.

Kamishnikov   Is it? Aren't you ashamed to say something so simple? A peace deal with Chechen rebels is good? How do you know, Alexander? Do you know all the details? Do you know all the Chechens involved? On what are you basing your tiny square of knowledge that a peace deal with Chechen rebels is good?

Sasha   My life.

Kamishnikov *cocks his head towards* **Sasha** *like, 'This one!'*

Sasha   I was in Chechnya. They are just defending themselves like our grandfathers did against the Nazis, you should –

Sergei   We are all fighting a war, Sasha.

Sasha   What war have you fought in?

Sergei   Metaphorically speaking. I don't mean to insult you in your own home but you are being obtuse.

Kamishnikov   Alexander Litvinenko. You must kill Boris Bereszovsky. Russia has fallen on hard times and there are people like him who are very rich who have robbed our Motherland; they have corrupted institutions and they are buying everyone in power.

Beat. What.

Sergei   I know what he's doing now, I can see it in his eyes. He is memorizing. He is memorizing what we are saying so he can note it down once we have left and be a good noticer . . . He doesn't care his friend Boris is at the trough.

Sasha　If Bereszovsky or anyone has wronged this country, a fair trial is the solution.

Sergei　Of course a legal route would be preferable. / Obviously.

Kamishnikov　/ Don't choose a dirty Jew over the Russian people, Sasha.

Sergei　It is necessary.

Marina (*to us*)　They were very clear with him, which is not always the way. I did not know all this at the time. Now I see how, after this, everything felt different. I thought maybe he was angry, or sad with me, missing his wife from before (?!) or I have done something wrong, you know? Stupid. He was in trouble and I was making things in my own head. What a waste of time.

She looks at **Sasha**. *The FSB men speak to us.*

Sergei　And since we're stopped you know, we never would have had this conversation in his house.

Kamishnikov　It would have been at work. If we had. Which we didn't.

Sergei　Never with the chance of being overheard. Never with the chance of being recorded. And never while drinking, we're not MI6.

Kamishnikov　It wouldn't be like this. If it happened. Which it didn't.

The FSB men collect their cards and lighters and leave.

Marina (*to us*)　So this tenseness goes on for weeks and weeks, but then, it breaks open. Something very bad. Like a box of Pandora. One night after we went out. This was not a joke.

Scene Five

The Street

Sasha　Come on, take my arm. Walk on the other side.

Marina *does. She's detached.*

Sasha   It was fun tonight, yes?

She nods. Her mind on something else.

Marina   You know there was another libel in the paper today. About your ex-wife.

Sasha   I know. I saw.

Marina   That you are not paying maintenance to her.

Sasha   I am paying maintenance to her!

Marina   That's why I said a libel.

Sasha   Yes. I heard that. Sorry.

Marina (*re: his face*)   What's wrong, it is like you are in pain, angry / all the time –

Sasha (*getting angry, an old fight*)   Just because I am quiet does not mean I am angry.

Marina   But you are angry, look! I'm right!

Sasha   Because you're accusing me of being angr – ! Marina, before we get back, put Anatoly to bed – I am in a position. You understand I want to tell you very little, yes? But you should know the situation, in case.

Marina   In case . . .

Sasha   I was asked to do something Boris, who I work for . . . might not like . . . and I told him about that. It was my duty. And today, the Lieutenant Colonel he took me aside, he said to me himself.

Gets out notes. Reads.

'You bastard, you're a traitor . . . If you don't shut your mouth we'll sort you out our own way.'

Marina   Sort you out?

'What do you think?' gesture.

Marina   Be specific, please.

Sasha   In case something happens –

Marina   Stop saying that. What did they ask you to do?

Sasha   Get rid of Boris.

Marina   Stop joking! This is . . .

What did Boris say?

Sasha   He didn't believe me either, Boris said he had been on holiday skiing with Yeltsin, they were friends! He couldn't believe someone he once went skiing with would try to kill him.

Marina   Well most of us would assume that. That's not a crazy thing to assume.

Sasha   I'm not making it up! I told him, cos I knew otherwise they'd quickly get someone else to do it and I would have been letting my friend be hurt as sure as if I'd done it myself.

Marina   Well. No. But OK . . . Is he, is Boris afraid?

Sasha   No, different from afraid. More, you know (*almost laughing*), when you discover someone really doesn't like you? You think why? What, what did I do? It was . . . he was hurt.

She nods, a hand hold.

Marina   I cut out that article about your ex-wife.

Sasha   Thank you.

She passes it to him to put in his notebook. He does. A moment between them. Thanks.

Hyatt   OK Edwin, so this was punishment for refusing to kill your boss? These stories in the paper?

Sasha   Yes but there was more. That was only very small –

*A **Youth** runs past the couple and barges into **Sasha** hard.*

Sasha   Damnit, yeah alright, wait.

Youth   What d'you say?

Sasha   That was not the worst. Watch where you're going.

Youth Two   I know this guy.

Youth   He bashed into me.

Sasha   That's not what happened.

Hyatt   Who are these guys then?

Marina *backs away towards* **Hyatt**.

Marina (*to* **Hyatt**)   We don't know.

Youth Two   I do, I know him. He touches kids.

Marina   OK, OK, you see the situation.

Hyatt   This is a mugging.

Marina   They are kids. They attack us on the street.

Youth Two   Don't fucking run, or we'll stab him.

Marina   One of them had a knife.

He has a knife.

Youth Two   I know I've got a fucking knife. Don't tell me what I've got.

Sasha   What do you want? Money?

Youth   You're in trouble, babe.

One of the youths dives and tackles **Sasha** *to the floor. Unprepared,* **Sasha** *goes down. Other youths surround him, swarming . . .* **Sasha** *protests, hidden.*

Marina   It has already happened. It has already happened so . . .

But it pains her still.

Youth Two   Shut up or we'll cut your tongue out.

Now **Hyatt** *is having to get involved, to keep them off* **Marina** *. . .*

Sasha   I'm FSB, you idiots!

Youth Three   Jew-lover.

Sasha *produces a gun we didn't know he had, standing. Almost fumbles it. The youths don't clear though. One just tries to wrestle it off him.*

Youth Two   Give us it.

Sasha *fires the gun into the air. This does scatter them somewhat.*

Sasha   FSB! Get back!

Did I hurt anyone?

Marina   No no, you OK?

Sasha   I'm OK.

Hyatt   You're saying this was not a standard mugging?

Sasha   No. This was one of many threats.

Hyatt   These kids were sent to kill you?

Sasha   No, in Russia it is more warnings, make your life impossible.

Marina   Don't make trouble. Is everything.

Youth (*to* **Hyatt**)   Mate, they gave us money. They gave us money and a picture. They didn't say he was police. They said we wouldn't get done for it. We've got no other work.

Sasha   This was the way of saying you are punished for refusing this order.

Youth (*to* **Sasha**, *leaving*)   Nothing personal.

Sasha   After this my gun got confiscated

Marina   His salary was stopped.

Sasha   When I asked at work, I was told that I had been suspended. But others denied this.

Marina *treats* **Sasha**'s *face.*

Hyatt So you believe you were being punished by the FSB or the Russian government for refusing to kill (*checks notes*) this – what's his chops – Boris Bereszovsky?

Sasha Yes.

Hyatt OK. And who is Boris Bereszovsky?

Marina *and* **Sasha** *look at each other. It is hard to believe someone doesn't know.*

Sasha He does not know.

Marina Oh goodness. You really do not know?

Sasha Why should he know? It's two worlds on top of each other.

Hyatt Give me a clue.

Marina (*to us*) And maybe you do not know! Boris – there is all this talk of him being killed and he has not even been introduced!

(*She turns to her husband.*) How would you – ?

Sasha *shrugs, big job. They giggle with each other. Where to start?*

Marina (*to us*) Love him or hate him, you cannot deny him.

Sasha (*to* **Hyatt**) Mathematician became . . . car salesman . . . became . . .

Marina Millionaire.

Sasha Billionaire.

Marina Media mogul.

Sasha Godfather of the Kremlin!

Marina The Original Oligarch.

Marina . . . Boris / Bereszovsky!

Sasha / Boris Bereszovsky

Boris Bereszovsky *has come on from the wings. Rotund charisma in a smoking jacket. We like him immediately. He smiles, carries two martinis and doesn't give a shit what you think.*

Boris *approaches and smoothly hands* **Sasha** *a martini, swapping for the gun which he pockets. The other martini goes to* **Hyatt**.

Hyatt   Oh, thanks very much.

We're all going to a fancy party at the –

Scene Six

Logo Vaz Club Hunting Lodge, Moscow

A whirlwind of Moscow's finest and some eccentric drinking types at a birthday party. There is some evening wear but the vibe is eccentric and characterful; ironed shellsuits too, '90s Russia style.
(Can be before or after the song.) **Boris** *picks a dazed* **Sasha** *up off the floor and dusts him off, concerned. He calls over some members of staff to see to the younger man's face, to provide him with a garish jacket, and* **Marina** *with a gown. It's warm and paternal.*
The party absorbs them.

Boris *performs Crocodile Gena's* Birthday Song *(preferably in Russian) to wish his wife happy birthday. A Russian song.*

Boris   Never mind that the clumsy pedestrians are jumping over rain puddles

And that the water is streaming down the street

And never mind that the passers-by can't make sense of

Why is it that I'm so happy on such a rainy day

Yet I'm playing my accordion

In front of everyone on the street

It's so sad that a birthday

Can only happen once a year

A wizard will suddenly appear

In a blue helicopter

And will show me free movies

He'll say happy birthday

And just before he flies away

He'll probably leave 500 ice cream cones for me.

Boris *ends on his knees offering his wife,* **Galina**, *a flower. She takes it.*

Boris   Happy birthday, darling. Now someone help me up!

Guests do, laughing.

Boris   I'm not much taller now.

Marina *comes back in in her gown.*

Marina   Shall we dance?

Sasha   All these people are here.

Marina   Oh no, and then all of these people will have seen you dance, what will we do?

His vulnerability is sweet to her.

Sasha (*re: bright jacket*)   I am wearing this, is it not enough?

Boris   Marina, you look beautiful.

Marina   Thank you, Boris Bereszovsky. Happy birthday, Galina.

Galina   Oh please, I do not acknowledge such things.

Boris   When are we going to stop living these lies and run away together?

Marina   Boris, stop being terrible –

Galina   He knows I am here.

Boris   I know this is the problem!

Galina   I hate you, darling.

Boris   I hate you too.

They kiss too much.

Boris   Sasha, you always look so serious! With your face.

Sasha   Happy birthday, Galina.

Boris   Come Sasha, let's have a picture together!

Boris *has his own photographers who he poses for as he walks. They snap one of him and* **Sasha**.

Boris   Sasha, I wish to apologise for how I reacted when you told me of the terrible threat to me.

Sasha   It's alright, Boris.

Boris   No no, I said 'Fuck off ' many times. In your face.

Sasha   It must have been a shock.

Boris   And I wept. I admit it. But you must understand.

I had been skiing with the president and his family.

Sasha   You said.

Boris   I consider him a friend. Like I do you.

Sasha   Anyone would have done the same.

No.

Boris   I think you are a piece of good fortune on my part. Listen. I have located the source of these commands against me, a jostle for power in Kremlin halls that shames us all. But not Boris Nikolayevich. Not Yeltsin. I never thought that could be. Everything will change now. We have spoken at length and he is sure to be re-elected.

Sasha   Can such a thing be sure?

Boris   Of course. Legally, democratically. My dear Sasha –

I have mastered mathematics, I have dabbled in oil, I have run the Russian skies, and with none of them comes the power of television. All Yeltsin. All the time. On my channels, on other channels. I have rearranged the situation.

Sasha But I thought Russia needs a new situation? Someone new?

Boris Exactly! But the opposite! We *are* to start again and only he can do that. New broom. Same man. He is grateful. He is vulnerable. That is how change happens. I know I talk loud, and I like a drink, but I'm not foolish. I have listened to every word you have told me about your life and your work and I have communicated all the corruption you found and the pressure you were getting, and pulled all the strings and an investigation is underway.

Sasha (*oh shit*) Into me.

Boris Into the FSB! Khokholkov has been transferred, and Kovalyov fired.

Sasha (*incredulous*) The director has been fired?!

Boris He was shaming Russia with these things. In his place, the FSB will be run by a young friend of mine, not a puppet, but a man of his word. Vladimir Vladimirovich. One of us. Now he's inexperienced, so he needs our help. He needs officers behind him. I told him you'd introduce yourself.

Sasha It is like my chest is . . . free again to breathe.

Boris You saved me first.

Sasha It's true. I've been waking up afraid and now I can live.

Boris For sure. Eat! Drink! I would say fuck but your wife is here!

Sasha I could do that with my wife, BB.

Boris You, sir, are an inspiration. Andre Luguvoi! You must meet Sasha Litvinenko. You're in the same business.

At the party is **Andre Luguvoi***, another tall, fair Russian. He is not yet the peacock he will later become.*

Luguvoi How do you do?

Sasha Hello.

Luguvoi Just for future reference the correct response is also 'how do you do'. In case you ever have to pass. Boris Bereszovsky, the women here are very beautiful and very rude.

Boris   Ideal surely?

Luguvoi   I asked for one's number she said what is *your* number, how much money do you have?! I laughed and said, 'OK, how big is your chest?' She made a face like a cat's arse.

Boris   Well never give up.

Sasha   Maybe give up.

Luguvoi (*to* **Sasha**)   Thanks for the advice, friend. I'm afraid I can't hear it over your jacket.

A statusy arm slap and **Luguvoi** *breaks away to cruise.* **Luguvoi** *re-approaches the young woman,* **Natalia** (*young but formidable*). *He has brought her a drink and offers it.*

Luguvoi   I bring you a drink, to apologise if you were offended by my wit.

Natalia (*takes it*)   Oh thanks very much.

Luguvoi   Are you having a good time?

Natalia   Mm. It's a bit old school. We are just going somewhere else. There's an American party in a loft somewhere East. My friend knows this man at the embassy.

She's off.

Luguvoi   Oh but you'll take the drink.

Natalia   I'm sorry?

Luguvoi   You'll take the drink.

Natalia   The drinks are free.

Luguvoi   Sure, that's why you're here, no?

Natalia   Oh I'm sorry, you want the drink back? Do you mind if I keep the glass?

She throws the drink at him. People around look. **Luguvoi** *tries to manage his humiliation. He succeeds. She leaves with her friend.*

Natalia   (I've never thrown a drink before?!)

Luguvoi (*to the room*)   No no, I deserved that. I deserved that.

Guests leave. Especially the women.

Luguvoi, *worse for wear and irked by rejection, approaches us. The party has degenerated into a few remaining male guests, slumped behind. In this light they could be passed out, they could be dead.*

Luguvoi (*to us*)   I don't think I did deserve that. I know it is the fashion now, ladies, when men humiliate themselves over you, to humiliate them some more. But I don't know how that's going to work out for you(!) (*He laughs, threateningly.*) Well perhaps I'll give *you* a number.

Twenty-five million. Twenty-five million men. Dead. For the Motherland. During the war. The waves of men that takes, you know. More killed at Stalingrad alone than the whole war took of your lot and America *combined.* There is pain here. There is trauma here. But it's different for Russia. Twenty-five million. Dead for being men. For being useful in that one way. They are the ones who discover the concentration camps. You know. The Russians reach them first, we know this. And there's this message back to Stalin, a complaint at some point, as they carry on their grim march across Europe, that these young soldiers are 'mistreating local women as they go'. And Stalin says, 'Yeah. I bet!' This is pain, this is trauma! And after the war, the US gives billions to rebuild to you, to France, to *Germany*! To *Japan*! But not to us. Twenty-five million. It is true we did not want it, that is true, but what sort of nation begs on its knees, to be controlled by whoever has the most money? Yes we have our pride. It is a virtue. You want men to be vulnerable? Oh, those young boys were shitting themselves. *Gorbachev* was vulnerable! He dismantles an empire for the greater good. 'Let us lay down our weapons.' Giving *away power*! *And you make us crawl.* 'We win!' 'You lose!' 'Get. On. Your. Knees.' (*He shakes his head.*) Shame on you. Twenty-five million.

Luguvoi *staggers, swigs, passes out among the other men.*

Scene Seven

FSB Office – 1998

Over the mess steps **Vladimir Putin**. *He is the new head of the FSB, trying to set up his new office. He is tidy, brittle, cautious. He is shorter than you'd think.*

Sasha *enters, with binders full of corruption.* **Putin** *is sat at his desk and there are a few moments before he notices (or chooses to notice)* **Sasha**.

Sasha   Comrade Colonel?

Putin *looks up, apparently surprised. Beat.*

Sasha   Or, Comrade Director.

Putin   Ah!

Putin *gets up, comes round and shakes* **Sasha**'s *hand, leading to uncomfortable shifting of all that* **Sasha** *is carrying.*

Putin   Yes, here we are.

Sasha   Can I – ?

Putin   Certainly, certainly.

The files get put on **Putin**'s *desk which he doesn't relish but doesn't have the nerve to deny.*

Sasha   Would it be appropriate to offer my congratulations, Vladimir Vladimirovich?

Putin   . . . Congratulate away.

Sasha   Congratulations. I'm Lieutenant Colonel Litvinenko.

Putin   I know! We have been meaning to see you for a while. We could not find you.

Sasha   I have been on suspension.

Putin   Oh dear.

Sasha   I think.

Putin   You wish to have your job back.

Sasha   Nothing so personal. I think we have a friend in common.

Putin   Oh, Boris!

He laughs. **Sasha** *laughs. Oh* Boris.

Putin   He has been something of a mentor to me.

A nod. A thaw. **Putin** *decides to sit behind his desk, leaving* **Sasha** *standing.*

Putin   I will sit here if you don't mind.

Sasha   I was keen to speak with you and Bereszovsky encouraged it.

Putin   That is why we are speaking.

Putin *stands. He isn't sure how to conduct himself. No easy confidence like* **Sasha**.

Sasha   I say it is not personal. Because there are bigger things, much more important.

Putin   That's true. I think we live in service to those bigger things.

Sasha   Exactly, that's why –

Putin   It does not matter what, I think: an ideology, a religion, a sense of country. But a man must have that larger sense.

Sasha   I think you will be interested and maybe even –

Putin   I remember I visited an official in St Petersburg, you'll like this. I think this as I'm trying to decorate my office. I visited him and noticed he had a very large cross behind his desk and as I looked around, every surface was saints and iconography. Jesus Christ and the Theotokos. The apostles. The Holy Mother in gold and wood. And I presented myself with piety and said, 'You are a religious man?' 'Oh very. Very religious.' 'And Russian Orthodox?' I said. 'This week,' he said. 'This week I am embracing of its power. I like to embrace something different each week, change the décor, let it inform me. As I said I'm *very* religious.'

He makes a gesture to indicate a wide spectrum on 'very.' A smile. A laugh.

Sasha   You must be minded to find your own vision for the FSB.

Putin   Do you wish me to present my vision for you?

Wait, who's in charge here?

Sasha   No, sir! You may discuss what you wish.

Putin   Yes well perhaps that is what I wish.

Pause. He doesn't have a vision.

Sasha   I think I can be of assista –

Putin   As I said it does not matter the type of cause but it must exist. People have to have a sense of past, and a sense of future. This is why you cannot just, say, draw a line under KGB then say this is FSB, this is new. You cannot make history a graveyard. You cannot be dead then alive, you see? You cannot replace the past with shame.

He rests a hand on the folders. **Sasha** *takes the opportunity to attack his purpose.*

Sasha   I have been awake all night preparing information. This is everything discovered about the connections we know between several large organized crime operations internationally and a few members of the FSB and government. This is a list of commercial companies who work to clean the money. This is specifically laundering.

Putin *looks at him.*

Sasha   Shall I continue?

Putin   Please. This is exactly your job.

Sasha (*pleased*)   This is a list of – wait, let me start here. There is a protection ring that operates within the FSB. I discovered they were receiving bribes from Central Asian drug lords to ensure the route of heroin from Northern Afghanistan to Europe via Russia. And all of those involved reported directly to, well sir, your predecessor who was taking his cut on the way. So if you have any fears of how you'll match up, sir, I wouldn't fear too much –

Putin   I have no fear of comparison to Khokolkov.

Sasha   You shouldn't.

Putin   No, I have no sense of competition.

Sasha   I don't mean to imply as much.

Putin   Good that I don't.

Sasha   . . . yes.

Putin (*pointing*)   And what is this?

Sasha   That's . . . that is just an arrow.

Putin   Yes obviously I know, what does it denote?

Sasha   Pointing to a link between a principal mob group and their area of activity, you see, here. That's just the arrow.

Putin   I understand that. I was pointing to the arrow – using my own finger as an arrow as it were – so that you might follow the arrow to the information and then describe it further for me, I was assuming you knew how an arrow worked.

Sasha   Yes. I drew it.

Something in **Sasha***'s simple confidence undermines his boss.*

Putin   This is neat and able work. We cannot go on as we are.

Sasha   Yes!

Putin   And this is good, this helps.

He is pointing at something which isn't particularly helpful. **Sasha** *isn't sure why. Is he stupid? Or trying to . . . impress him?*

Sasha   There's a lot of detail. Would you like to keep the scheme, to examine further?

Putin   No, it is your work, you should keep it. No, actually, I will keep this file, the others seem in the same vein. So, to start with.

Sasha   Absolutely.

Sasha *takes the rest of the files back.*

Putin   And maybe . . . give me your number, at home, and when I have more questions I can –

Sasha   Sure. It's 495.

Putin *doesn't write it down.*

Putin   495.

Sasha   892

Putin *nods and doesn't say it back.*

Sasha   Sorry I thought you were / going to –

Putin   892 –

Sasha   Sorry, yeah / 9482

Putin   / 495 892

Sasha   Sorry.

Putin   Go on.

Sasha   892 9482

Why doesn't he write it down? Trying to impress with memory.

Putin   Great. OK. I'll be in touch.

Sasha   I appreciate your time.

Putin   All the best. Wishes.

Handshake. Really? All the best wishes? **Sasha** *salutes. (If he does salute he must be wearing a hat.)*

Sasha   Commander.

Putin   Absolutely.

Sasha *leaves. Weird.*

Putin *goes to his desk. He opens a drawer and takes out a real telephone, which he uses to make a call.*

Putin   I want to monitor and inconvenience a subject. An officer, rank Lieutenant Colonel. Name Litvinenko. Telephone 495 892 9 – sorry yeah 924 – wait I'll finish! 8. 48. 9482. I'm repeating the last sec – you're making me forget! – OK. Keep me informed.

Scene Eight

The Litvinenkos' Moscow Apartment

Marina *is waiting up at night, in pyjamas, smoking. (If stagehands construct the flat, maybe they leave a book out, deliberately.* **Marina** *comes back into the space noticing something has been moved. Did she get that book out? She replaces it.)*

The sound of the key in the door. **Sasha** *enters.*

Sasha   Hey.

Marina (*deliberately cool*)   Hey.

Sasha   I'm sorry I'm late.

A small shrug from **Marina,** *who is annoyed by her own fear.*

Sasha   Can I talk to you?

Marina   We are talking.

Sigh. She looks at him.

Marina (*where fear becomes annoyance*)   Oh God what?

Sasha   You know I don't often talk to you about work. Things.

Marina   Yes.

Sasha   Can we go outside?

Marina   No, Sasha! I am not going outside anymore!

Sasha   Why?

Marina   Because it is midnight! I'm in my bed things! Because three days ago me and Anatoly found teeth on the pavement out on the street.

Sasha   What, what teeth?

Marina   I don't know, adult teeth!

Sasha   Where were they from?

Marina   I don't know, he picked them up, how would I know?! They were teeth.

Sasha   OK.

He turns the TV on.

Marina   So it is not about waking Anatoly. You think someone is listening. Who is listening, Sasha, why?

Sasha   If you just shout, then I just have to turn it up more.

Marina   Then I will shout over the TV.

Sasha   OK, great, fine.

Marina   I don't know if you are going crazy which is – I don't know what to do, *or* you have put us in a situation where we are not safe and people are listening to us, which is it?

Sasha   Fine.

Marina   Which sort of man are you?

He doesn't take the bait. He nearly does.

Marina   Do you really think we are being listened to? Yes or no.

He understands the question. He takes a quick look at how he knows it would be done. Maybe a screwdriver to a light switch, leaving it hanging off. No sign of tampering.

Which tips him into an over fifty per cent likelihood of . . .

Sasha   No.

Marina *nods.*

Sasha   We thought that things were going to change. With work. Get better. But they won't.

Marina   You're in trouble again?

Sasha   *They* are in trouble and don't want us pointing it out.

Marina   Let's go then. Let's leave.

Sasha   Leave? Where?

Marina   Somewhere different. Let's go somewhere warmer. And live there.

Sasha   I can't do that.

Marina   Did they ask you to do something more?

Sasha   Yes but that's not . . . This new guy is worse. My work, if I see something is wrong, I investigate. Something happens. Results. But now, when I find something. They say to me, 'Sasha, no that's not right. We have more information. You are mistaken.' And if I continue, if I say, 'Look, no, here is the evidence', they put me somewhere else. Look over there.

He whistles.

Sasha   It's . . . makes me feel like I'm –

Marina   Going crazy.

Sasha (*no*)   Useless.

Myself and others, it is not just me, we are going to say something publicly. About what is happening. There is not a divide anymore between who is committing crimes and who is meant to be solving them.

Marina   And it must be you that says something?

Sasha   Or who?

Beat.

Marina   We will lose everything?

Sasha   I haven't had a salary in months, we are already lost anyway! What if all the good men leave?

Marina   ('. . . the good men . . . ?!') You sound like an American song? Who cares about your pride? Who cares, Sasha?!

Sasha   Me!

Beat.

Marina   And what will you say?

Sasha   Just. These people do not behave well.

A nearly smile at his understatement.

Marina   So what you will write, a letter?

Sasha   I already wrote a letter.

Marina   Sasha!

Sasha   It makes no difference to go upwards. If people knew, they would change things. Television is the only thing everyone sees.

Marina   You're crazy!

Sasha   We will do a press conference, the major channels, / Bereszovsky says –

Marina   / You have a son! They will kill him!

Sasha   You see that is not normal! That is not a normal response! To telling the truth.

Marina   I think you want the whole world to look at you.

Sasha   You have known me five years every day.

Marina   Six years.

Sasha   Six years. You think I want infamy.

Marina   Yes. Are you so different to everyone else?

Sasha   Not because I think it is right.

Marina   Both things, both men are available to me.

Sasha   No, one thing. It's important, you think this?

Marina   Oh God, Sasha!

Sasha   I love you.

Marina   I know you do.

I'm afraid. I hate it.

Sasha   I am too.

This impresses her.

I love you both so much. I love you.

He is kissing her.

It's going to be OK.

Marina   Don't lie. They will arrest you or they will kill you.

Sasha   Sorry.

Marina   Do it, don't do it. Don't be sorry.

They refind each other. They start to make love.

You aren't worried someone is spying on us now . . .

Sasha *shrugs.*

Marina   Oh yes. Good. YOU'RE SO GOOD. YES. YES! GIVE IT TO ME!

She laughs.

Sorry. SORRY!

Sasha   No no, that's OK. I don't mind that.

Laughter. Love. Bed.

Scene Nine

NTV/the Moscow apartment/Putin's inauguration

Out of the darkness

crawl puppets. Kukli puppets.
Gorbachev, Yeltsin, Brezhnev. From the TV world. A red neon sign
somewhere displays 'NTV.'

They sit on the apartment sofa where the Litvinenkos were before
and watch a video of real humans. The world of the real and the
onscreen swapped around.

They are watching the video of **Sasha** *and colleagues giving a press*
conference in 1998, detailing corruption in the FSB. Maybe we only
hear it.

Sasha (*voice only, from the TV*)   (My name is Alexander
Litvinenko, and me and my colleagues work for the FSB. Certain
official personnel within the FSB are using the organization for
non-constitutional purposes: instead of protecting individuals and
the state, they are using the FSB for their own political and private
business ventures. Corruption in the secret service and law enforce-
ment agencies are not just isolated incidents. It is a system. / Me and
my colleagues have been working in the most secret departments of
the FSB and have learnt when we have recently got our orders, that
they include extra-legal killings. Murders. The task of some units
is to act on orders of top officials not just to make them money, but
to dispose of anyone they found disagreeable. We are discovering
among other FSB officers crimes of kidnapping, armed robberies,
killings, and our superiors know all about them. In fact, they are
often orders from our superiors, who operate a protection racket
giving cover to commercial companies and international drug
dealers.)

Marina (*to us*)   / Sasha did a press conference on television.
I didn't go. He didn't want me there.

FSB Officers *enter in ski masks. They stand behind the puppets.*
Marina *continues to talk over the TV . . .*

Marina   But you know, a lot of people watch television. There was
one channel, everyone watch, called NTV, that showed comedy like
Kukli, also show news, real news. Bad things the government was
doing. The war in Chechnya. And then one night, the headquarters

of NTV, has visit from 'the tax office'. They are there twelve hours. After this, not so funny.

The **FSB Officers** *swarm the stage.*

FSB Officer One   We are from the tax office and we have the right to search the premises of NTV and any other subsidiaries of Media-Most company.

FSB Officer Two   We have been granted this permission by the highest levels of government.

FSB Officer Three   Look at this shit!

FSB Officer Two   These rootless cosmopolitans think it's funny.

FSB Officer Three   These are great men. Reduced.

FSB Officer One   Don't look at me!

FSB Officer Three   Grotesque.

FSB Officer Two   They think it's funny, to mock people who gave their lives for Russia.

FSB Officer Three   These fucking traitors.

FSB Officer One   Stop fucking looking at me!

FSB Officer Three   I'm not *offended.*

FSB Officer One   Stop fucking looking at me!

The puppets are destroyed. The NTV sign is shattered or fizzles out. The **Officers** *leave.* **Sasha** *and* **Hyatt** *come on, picking their way through the damage.*

Hyatt   So Edwin, would it be fair to say your television press conference did not go down well?

Sasha   Yes that would be fair.

Hyatt   Are you operating under the belief that events now may be tied to your decision to go on television eight years ago?

Sasha   But they already punish me for this.

Marina   They came very late at night. They dragged him out of our bed.

Sasha   They put me in the back of an unmarked van and four or five men beat me. Over and over. Many hours.

Anatoly, *a small child, emerges from his 'bedroom' in pyjamas.*

Anatoly   Mama. Where is papa?

Marina   Oh, Anatoly. It's OK. He is away for work.

Sasha   Then they take me to a prison. One of the worst in Russia.

Anatoly   At school they say he is in prison.

Sasha   They put me in a room so small, I could not sit down, I could not lie down.

Marina   It's not his fault. There is a man in charge at the FSB who does not like him.

Sasha   They spit on me and threaten me.

Anatoly   But Papa is good at his job.

Marina   Yes.

Hyatt   But what was the charge? Or was there one?

Sasha   They charge me with abusing my position, but then when they realized that is not a real thing, they charged me with stealing vegetables from a warehouse. I don't know where they get this one from.

Hyatt   But wait, you're in prison? So was there a trial?

Sasha   No, in Russia sentence comes before trial.

Anatoly   Papa should be made the leader of the FSB.

Marina   Well, soon we will have an election and there will be a new president. And that president will understand what has happened and he will get rid of the bad man in charge of the FSB and that will make it all better.

Anatoly *can hear the newly reinstated Soviet national anthem.*
Marina *looks. She realises. Oh no.*

Everyone is arranged on stage for an inauguration.

The inauguration of the new President, Vladimir Vladimirovich
Putin. *From the back centre of the stage, a procession begins, grand
and loud and regal.*

*Smoke on his entrance. Strong, confident, but charmingly sly, he
doesn't seem to take the things too seriously. The awkward office
manager has gone replaced by an excellent impression of a Blair-ite
leader.*

*He smiles at us. Maybe he is miked up, but in a way that makes him
sound more intimate and real, not distantly powerful.*

Putin Ladies and gentleman, you've been very patient. Of course,
of course all roads lead back to me, that is how it is now, I see.
But you are too smart to believe this. A theatre audience. You know
better. You know that as soon as anyone starts telling a story they
start telling a lie. And so, if you will indulge me for just a moment
before a break, I will tell you a short story. You may remember, in
2002, in a Moscow theatre much like this one, they were performing
a musical. Because, like here, the Moscow theatre needs to put
musicals on sometimes or you shallow bastards won't come out.
And during this musical, with absolutely no warning or expectation,
between forty and fifty men and women walk in and start shooting
into the air. At first they thought it was part of the play. You know,
that embarrassing thing when it comes out into the audience. But
pretty soon it's clear.

People start screaming and barging, they see explosives attached to
the intruders' bodies. And so starts the Moscow theatre siege. For
four nights, Chechen terrorists hold hundreds of people hostage in a
theatre. They use the orchestra pit as a toilet.

On the fourth night, the hostages wake to see a grey mist spreading
throughout the auditorium. Our special forces have slipped something into the ventilation system and, cunningly, it knocks out the
Black Widows, as they call themselves. Of course it knocks out the

hostages too. And then, in creep Russian soldiers in gas marks, we kill all the Chechens. Without firing a shot. But this is a very secret mission, and the arriving medics have no idea what antidote to use for the gas. And so some people are convulsing, carried out, choking on their tongues, their vomit, barely able to breathe, laid out on the steps of this beautiful theatre, cameras capturing everything on the pavement outside. And TV showed this. Every detail. One hundred and thirty hostages died. And the country saw everything on the news. The fuck up, the pain, the sickness. The corpses propped up in a bus we brought to get them off the street. And it didn't help, it didn't bring anyone back. It was just another terrible terrible fucking awful tragedy born of some people's pain causing more people pain and it won't ever stop and now you have to live with it too.

Because how much can you take, how much can you feel? In this one life? To know so much suffering and do nothing. You are not equipped to be kind and thoughtful to the people around you and *still* feel like a failure, still feel impotent, still have the death of a child on your mind, every moment, every day. It is exhausting.

You cannot die with every death. You can't. You can't. And luckily this story has a happy ending.

And so, from then on, Chechnya was a happy place. There was infrastructure built, and there were community projects, and a centre for Chechnyan Russian relations was built. And they voted ninety-eight per cent for me, the man who saved the hostages. Oh, and the Litvinenkos? That little story? Alexander Litvinenko retired with his family to *a dacha* on the beautiful banks of the Volga. And they lived out many years there, happily. With their son and their cat called Yuri. (*A dog barks. Oops.*). And who among us could want more than that?

Ushers open doors.

The doors are open ladies and gentleman. Enjoy your drinks. There is no need to return.

End of Act One.

Interval.

Act Two

Scene One

An ornate font announces:

Professor Dombey's Report Into the Origins of Polonium

Commissioned by

Marina Litvinenko

Originally, the following poem was also performed as a shadow play.

Dombey

All Russian children know from when they're young

By heart, a tale of love and fire that's sung

Of Ruslan and Lludmilla, hearts entwined,

She's kidnapped, while her love is left behind.

The Prince's epic journey and their fate

That make up Pushkin's tale I won't relate

But know that from the lovers' burning flames

Two nuclear reactors took their names

So Ruslan and Lludmilla came to be

Built by a secret town, in secrecy

Behind the Ural mountains by a lake

A dangerous atomic love they make

A substance first defined in Paris, France

When Marie Curie made a strange advance

Uranium experiments had shown

Existence of an element unknown

She named it for the country of her birth

One of the rarest elements on earth

She named it after Poland, then unfree,

Partitioned, sat at Mother Russia's knee.

And after battles, strikes, The First World War

An independent Poland *was* restored

And Curie saw her newly reborn nation

Before she died, from years of radiation.

Curie *'s eaten away by radiation.*

Scene Two

Putin's Box / Moscow Sheremetyevo Airport

Putin   *is in the box, commenting on the play. He grabs our attention.*

Putin   A fairy tale. I love a fairy tale, don't you? You must, you have returned. That shows a certain lack of trust. Hurtful. Well, if you must absorb the rest, that's your choice, your risk. But I think you'll find the only criminal thing here is charging four pounds for a program. Bring on my next act!

Luguvoi   *(40s), a Russian Anglophile, hurriedly makes his way through the auditorium to get up onto the stage. He is tall and lean, dressed by Harrods, dragging a small croc-skin suitcase.*

Luguvoi   *(at the stage)*   I'm coming! Hold please. One moment.

A female member of **Cabin Crew** *is welcoming him at the gate.*

Lugovoi *makes his way up onto the stage.*

Luguvoi   Sorry, sorry.

Cabin Crew   *(taking and checking papers)*   Travelling to London Heathrow?

Luguvoi   Yes.

Cabin Crew   Thank you, Mr . . . Andre Lugovoi. Just in time.

Luguvoi   Just check for me, I'm sure he is, but I'm travelling with a friend, should be next to me, he's boarded already, yes? Kovtun, Dimitri Kovtun?

Cabin Crew   Let me just, the plane is rather full. Next to you?

Luguvoi   Seat 14F, next to me, yes.

Cabin Crew   Ah yes, Mr Kovtun. No, Mr Kovtun has not joined us yet, I'm afraid.

Lugovoi *expresses his annoyance.*

Cabin Crew   We're nearly at gate closing. Ah. Wait.

Luguvoi   Yes?

Cabin Crew   We're doing a random hand baggage check and you're selected. We'll be quick as we can.

Brief panic then . . . actually –

Luguvoi   No of course, fine. Very good.

Lugovoi *checks his watch, we notice it's big and expensive. He looks all around the theatre / airport, trying to catch sight of his friend. Nothing.*

His expensive suitcase is unzipped on a table to be looked through. Everything in it is neatly pressed. An aftershave comes out. She sprays it in the air to smell it.

Luguvoi   That's –

Cabin Crew   Lovely.

Luguvoi   Expensive.

Cabin Crew *thoughtfully unpacks his folded underwear, laying them gently down.*

Luguvoi   Take your time.

From the auditorium –

Kovtun   Andre!

Lugovoi *looks out, eventually spotting* **Kovtun** *waving frantically from an unlikely part of the auditorium* (*Circle / Box*)

Kovtun   Andre, Andre, I am here!

Kovtun *is a shorter, rounder man. He looks permanently sweaty and smiley and has a large leather travel bag diagonally across him. He is waving with both arms, revealing almost comically large sweat patches.*

Luguvoi   Dimitri! Why are you over there? Come here, you're late!

Kovtun   You said to be late!

Luguvoi   No, I said be very last minute.

Kovtun   I am very last minute. This is the last minute.

Luguvoi   Don't start, Dimitri, I am already regretting this. Why are you over there?! Come here!

Kovtun   It just seems like a big drop, Andre.

He looks about haphazardly.

Wait, wait, I have an idea.

Cabin Crew   You did pack this yourself, sir?

Luguvoi   Yes I did. Have you read it?

He's referring to a book, a Sherlock Holmes.

Cabin Crew   No! This is Arthur Conan Doyle? (*She mispronounces Conan.*)

Luguvoi   Arthur Conan Doyle. He's very good.

Cabin Crew   I just watch that on the television, Baker Street.

Luguvoi   Ah, no, the books are better. Have you ever been to London?

Cabin Crew   No.

Luguvoi   Oh you must. Everyone's there now. The food is much improved.

Cabin Crew   OK –

Luguvoi (*buying time*)   No no, take your time. There are many pockets. I don't want to seem guilty but I also don't want you to get in trouble for not being thorough.

Kovtun *has found a ladder and erected it to get down from the Circle / Box into the main auditorium.* **Lugovoi** *turns to see him.*

Luguvoi   Dimitri, what the fuck are you doing?

Kovtun (*right at the top of the ladder*)   I am coming, Andre!

Luguvoi   That's so dangerous!

Why don't you go around?

Kovtun   Around how?

Luguvoi (*indicating the stalls*)   Just out the back and down into the . . . stalls!

Kovtun (*frozen*)   Oh.

Luguvoi   Well come on now, everyone's staring at you!

Cabin Crew   Sir –

Luguvoi (*a rictus grin*)   Just . . .

Kovtun   . . . I can't.

Luguvoi   You can't what?

Kovtun   I'm stuck. You said it's dangerous.

Luguvoi   Well of course it's fucking dangerous, it's getting more dangerous the longer you sit there –

Kovtun   . . . I can't.

Luguvoi   Dimitri!

Cabin Crew   *Sir.*

Luguvoi   Just – !

Kovtun   Don't shout at me, it doesn't help if you shout at me.

Luguvoi   Dimitri old friend. All you need to do is keep climbing down. It's very simple

Kovtun   I'm just holding on.

Luguvoi   One foot down, then the other, just like with stairs. At home.

Kovtun   I live in a bungalow. You know that.

Luguvoi   I temporarily forgot. When I count to three, OK, pretend you're being shot at.

Kovtun   WHAT?!

Luguvoi   Oh my God, you're being shot at! Left leg, right leg, Dimitri hide! There's a man with a gun!

Kovtun *manages it out of fear.*

Cabin Crew   Sir, the plane is leaving without you.

Luguvoi   No it isn't. NO it fucking isn't. And I'll explain to you why it isn't, and I'll do that while you're shut in an FSB waiting room with no sign on the door and no clock on the wall and man after man will come in and explain to you over and over again, until everyone really really has a good understanding. OK. Don't make me use further proof of this.

Cabin Crew *senses the truth of this.*

Kovtun *emerges into the stalls with his bag. He needlessly climbs over members of the audience and passes through a row, apologizing. His bag dragging against them. He tries passing front facing them and back facing them and chats through the pros and cons of each.*

Kovtun   Sorry, sorry, sorry. Oh lord, it's arse or crotch isn't it, arse or crotch, what's worse, you choose.

Eventually he reaches the stage.

My friend!

He opens his arms to embrace his friend, showing us the full glory of his sweat patches.

Wearily, **Lugovoi** *acquiesces to a mean hug.*

Cabin Crew   Gentlemen I can't –

Luguvoi   We're going.

Luguvoi *himself packs up the last of his searched clothes.*

Kovtun   What are we waiting around for, come on.

Luguvoi   Because they searched my bag, Dimitri. Just to be safe.

Kovtun (*panicked*)   Oh no!

Luguvoi   No obviously it's fine.

Kovtun   Oh yes! Absolutely. Fine. Search mine if you –

Luguvoi (*panicked*)   No! The plane is leaving!

Kovtun   Oh no! We should get on it!

Luguvoi   Mhmn.

Thank you. Allow me to show my respect.

He awkwardly tips her, which she coldly refuses. It falls to the floor. **Luguvoi** *bends to retrieve the money from the floor, but* **Kovtun** *has got there before him.*

Kovtun   That's free money! Crisps on the plane! Suit yourself!

Kovtun *briefly tries to go through the wrong exit before* **Luguvoi** *corrects his passage and they head off onto the plane. The* **Cabin Crew** *follows them.*

Curtain up to reveal London and the Litvinenko's London flat.

Scene Three

Welcome To London, the London flat and environs. 2000.

Everything in the flat is smaller and cheaper-looking than before. **Marina** *stands in front, with a suitcase, not yet inside.*

Marina (*to us*)   It was impossible for us to live in Russia. The only thing to do was to escape. After his press conference, Sasha was in prison over and over for nothing many times, I was sure he would one day suddenly be dead. So, there had to be some plan. Sasha escaped across the Black Sea on a boat, then travelled to Turkey, on a plane.

Putin   How exciting! What an adventurer! Oh, the plane was billionaire Boris Bereszovksy's private jet.

Marina   He told me to book a normal package holiday for me and Anatoly to go to Spain, and he would meet us there.

Putin   You know, like a coward would.

Marina   And we did and when we were all together, eventually, we decided to come to London.

Putin   Actually, first they tried the American Embassy. That was Litvinenko's first choice. The US. Which you can understand, weather-wise. They rejected him.

Marina   And so we came to London Heathrow and asked in the queue for immigration if we could apply for asylum.

Putin   Defection, of course, would be another word.

Marina *makes her way toward the London flat.*

Putin   Come on my dear, these people have trains to catch.

Perturbed, **Marina** *joins the scene.* **Sasha** *and* **Anatoly** *are inside it.* **Sasha** *gets a can of Tango out for* **Anatoly**.

Sasha   Guess how much it was for that?

Marina   . . . I don't know. One / pound?

Sasha   / One pound!

Anatoly   Tango Tango! Which is my room?

Marina (*after him*)   You may have to sleep with us tonight, Anatoly.

But he's gone. Something immediately breaks – a chair or the front of a drawer comes off, something like that.

Marina   Are you tired?

Sasha   It is very complicated, the asylum application. And I don't think I can work here until it's done.

Marina   Well I can teach. I can do dance.

Sasha   That won't be legal.

Marina   But put it in the paper or something. Just small amounts of money. People who are getting married maybe. The floor is good.

Sasha   There is no space in here.

Marina   Yes here is enough. Move the table, I'll show you.

She is trying to lift the mood by getting him to dance with her.

Sasha   Not now.

He is going through the hefty asylum application he has started.

Sasha   It says we need a marriage certificate, they don't give you a certificate when you get married.

Marina   Yes they do.

Sasha   But we don't have one.

Marina   Yes we do. But at home.

Sasha   And what is a police registration number?

Marina   Can Boris help?

Sasha   *I'm* doing it.

Marina *comes over and puts her fingers all over his forehead.*

Sasha   What are you doing . . . ?!

Marina   I am trying to uncrumple your face.

This only crumples it further. **Marina** *flounces off, chucks a bag of sweets at him.*

Marina (*giving M&Ms*)   You're in a bad mood because you're hungry.

Annoyed at first, he then relents and eats some M&Ms. His mood almost immediately improves. He has a London A–Z he picks up.

Sasha   I think we should choose a different name. Just to be safe. In case. The solicitor tomorrow is on Carter Street. I like it. I think it solid and British. Carter. And for my name I am thinking something robust and male, like Edwin.

Marina   'Edwin'.

Sasha   'Edwin Redwald'.

Marina (*deliberately macho*)   'Edwin Redwald'. Yes. But what about me?

Sasha   What about you, Mrs Carter?

Marina   I think maybe . . . 'Maria'!

Sasha   'Maria'. Wow. You're crazy.

Marina   What? / Is easy to remember!

Sasha   / That is so confusing and different, Marina! Oh my god.

Marina   Maria Anna Carter!

Sasha   Your imagination!

Marina   Shut up and give me the other one of those cans.

Sasha   Oh. No. I drank it.

Marina   When did you have that?

Sasha   You saw me! Outside.

Have water from the tap. It's good for you here.

She shoots him a look. Maybe she sips and says 'Mmmm'. **Sasha** *returns to the formidable forms.*

She leans over the forms, to help.

Marina   You need better English. I mean for this.

Sasha   I know.

Marina   Anatoly is good now. Better than us! He will be fine at school, I think.

Sasha   I don't like him just going into a strange building on his own.

Marina   Don't say that! It's good. He will just say bye bye and in he goes. Lots of children from many countries. Come on. Would you like a cup of tea?

Sasha   'Would you like a cup of tea?'

Marina   No, 'would you like a cup of tea?'

Sasha   'Would you like a cup of tea?'

Marina   No I am really asking you if you would like a cup of tea?

Sasha (*embarrassed*)   Oh no. Thanks.

Anatoly *comes back in his school uniform. Burgundy. Smart. A tiny bit heart-breaking. This is another day bleeding in.*

Marina   Look at this!

Sasha   Well.

Marina   So grown up!

Look at his bag! Show him.

Anatoly *opens his schoolbag so his dad can see inside.*

Sasha   What is in there? Feels like something. Very deep inside. What's that . . . Oh no my hand, it's got my hand! No I am serious, I am not joking with you!

He is pretending his hand is stuck in the bag. Eyes are rolled but he commits.

Sasha   No! Really! Something is in there!

The bag comes off as it attacks **Sasha**. *He rolls around on the floor.* **Marina** *watches, amused. The bag goes for his throat.* **Sasha** *fakes* *dying.* **Anatoly** *tries to take the bag back, joining his father in play. Not too grown up for this.*

Hyatt *joins the scene from the future.*

Hyatt   Mr Carter? Edwin? Are you able to talk?

Sasha *sits up from his pretend dead state.*

Sasha   Of course, detective.

Hyatt   Can I introduce you to my colleague, DS Hoar, who has been assisting me in the enquiries.

Hoar   Nice to meet you, Edwin.

Sasha   Hello, Detective Sergeant.

He makes a point to shake his hand.

Hoar   I've been to your flat. In Osier Crescent.

Sasha   Ah. Good.

Hyatt   Where he retrieved the notebooks and SIM cards you mentioned.

Hoar *retrieves them from around the flat.*

Hoar   Now we've gone through the contents but they're either written in a deliberate code, or else somewhat vaguely.

Hyatt   I suppose the questions the notebooks raise, as well as the use of two different SIM cards, is what is it you actually did for a living once you came to London?

Sasha   I continued my work investigating and exposing issues of the Russian state.

Hyatt   Right. Cos I would have thought, having escaped with your life, that you might settle down a bit, take it easy?

Sasha   Absolutely not.

Marina   Absolutely not.

Hyatt   And what form did your fight against the Russian state take?

Marina   No no, wait, he is not fight *against*, you understand? It is fight *for.*

Sasha   I did not escape Russia to watch DVD box sets and go to London Zoo.

I come to a country that has freedom of speech, is not 'Haha we are fine now!' If I did not use that to say what is happening back in Russia, for truth, then I am dead, that is the same thing that they want.

Hyatt   So describe to me the nature of your work.

Sasha   Sometimes journalism yes, not to be paid, obviously there is no money in that. But I would meet with people and talk to them, write.

Marina   I would say to Sasha he should go out and meet people. He was shy, not like me –

Sasha   Marina –

Marina   It's true! I was worried he would get depressed, go out, you know, Vitamin D!

Sasha   I like people to come to the flat.

Marina   Journalists would come.

Sasha   My friend Anna Politskavya. Very good journalist, very important.

Marina   Anna would sit on the floor and play with Anatoly.

Anatoly *sits and plays with no one.*

Hoar   This Anna Politskavya, she would come back and forth from Russia, she was a source?

Sasha   She was my friend.

Hyatt   Did you have any contact with her? Before you got ill?

Sasha   No.

Marina   No.

They look at each other. Something going on.

Hyatt   You sure?

Marina   Yes.

Sasha   Because Anna Politskavya was shot and killed in her apartment block one month ago.

Hyatt   Bloody hell.

Anatoly *stops playing.*

Putin   Duh duh duh! A lot gets made of this. Look, I don't know who killed this Anna Politskyvaya. She wasn't a big name till after she died. And don't pretend you care, you haven't even met her, she's not even in it! But I'll tell you this: when women get killed in their homes, there's normally a few other men to take a look at before you get all the way up to the President. Grow up.

Marina *steps out to speak to us.*

Marina (*to us*)   I can see them not be sure. If somebody says this person was murdered by the state, how are they are supposed to believe it? I was like that myself also. With Sasha. When he would say things. I did not know if the scales were falling from his eyes or somebody was . . . putting scales into his eyes. I would listen to Sasha talk with Anna and with his dissident friend Bukovsky and think, hmm, too much. But then. It would all come true.

Scene Four

The London Flat, Christmas

Marina *comes in to the flat.* **Sasha** *is putting up cheap Christmas decorations. She has a pamphlet-style newspaper she has read and presents it to* **Sasha**.

Marina   What is this?

Sasha   It's a piece for the *Chechen Press*. I wrote it.

Marina   I know, this part. Saying Putin might be abusing children? A paedophile?

Sasha   What? This is what he does. He accuses people and ruins them and shames them. And here he is lifting up that little boy's shirt and kissing him, you know. It is not a joke exactly but it is what he does, back to him. That is the point.

Marina   That is not the point.

Sasha   He plants child pornography in their homes and tapes them with women he's paid, blackmails them.

Marina   I know, I don't care about that.

Sasha   We need money, I have a family!

Marina   Yes, that's me.

He mistakes her anger for fear.

Sasha   We're in London now. We are safe here.

Marina   You think I'm scared! I am the one who said come here, I'm happy here! I'm the one with friends. You're scared, obsessed with / home still –

Sasha   / Oh, 'the things you know'! You have no idea what is going on –

Marina   Oh OK –

Sasha   Stupid thing to say. You have no idea –

Marina   I chose to love a man who told me he had to tell the truth. Don't spit in that. Or you are no better than him.

Sasha   Fuck you.

Too far.

Marina   Don't make what I chose to love not true.

Sasha   Alright! Words.

Marina   Yes.

Pause. In this silence **Sasha** *makes some tea. There is real tension as to whether he is going to make some for* **Marina** *as well. She watches, pointedly. At the last moment he does get another mug and makes two teas. But it's tense for a while there.*

He gives it to her.

Sasha   I miss Yuri.

Marina   No you don't! You hated Yuri! You said he shit every-where, you said.

Sasha   No he didn't, he shat in one place once, under the bed, we just didn't find it for ages. That's our fault, not Yuri's fault.

Marina   That is what I said to you at the time!

Sasha   Who looks after him now?

Marina   My mother has him.

Sasha   I can't believe I did not ask you that before.

Marina   No, I cannot believe it either.

He reaches out to her somehow.

Marina   You know Boris is moving to London?

Sasha   What? How do you know this and I don't know this?

Marina   Galina called me. He thinks someone is trying to kill him.

Sasha   Boris never thinks *anyone* is trying to kill him?!

Boris *enters.*

Putin (*on mic, from the Box*)   Boris Bereszovsky, public enemy number one, WAIT! Not over my lines.

Putin *has halted the scene change.*

Putin   Boris Bereszovsky, public enemy number one, fled Russia in 2000 with the millions he had made there. And proceeded to set up a little Moscow upon Thames –

Boris *waves the scene change on.*

Putin   – devoted to unseating the democratically elected leader of that country, me.

Scene Five

Table, Scott's Restaurant, Mayfair

At an upmarket table in London, **Sasha** *lunches with* **Boris**.

Boris   Can you believe this midget cunt prince?! I MADE HIM! I gave the little bastard everything he has! We swam in France together! That Chekist prick. He was my friend!

Sasha   I don't know what to say.

Boris   He's a shadow, he's a sketch of a man. He told me one time the whole reason he joined the kontora was because of that stupid TV show, *The Shield and the Sword.*

Sasha   Perhaps he should have been an actor.

Boris   He lacks the charisma.

I don't know why I put my faith in people, I don't.

Sasha   We are very grateful, BB. For everything. For helping us get out. For Anatoly's school.

Boris *waves it away, a bit awkward.*

Sasha   Boris, we need to look at all the staff at your offices. Bukovsky and I know half of them are moles.

Boris (*waves away*)   Oh they are good people. No trouble.

Sasha   You're paying me for security advice.

Boris   Did you hear Roman Abramovich gave him a fucking yacht?

Sasha   Can we talk about your office staff?

Boris   He's a gangster. And Abramovich is going to buy this football team, you see! Like protection. 'I am a nice guy I am a hero', you are a gangster! Good luck your eleven fit young men protecting you, you shit. Maybe I should buy another team and beat his relent-lessly. Who is the best one? No, I have no money.

Sasha   It's Chelsea.

Boris   And a yacht is a terrible gift. You have to moor it, you have to clean it. Pay crew. You use it for one week a year. It's not a gift, it's a burden. It's a job you're giving someone.

Sasha   If you want for me to help with your London security, Boris, we have to talk about your tendency to give jobs to question-able individuals.

Boris   Did I tell you Galina wants 150 in the divorce?

Sasha   Million?!

Boris (*nods*)   I can tell you one thing, get a pre-nup. Did you two get a pre-nup?

Sasha   I'm not sure it's really relevant for us.

Boris   But you're right. I do have to talk to you. How is little Anatoly?

Sasha   He is healthy, thank you.

Boris   Remember that, Sasha. Family. That's all there is. But get a pre-nup.

As I said, it is time to revisit some of the shape of the expenditure flowing between us.

Oh. He didn't say.

Sasha   . . . OK. I don't want your money, Boris, I just am trying to live.

Boris   And yes yes yes, you let *me* live.

Sasha   No! I want to do a job of work for you but you don't seem interested in my advice.

Boris (*waving away*)   You're my friend. I don't care about the money.

But you don't seem to know your abilities. Or your contacts. Don't you see what you can monetize here? Look around you, Sasha. Look where you are.

Sasha   An over-priced restaurant called Scott's?

Boris   Mayfair. Private intelligence, Sasha. Sometimes I get these moods. But then I just walk through this part of London, I look around and I think to myself . . .

He inhales dramatically.

Sasha   Oh God, are you going to sing?

Boris (*a song probably, yes*)

> There's a village in London, and it's right at the heart
>
> Surprisingly peaceful, prestigious and smart
>
> If you want pure location, and you're prepared to pay
>
> Take a look out the window, it's a beautiful day.
>
> The golden triangle, Mayfair to the West
>
> Is an oligarch's playground, and the swings are the best
>
> One day it's dictators, then the oil billionaires
>
> But today it's the Russians, it's a market of bears.
>
> It's the wealthiest district, dark blue on the board
>
> And the business is knowledge, which the rich can afford
>
> Through the large Georgian windows, you ask who they are
>
> 'Is it lawyers or hedge funds or swanky PR?'
>
> But you don't know your country, it's the best at one thing
>
> And that one thing is spying, of that you're the king
>
> And if London's the kingdom, then the palace is here
>
> Yes Mayfair's the crown jewels of espionage, dear.
>
> Private intelligence, makes the world go around

More British than Harrods, stronger than the pound

Nothing is private, so there's plenty to glean

Yes Mayfair's a quiet information machine.

And it's perfectly legal, as I'm sure that you know

So go take some meetings, down towards Savile Row.

One day it's dictators, then the oil billionaires

But today it's the Russians, it's a market of bear....eszovsky!

Bereszovsky is offski.

Boris *leaves.*

Putin (*to us*)   Oh you like him, do you? You know why you lot standing at the top can't afford a house, don't you? Cos 'people like Boris' own five.

Scene Six

These smaller scenes run on from one another, and should flow seamlessly.

1.   Table, Itsu, Piccadilly

Sasha *greets* **Luguvoi** *and* **Kovtun** *and make their way into a restaurant for lunch.* **Luguvoi** *has with him Bond Street / Harrods shopping bags.*

Luguvoi   Better than it should be, this place.

Sasha   I like it.

Luguvoi   The first one was in Chelsea you know.

Sasha   That meeting went well, I thought.

Luguvoi   Excellent.

Sasha   You looked quite the English gent with those bags.

Luguvoi   How very dare you, sir?

Sasha   Why do you go to Harrods? It's so overpriced.

Kovtun *joins them, having got the boxed Itsu food which he doles out. They eat with chopsticks.* **Kovtun** *particularly disgustingly.*

Kovtun   Boom. Boom. Boom. I like these. You know why I like them? All boxed up. Boxy boxy box. All sealed and ready fresh in a box.

Luguvoi   It's a bit salty though. Can make you thirsty. I find.

Sasha   Are you doing anything else while you're here?

Luguvoi   Oh we have vague plans. Maybe *The Lion King*. There are some architectural sights I'd still like to see. Kovtun doesn't know London.

Kovtun   I know it a bit. It's big.

We have known each other a long time. We grew up in the same apartment block.

Luguvoi   We did.

Kovtun   Andrei was always very popular. With the girls and the boys. With everyone really.

Luguvoi *frowns at him. What?*

Kovtun   Sorry. OK.

So you are long time colleagues?

Luguvoi   We met in Moscow. Boris parties.

Sasha   We only started working together last year, after I 'moved' here –

Luguvoi   I love it here.

Sasha   We met to talk about a job. Just stupid corporate thing –

Luguvoi   Ever since the food got good, it's a world class city.

Kovtun   Mhm. What job?

Sasha (*decides to trust*)   There is a vodka company, based here. They have disagreements with our ministry over who owns the recipe. Stolichnaya. It's OK. He's your friend. We just did some sniffing around. It's all very Russian.

Luguvoi   Yes, a vodka company and an agricultural minister. It is embarrassingly Russian. Anyway, here's to developing more with Sasha's friends here in Mayfair.

Kovtun   Ah.

A clink of glasses.

Luguvoi   And how is your son?

Sasha   Very well. Yours?

Luguvoi   Excellent.

Sasha   Excuse me.

Sasha *goes to the loo / to talk to* **Hyatt**. *The two Russians talk / argue.*

Hyatt   So you were trafficking in information about Russia, to British companies?

Marina   Were you?

Sasha   Yes, it is stupid, business. For money. But it is not like you say. That was not my main work.

It is like if you drove a taxi at night you know, on top of being policeman.

Hyatt   Yeah, that's not totally off the cards, to be honest.

Marina   I did not know you were selling vodka.

Sasha   That is not it, Marina. These companies had done deals in Russia from last century and they did not always know not who to talk to, what the deals were. They pay for advice. People think Russia – dangerous, frightening.

Hyatt   Well frankly I'm starting to see their point.

Marina   Why is it so late now that we talk about this? Why were you just silent so many nights, saying nothing to each other, reading books?

Sasha   We are getting distracted.

Hyatt   Edwin. I need you to take me through your exact movements on the day in question. I need to know every person you had contact with in the twenty-four-hour period leading up to you feeling unwell?

Marina   The day before he was ill, was 31st October, he left the flat in the afternoon, I was teaching.

Sasha   Four pm I had a meeting with a person. Now I cannot tell you anything about them, how they look or their name or anything.

Marina   Sasha this is stupid, tell them.

Sasha   I am but I can't!

Marina   You are turning me into some poor, foolish wife. Is that how it is?

Sasha   No, Marina.

I like the silence. I like the books.

Marina   I'm going to get a drink.

She goes. **Hyatt** *sends* **Hoar** *after her.* **Hoar** *goes.*

Hyatt   She's got a point. If it's relevant to your condition, it could be absolutely vital you tell me who this person is you met the day before.

Sasha   I cannot betray their identity.

Hoar *comes back in.*

Hoar   Edwin's got a visitor.

Martin *appears.*

Martin   Hello, I'm Martin. 'MOD'.

He actually does the air quotes. Posh, smiley, nice, polite.

Hyatt   Was it him?

Sasha   Yes.

Martin   I'm sorry we took so long. It would have been too compromising to turn up for a stomach bug.

Sasha   Hello, Martin.

Martin   Hello, Sasha.

Sasha   This is Detective Inspector Hyatt. This is. Martin.

Martin   How do you do.

Hyatt   Alright.

They shake hands.

Sasha   I was told you are supposed to say 'how do you do' back again, and that's how you know someone is truly English.

Martin   Oh yes, you've cracked the code.

Hyatt   *Are* you?

Sasha   / Yes.

Martin   / Yes.

Hyatt   You say how do you do back to someone when they say how do you do?! Did you know this?

Hoar   Yeah.

Hyatt   (Piss off?!) Alright. So. On the day in question. October 31st.

2.   Table, Waterstones Café, Piccadilly

Sasha   Me and Martin met at Waterstones Piccadilly. Like we did from the first time. I didn't know there was a café there, but it / turns out hardly anyone does so that is why it is good –

Martin   / Yes it turns out hardly anyone does so that's why it's good – I always wonder if you're allowed to just take one of the books and read it here like a library. I wouldn't. I rather like their shortbread and I'd get the pages all sugary.

I'm aware of your recent troubles, have things calmed down a bit?

Sasha   It is just threatening messages. It is OK.

My friend Anna she told me that she had been brought in by the police in Moscow and they had taken her to a shooting range, and made her shoot a gun. And the target was my face.

Martin   Oh dear. That's a bit much. Are you alright? You still wish to help us out?

Sasha   Yes. It is important.

Martin   Because really, strictly speaking, there's not as much need as there was, we are on relatively good terms at the moment.

Sasha   Well, we should not be. And we should probably meet somewhere else now.

Martin   What? Why's that?

Sasha   Here has just been bought by Alexander Mamut. You know?

Martin   Oh Waterstones, yes, I saw that, in the *FT*. That's a problem is it?

Sasha   He's one of the oligarchs.

Martin   Do you suppose they will tape wires to the bookshelves, record us?

Sasha   Not that maybe.

Martin   But could look a bit daft if something were to happen.

That wasn't **Sasha***'s concern but OK.*

Martin   Yah, well, I'm glad someone's parachuted in. I don't want Amazon to become the only place for books, you know.

Sasha   Sure.

Martin   So I hear you've also been providing help to the Spanish.

Sasha   How do you know that?

Come on.

Sasha   I think I will testify. The cartels, the drugs and the money out of Russia. Spain is the only place addressing it. They are actually having a trial.

Martin   It won't go down well.

Sasha   They asked me.

Martin   Don't do anything silly.

Sasha   They ask.

Martin   Well. Maybe you know what you're doing. Here, have some shortbread.

Hyatt   Did you have the shortbread?

Sasha   Yes. A bit. Was dry.

He does.

Sasha (*to* **Hyatt**)   Next day, 1st November I get a bus from my home in Muswell Hill then the tube to Oxford Circus. I meet an associate of mine at the statue of Eros, Piccadilly, Mario Scaramella.

Hyatt   Scaramella? You're serious?

Sasha   Yes. We work together on links between Italian government and KGB.

Hoar   Isn't that a name out of a Bond movie?

Sasha   I don't know. I don't watch. They're stupid. But Mario, he loves all this, he thinks his life is going to be James Bond. I took him for lunch at Itsu, Piccadilly.

3.   Table, Itsu, Piccadilly

Mario Scaramella *is rotund and almost deliberately Italian.*

Mario   Here he is, here he is! My favourite secret service member. Double oh yeeeeaaahh. Ahh not really, not really. I tease.

Sasha   Mario. Stop.

Mario   Well then you should tell me. What MI are you? Is it the one with all the glass? Or the one near Whitehall with the shit offices? Ahhhh I tease you.

Sasha (*irritated by his volume*)   Mario. If I did I would not tell you, if I said I didn't, you would not believe me.

Mario   They try for me constantly. They're drunks. They always want to meet in the pub.

Sasha   Well that's up to them.

Mario   But Sasha in all deadly seriousness. There is something I have brought you.

Sasha (*to* **Hyatt**)   He gave me a list of names he thought would interest me.

Mario   These are people who are in trouble. It comes from someone who knows in FSB.

Mario *is offering the piece of paper.*

Sasha (*to* **Hyatt**)   But I remember it is grubby, crumpled, I did not want to take it. When I make notes they are ordered, clean.

Hoar   We know, we've seen your notebooks.

Hyatt   Exactly what you'd want. Made our life a lot easier.

Mario   Come on, you should see.

Hyatt   Did you take the paper, Edwin? Touch it?

He takes them.

Sasha   Yes.

Hyatt   And then what?

Sasha   I was getting many phone calls from colleague of mine, wanting me to meet him at his hotel. Andrei Luguvoi. In my notebooks, he is listed as 'Friend 2'. He calls me to ask to meet at Millennium Hotel. I go north, Old Bond Street, Grafton Street, then Berkeley Square.

4.   Table, Millennium Hotel, London

Luguvoi *enters and greets* **Sasha**.

Hyatt   Could you describe the gentleman you were meeting?

Sasha   Andrei, I mention before, Russian, private intelligence, ex FSB, like me. I am one metre seventy-seven/seventy-eight so he is maybe one metre seventy-six. Two years younger than me. Light hair with a small bald patch.

Hyatt   And did you meet?

Sasha   Yes, he was with his whole family, come to see a football match. I remember because Moscow were playing Arsenal and he had brought his son to see it. He made him shake my hand. I arrived around four pm and we went to the hotel bar. He had already ordered drinks. There were glasses and mugs and a teapot.

I think three or four cups.

Hyatt   And did you drink any of the tea?

Sasha   Yes, although there was only a little left in the bottom of the pot and it made just half a cup. Then his friend came over and took a place at the table on right side. He seemed depressed.

Kovtun *enters and does this in a football scarf.*

Hyatt   Did they seem insistent you drink?

Sasha   No. I could have ordered a drink myself. I don't like when people pay for me but in such an expensive hotel, forgive me, I don't have enough money to pay for that. So I . . . had what was left.

Hyatt   OK. And then . . .

Marina's *back.*

Marina   He came home.

Sasha   I come home.

He comes home. Greeting. Domestic bliss.

5.   The London Flat

Sasha   Marina had prepared a special dinner.

Marina   A chicken. It's easy. Nigella.

Sasha   Because it's six years to the day since we come here. And just recently I had become British citizen.

Marina *and* **Anatoly** *and* **Sasha**. *It is beautiful, wholesome. Safe.*

Sasha   Look at that!

He puts his passport down on the table.

Pick it up! Pick it up!

Anatoly *picks it up.*

Sasha   Careful! Don't –

Marina *pours fizzy wine.* **Anatoly** *eats crisps.*

Anatoly   Can I have some?

Marina   Twelve is too young.

Anatoly   I just want a sip!

Marina   Not if you are going to eat crisps instead of your mother's cooking.

Anatoly   I eat both.

Sasha   Look, let me show you what we do in Britain.

Anatoly   I know what to do! I am in Britain.

Sasha   I know but I am a British citizen so I know. Look this is how you open up the crisps, you tear down here, you don't just eat them like that, you put them here on the table, so everyone can have some.

Anatoly   Ugh. That's Communism.

Marina   Anatoly!

Anatoly   Why does Mum shout at me when you're not here?

Marina   OK!

Anatoly   You do. Like a dog. 'No!'

Marina *gasps with pretend offence.*

Sasha   Anatoly. Do not speak to your mother like that.

Sasha *gives* **Anatoly** *the crisps back when* **Marina***'s back is turned, serving dinner.*

Marina   He was asking me why do we still have the flag up outside?

Sasha   Why not?

Anatoly   The World Cup's over. It's embarrassing.

Sasha   It just hangs off the house! What's wrong with that?

Anatoly   Nothing.

Sasha   You support England!

Anatoly   Yeah but now it's the league.

Sasha   Who is there to support in that then?

Anatoly (*shrugs*)   Dunno.

Sasha   Well pick one. We're in London.

Anatoly   . . . I don't know maybe . . . Chel/ –?

Sasha   Anyone except Chelsea.

Anatoly   OK. Maybe Arsenal.

Sasha   OK, We'll get you a t-shirt.

Anatoly   It's not called a t-shirt, it's just called a shirt.

Marina *and* **Sasha** *exchange a look. Family harmony. They eat.*

Hyatt   Edwin? We've got a lead in the investigation. It's time sensitive I'm afraid.

Sasha *doesn't want this moment to end.* **Emmerson** *comes from the other side, another timeline.*

Emmerson   Marina, we have some news about the enquiry.

She doesn't want to leave either.

Gradually, they both push away from the table.

Hyatt (*to* **Sasha**)   We believe the one . . . advantage . . . of your situation is that the radiation that's poisoned you leaves a trace. We can revisit your locations that day. And find where it was deployed.

Sasha   It has a trace? We can track it?

Hyatt   Yes.

Sasha   Then we must.

He stands.

I love you, you know.

Marina   That's nice to hear. Been a while.

They smile at each other.

Marina   I love you too /

Emmerson (*to* **Hyatt,** *trying not to intrude*)   / Sorry, we haven't – Ben Emmerson.

Hyatt   DI Hyatt, yeah, well we exist in different . . . timelines, don't we?

Emmerson   Yes, quite. We appreciate the thorough investigation, they aren't always that way–

Hyatt   Yeah well, we have to do that now, dot every 'I' cross every 'T', if we don't, you'll go and get 'em off, won't you?

Emmerson   We represent who we're given to represent.

Hyatt   Must be nice. Nice clean hands.

Emmerson   It's not perfect but it's the best system we have –

Sasha   Detective. We should check in here, in case. For the source of radiation.

Hyatt   Of course.

Hyatt *produces a radiation tester. The room, the meal is tested for remaining Alpha radiation. (Suggest something hand-held by* **DI Hyatt** *that reveals ultra-violet markings. Perhaps also a sound FX when it detects.)* **Hyatt** *shakes his head.*

NO RADIATION.

Hyatt   Nothing.

Sasha   I am glad to see it wasn't you.

Marina (*near tears*)   No darling.

Marina *and* **Sasha** *don't want to part.*

Hyatt   Waterstones, yep? The shortbread.

Sasha   Yes.

They go over to the table at Waterstones, Piccadilly, where short-bread was shared with **Martin**. *They test.*

NO RADIATION.

Sasha *nods.*

Sasha   Not here. Yes, right.

That seems correct.

Hyatt   Now Itsu. Your Italian bloke.

They go over to the table at Itsu, where the list was handed over from Scaramella. RADIATION FOUND.

They all look at each other.

Sasha   Scaramella. Mario Scaramella poisoned me.

Hyatt   Where he handed over the paper. Here. Do you still have that piece of paper, Edwin?

Sasha   No, I destroyed it, after noting its contents down.

Hyatt   Where did you destroy it?

Sasha   At home.

They go off to find the evidence.

Putin (*on mic, from box*)   Apropos of nothing, I just want to say, I don't mind enemies. I've got no problem with not being liked. It's traitors I can't bear. You can respect an enemy. I'd rather be a bastard than a traitor. Rather be an idiot. Speaking of which. The state of this.

Meanwhile . . .

6.   Kovtun's Best Western Hotel Room, 16th October 2006

Kovtun *comes out of the toilet. He is not wearing a shirt.*

Knock on the door. **Luguvoi** *enters. Dressed like a Novarusski in a suit with checks (nouveau riche).*

Luguvoi   Jesus Dimitri, you haven't even locked the door.

Kovtun   I was about to put the do not disturb.

Luguvoi   I just wanted to see if your room is a shithole too and it is but it is a shithole facing the other way. Are you ready?

Kovtun (*showing new packaged shirt*)   I'm thinking this.

Luguvoi   I don't care. I mean have we prepared the solution?

Kovtun *shows him a boxed fountain pen.*

Kovtun   Yes, it will stay in the pen and then I will take out like a cartridge.

Luguvoi   OK OK, if we need to refer to it do not say the solution, we will say the matter in hand.

Kovtun   The pen?

Luguvoi   Or the pen. But better the matter in hand.

Kovtun *sprays himself with anti-perspirant for a bit too long on the underarms.*

Luguvoi   Did you – ?

Luguvoi *starts to say something but then* **Kovtun** *is spraying over his enquiry. He stops.*

Kovtun   Sorry.

Luguvoi   Sorry.

Just as **Kovtun** *starts up again –*

Luguvoi   Did you contact –

The same occurs.

Kovtun   Sorry, Andre.

Luguvoi   Please put a shirt on.

Kovtun *begins putting on a pink shirt, silvery metallic tie. During:*

Luguvoi   Have you contacted your cook friend?

Kovtun   I am assured he will contact me.

Luguvoi   And how have you arranged he be paid?

Kovtun   Paid?

Luguvoi   Presumably he wants to be compensated for the trouble?

Kovtun   I assumed our employer . . .

Luguvoi   Dimitri. We've been employed to do a job. If we ask someone else to participate, their part comes from us.

Kovtun   What?!

Luguvoi   Of course.

Kovtun *is shattered.*

Kovtun   No no no. This is – No. He's not even a very good cook. No.

Luguvoi   Someone needs to ad/minister the solu –

Kovtun   / Andre, understand this and understand it well, I am interested in money and money alone in this life.

Luguvoi   Fine, don't threaten our success out of meanness.

Kovtun *is finishing dressing.*

Kovtun   May I ask you one thing, Andrei, and do you promise not to lie?

Luguvoi *starts dialling on phone, ignoring.*

Luguvoi   No.

Kovtun   It is very important to me. I want to ask if you think realistically I could star in pornographic movies.

Luguvoi (*dialling*)   I'm going to call that red-haired girl I met here last time. We'll want some entertainment tonight.

Kovtun   I'm asking because I know I can do it physically, and the money's good. My ex-wife has agreed to pose with me for a magazine which I think's a good beginning but live action. That is where many men fall down.

Luguvoi   Hello sweet girl, it is Andrei here. I took your number last time when we met in the Oxygen Bar. I am in town on important business for a few days only and we are going to have some great food, some great drinks.

Kovtun *waves manically.*

Luguvoi   I also have a friend with me. Let's go spend some money, yeah? Ping me.

Luguvoi *hangs up.*

Luguvoi   You can't just expect attractive women to wander into your bedroom and say 'Hello there', that's not how it works.

A **Cleaner** *comes in. She is a young attractive woman* (*Australian*).

Cleaner   Hello there.

Sorry do you want me to come back?

Luguvoi   No, sorry. Yes. Hello.

Kovtun   Hello!

Cleaner   I'm just turning the room?

Luguvoi   Brilliant, excellent. Everything is in order.

Kovtun (*trying to be friendly*)   Just . . . get on with it!

Cleaner   OK.

Luguvoi   So, do you clean a lot? At home?

Cleaner   Not really, I'm a student. I'm making some money to go travelling again.

Luguvoi   Oh, you travel?

Cleaner   Just been to Sardinia. Beautiful.

Luguvoi   I have been there! The capital, Cagliari.

Cleaner   Oh no way? Yeah! Where are you from?

Luguvoi   Russia.

Cleaner   Ah right. So what, are you guys KGB?

Horror.

Luguvoi   Excuse us.

Cleaner   I just meant as a joke.

Kovtun   Very offensive. Very . . . offensive. Russian stereotype. Come on.

Luguvoi   Strange thing to say.

Kovtun   How do you do.

They make their way out.

Kovtun *remembers he has forgotten the pen. Swearing under his breath, he doubles back for it. And leaves.*

7.   London Flat

Sasha, Hoar *and* **Hyatt** *pass the radiation tester over a bin, presumably containing the remains of the Scaramella note.*

Hyatt   You're sure this is the bin in which you disposed of Scaramella's paper?

NO RADIATION.

Sasha Yes.

Hoar Nothing.

Sasha Yes, I would not expect Mario to behave in this way. Perhaps we should also check the hotel bar. Where I went after. Where I had tea?

Hyatt Why, do they know each other?

Sasha Scaramella and Andre Luguvoi? No. Unless. No.

Hyatt We've already found the radiation trace, Edwin, here, in Itsu. Scaramella's paper?

Sasha Yes but we should check all locations. To be complete.

Putin No you fools, it's Itsu! Everyone knows it's Itsu! The Italian man with the stupid name. Absurd performance.

The detectives go back to the table at the Millennium Hotel with the teapot. They test it. RADIATION FOUND.

Sasha Both places. Itsu and the Millennium Hotel.

Sasha *paces, solving. He is suffering.*

Hyatt Are you alright? Do you want to take a break?

Sasha We cannot take a break. Need to solve this. Or it dies with me.

Hyatt Edwin, I promise you I will do everything in my power to get this done properly, whatever happens.

Sasha Thank you.

The meeting with Mario. Itsu Piccadilly. That is somewhere I would go often. I had been there before.

Hoar Before the day you were poisoned?

Hyatt Why would that be relevant?

Sasha The last time was two weeks before I fell ill.

8.   Erinys Private Intelligence, 25 Grosvenor Street, Mayfair

Sasha   That day I met up with Andrei and his friend. It was normal for me to meet Andrei for work. This time I was introducing him to private intelligence firm, Erinys, they were looking to get contract with Gazprom. I was being matchmaker.

Tim (*posh, white, obv*) *enters a small board room with* **Sasha**, **Luguvoi** *and* **Kovtun**. *They all greet.*

Luguvoi   Dimitri is old friend, we now do business together.

Sasha *meets* **Kovtun** *for the first time.* **Kovtun**'*s armpits are already massively sweaty.*

Tim   How do you do.

Luguvoi   How do you do.

Kovtun   It doesn't feel like England today, it's so sunny.

Tim   Ah, you've been lucky.

Kovtun   Sunny as the sun.

Tim   Well wait five minutes, you know.

Sasha   I have always liked the British weather.

Luguvoi   While we are being English, shall we have some tea.

A trolley has been / is wheeled in, on which to make their own coffee / tea.

Tim   I'm fine, it's a bit warm for tea.

Luguvoi   I thought you drank nothing else here, Alexander, you will have some tea.

Kovtun   I will! Damn sure as marmalade.

Tim   Any other plans while you're in town?

Kovtun *makes/passes the tea. Perhaps he fiddles with a pen at some point. We don't notice, exactly, we're in* **Sasha**'*s memory / POV.*

Sasha *doesn't drink the tea.*

Sasha   We talked business. I remember when we talked about being able to work here, the small man says he had a visa.

Kovtun   I have a visa you know.

Putin (*on mic, from box*)   Let me tell you about Dimitri Kovtun's visa. It was sponsored by an English earl, the honourable Charles Balfour. If you really want to look at the mess the world is in, I would suggest starting with the British aristocracy.

Kovtun   I would like to be Dimitri the Honourable. How much for that?

Tim   Haha yah, it doesn't work like that, I'm afraid.

Putin (*on mic, from box*)   It absolutely does.

Kovtun *watches* **Sasha** *ignore the poison.* **Sasha** *stands.*

Sasha   The reason I say all this is then we go for lunch.

Everyone leaves except **Sasha** *and the detectives who scan the Erinys table for radiation.*

RADIATION TRACE FOUND. SHITLOADS OF IT.

Sasha   These bitches' sons . . . Sorry.

Hyatt   That's OK, Edwin. You're entitled. Did you consume anything here?

Sasha   No.

Hyatt   So this was the first time they tried to get you.

Sasha   And then we go to Itsu.

Luguvoi, Kovtun *and* **Sasha** *are now in an Itsu. We repeat the scene from earlier but now it is loaded with clear attempts to poison* **Sasha**.

9.   Itsu Redux

Luguvoi   I recommend the super salmon three ways.

Kovtun   Super salmon three way is a good name for a film.

Luguvoi   Go on, I think this is an opportunity for you to be useful.

Kovtun   I do not like the implication that I have been useless. Quite the contrary. Ohhh.

Sasha   I will go.

Luguvoi   No no!

Kovtun   I go.

Luguvoi   Look at that. He's like a donkey with a saddle.

Kovtun *has gone.*

Luguvoi   You understand, our fathers were friends. Better than it should be, this place.

Sasha   I like it.

Luguvoi   The first one was in Chelsea you know.

Sasha   That meeting went well, I thought.

Luguvoi   Excellent.

Sasha   You looked quite the English gent with those bags.

Luguvoi   How very dare you, sir?

Sasha   Why do you go to Harrods? It's so overpriced!

Kovtun *joins them, having got the boxed Itsu food which he doles out. Pissed off they are sealed.*

Kovtun   Boom. Boom. Boom. I like these. You know why I like them? All boxed up. Boxy boxy box. All sealed and ready fresh in a box.

Luguvoi   It's a bit salty though. Can make you thirsty. I find.

Luguvoi *pours water meaningfully. They eat with chopsticks.* **Kovtun** *particularly disgustingly.*

Sasha   Are you doing anything else while you're here?

Luguvoi   Oh we have vague plans. Maybe *The Lion King*. There are some architectural sights I'd still like to see. Kovtun doesn't know London.

Kovtun   I know it a bit. It's big.

Luguvoi *is subtly trying to indicate* **Kovtun** *should poison the water.*

Kovtun   We have known each other long time. We grew up in the same apartment block.

Luguvoi   We did.

Kovtun   Andrei was always very popular. With the girls and the boys. With everyone really.

Luguvoi *frowns at him. What? DO IT.* **Kovtun** *is in his own little world.*

Kovtun   Sorry. OK. Ooooh.

Luguvoi *'cheers' him.* **Kovtun** *gets it. During the following,* **Kovtun** *is trying to find a way to subtly dangle his hand over* **Sasha**'*s water.*

Kovtun (*trying to administer the poison but not subtly*)   And so you are long time colleagues?

Luguvoi   We met in Moscow. Boris parties.

Sasha   We only started working together last year, after I 'moved' here –

Luguvoi   I love it here.

Sasha   We met to talk about a job. Just stupid corporate thing –

Luguvoi   Ever since the food got better, it's a world class city.

Kovtun (*keeping edging towards it*)   Mhm. What's the job?

Sasha   There is a vodka company, based here. They have disagreements with our ministry over who owns the recipe. Stolichnaya. It's OK. He's your friend. We just did some sniffing around. It's all very Russian.

Luguvoi   Yes, a vodka company and an agricultural minister. It is embarrassingly Russian.

Kovtun *'s managed to poison the drink.*

Luguvoi   Anyway, here's to developing more with Sasha's friends here in Mayfair.

A clink of glasses. The water goes down without being drunk. Shit.

Luguvoi   And how is your son?

Sasha   Very well. Yours?

Luguvoi (*trying to cheers again*)   Excellent.

Sasha *does not drink.*

Sasha   Excuse me.

Sasha *gets up and goes to the toilet.*

Sasha   A second time!

Luguvoi   You're a fucking idiot, Dimitri, you do it right there in front of him, he could be on to us!

Kovtun   He didn't see a thing! I've been very careful to make him think I'm a moron.

Luguvoi   Oh, how on earth did you manage that? What an ingenious ploy! You have managed to poison every single part of London except the man we are supposed to be taking down!

Kovtun   Well am I wrong for trying too hard or for not trying hard enough, Andrei? You are hurting my feelings when all I am doing is my best!

Luguvoi (*thinks he sees **Sasha** coming back*)   Shh! No, it's not him.

Sasha *emerges from the bathroom.*

They do a radiation test on the table again. RADIATION FOUND.

Sasha   It was still there from then. They tried to poison me before and failed. It wasn't Mario at all. I just met him in the same restaurant a few weeks later, same table, and the radiation was still there. Damn!

Kovtun *grins at him.*

Kovtun We are going out on Oxford Street this evening, friend! You will come, won't you! Meet outside Nike at seven!

Sasha I'm afraid I'm not available.

Luguvoi You must!

Kovtun You must! For me.

Sasha Goodbye, Dimitri. Goodbye, Andrei.

The two failed assassins leave.

Sasha (Bastards.) I thought Andrei was my friend.

Hyatt Edwin, we have made enquiries about the movements of those two gentlemen. We found that they returned to their Best Western Hotel.

Hoar Where we found extreme levels of radiation running down the drain in the bathroom of one of the rooms occupied by the two Russian gentlemen.

Luguvoi Where is somewhere fun that we might meet some girls?

Hyatt A concierge recommends a well-known brothel in Beaufort Gardens.

Luguvoi *and* **Kovtun** *look at each other, uncomfortable at the idea of visiting a brothel together.*

Kovtun Do you wanna – ? Might be fun?

Luguvoi Not with you.

Hyatt For some unknown reason the men instead head to Soho.

They take a rickshaw, again asking the Polish driver what he knows about meeting girls. The man recommends Hey Jo's in Jermyn Street –

Hoar A private members' club renowned for its Russian clientele.

Hyatt   Turns out this is an erotic club founded by one Dave West, a former fruit and veg stall owner from Essex.

A man in a pink suit salutes, goes back to his laptop.

It is described as having mirrored walls, frilly pink cubicles and waitresses dressed up as naughty nurses.

*A **Waitress** fills drinks.*

Kovtun   Why don't they just dress them as naughty waitresses? That would be just as good.

Luguvoi   Because I like the idea if I have a heart attack from one of these lovelies, they are trained in CPR.

Waitress   I have to legally tell you I'm not trained in CPR.

Kovtun   We'll see about that!

Waitress   No, I'm not. I have to say that.

Hyatt   It is also apparently famous for a huge bronze phallus that decorates the dancefloor.

And so it does.

*Bad music and a glitterball on a quiet night in Hey Jo's. There are pathetically few women. **Luguvoi** gets off a call.*

Kovtun   Is it still too early for the women, Andrei?

Luguvoi   I don't know, do I? I don't know when they come out. They're not bats.

Kovtun   There is no reason to be surly.

Luguvoi   Do you know the blasting I just got on the phone? There are two of us precisely so we don't fail.

Kovtun   Well you know what, I feel relieved.

Luguvoi   *What* do you feel?

Kovtun   I am having a lovely time in London, and I tried my best, but also I do not have something on my conscience that would make it harder to enjoy this drink.

Luguvoi   You know we don't get paid a thing if it doesn't happen?

Kovtun   What?

Luguvoi   No conclusion, no money.

Kovtun   Oh no. No no no.

Luguvoi   That's the job! Now we have to go back, refuel and then in a few weeks we fly back again for a football match and try again.

Kovtun   So what do I do with . . . you know . . . / remaining . . .

He turns the bag round again to his front.

Luguvoi   / Chuck it down the toilet, I don't care.

Kovtun   But isn't it expensive.

Hyatt *now in this reality. Investigation smashes into farce.*

Hyatt   Excuse me, sir. I'm interrupting this scene to say that the London Metropolitan Police have reason to believe you are responsible for the murder of Alexander Litvinenko on November 1st at the Millennium Hotel in Mayfair.

Luguvoi   What?! Ridiculous.

Sasha   You mean *attempted* murder?

Hyatt (*to* **Sasha**)   They flew back to London under the guise of attending a Moscow–Arsenal football match, with the intention of poisoning you in the bar at the Millennium Hotel.

DS Hoar *carefully sets up a table and chairs in the centre of Hey Jo's dancefloor, to redo the scene at the Millennium Hotel.*

Emmerson   The Crown Prosecution Service saw fit to charge Andrei Luguvoi in May 2007 and then Dimitri Kovtun. They were charged with the murder of Alexander Litvinenko.

Sasha   Detective Inspector, he means attempted murder, yes?!

Sasha *is forced into his chair.*

Luguvoi   This is purely hypothetical!

Kovtun   Ridiculous!

Hyatt   We have witnesses attesting to the presence of these two gentlemen in several key locations.

Emmerson   Miss Christina Barton.

Cleaner   It's weird because I was trying to make a joke, I just thought they looked kind of trashy – but the way they freaked out when I said it . . . ?! Then I thought maybe they *are* KGB!

Tea and teacups are put out. Football scarves are put on **Kovtun** *and* **Luguvoi** *as they wore on that day. The assassins are forced back into their places / seats in the scene.*

Emmerson   Allow me to introduce Professor Dombey, Professor Emiritus of Theoretical Physics at the University of Sussex –

Dombey   Hello again. A highly unusual substance like Polonium emits Alpha radiation. Most likely they gave two useful idiots the substance to carry, because no one would knowingly handle something so dangerous.

Luguvoi   This is typical British provocation.

Kovtun   Excuse me, how dangerous?

Luguvoi   Anyone could have done this. But you are always with the Russians.

Dombey   The Polonium 210 used to murder Mr Litvinenko could only come from one isotope-producing reactor in the world, in Mayak, affectionately referred to as Lludmilla. The security services say it could only be obtained by a state actor.

Martin   Yah, hundreds of lives put at risk. Not great. The aeroplane they travelled on, through the streets of London, into the bathroom at the Millennium Hotel where the poison was placed into a teapot, poured into his cup, where the victim proceeded to ingest it.

They all look at **Sasha**. **Sasha** *is sat at the reconstructed table. Everyone watches.* **Hyatt** *puts a hand on his new Russian partner's shoulder.*

Hyatt   (I'm sorry, Sasha.)

Sasha *sips from the teacup, knowing it will kill him.*

Hyatt   Andrei Luguvoi and Dimitri Kovtun, you are charged with the murder of Alexander Litvinenko using Polonium 210 in a pot of green tea in the Pine Bar at the Millennium Hotel on November 1st 2006.

Kovtun   This isn't proof! This is just some people standing around saying words. You can't prove it!

Emmerson   Can we get the lights, please!

The lighting state changes and a spotlight follows a trail of radiation from **Kovtun***'s bag, following his steps through the theatre, ending up at where* **Kovtun** *came into the theatre.* **Putin** *is there, not expecting to be caught out.*

Putin   Oh for fuck's sake. These people don't want to watch an enquiry. They came here to be entertained. So come on, show them what's in the bag! Show them!

Kovtun *opens his bag slowly.*

And then, out of the bag, steps a dancing girl, and then another, and then another. They begin a distracting and brilliant dance routine across the stage, which sweeps everyone and everything up into it.

Everyone dances. The police investigation, the QC's account, blend together. **Marina's** *story,* **Sasha's** *story, become one and the same.*

A MASSIVE NUMBER SO EFFECTIVE IN ITS JOYOUS CHOREOGRAPHY THAT IT HAS US THOROUGHLY DISTRACTED.

The two assassins manage to escape underneath a big, high-kicking dance routine. The whole ensemble take part.

It ends with **Marina** *and* **Sasha** *finally dancing together. They spin around the stage, in a Viennese waltz, until in one move* **Marina** *and* **Sasha** *turn and when he returns, she is not there. No one is.*

Only **Sasha***'s hospital bed on the stage.*

The dance is over. He has to get in the bed. The story demands it. And we are back in the real world. In hospital. And **Sasha** *is dying.*

Scene Seven

Hospital

Everyone has masks and gloves.

Marina   I don't know if this is a good idea.

It takes tremendous effort for **Sasha** *to speak.*

Sasha   If . . . they . . . see . . . they'll do something.

A nurse lets in a photographer, also masked and gloved. The **Photographer** *is even a little bit shocked.*

Photographer   Hello, hello, Alexander. OK. So we're just taking straight on, yes?

Sasha   Go.

We all watch the **Photographer** *work.* **Sasha** *looks hard into the lens.*

Photographer   Thank you.

The **Photographer** *goes.*

Sasha *is surrounded by suited, masked professionals.*

Sasha *breathes a certain number of times. In. Out. In. Out. In. Out. In. That's all.*

When they disperse, **Sasha** *is gone.*

Marina *gets into the empty bed alone. She covers herself in his memory. Grief. Eventually. A* **Nurse** *comes back on.*

Nurse   Marina. Marina. We need to destroy the bed.

The bed gets removed. She is left with nothing.

Act Three

A Nightmare

Putin (*on mic*)   I'm sorry for your loss.

Silence.

Putin   I'm sorry for your loss.

Silence.

Putin   All death is tragic.

Silence.

Putin   He knew what he was doing.

Marina   No.

Putin   He knew there is a playground where borders do not matter. Everyone knows that. And he chose to play there.

Pause.

Putin   You must be tired.

Marina   I hate you.

Putin   I'm a convenient villain.

Marina   He was a British citizen.

Putin   Not *really*. We're not like them. You know that. They know that.

Marina   . . .

Putin   I would protect you.

Marina   You'll see.

Putin   That's vengeance, Marina. Nothing brings him back.

Marina   I hate you.

Putin   That's OK.

Marina   Leave me alone.

Putin   Give up. Let go. Come home.

Marina   Shut up.

Putin   Come back to Russia. All will be forgotten.

Marina   Where are you?

At some point **Marina** *gets up, infuriated.*

Marina   Stop this! Where are you?

Where are you?!

Marina *looks for him in the boxes. When she turns back, she finds he is right there with her, centre stage.*

Putin   There's no place like home.

Marina   Get out of my house! Get out!

Beat.

Putin (*looks round, on mic*)   You're being disappointingly literal about this, Marina.

Marina *wrestles his mic off him.* **Putin**'s *instinct is to fight but then can't when he remembers he's being watched. He decides to turn it into a monologue . . .*

Putin   Of course, the in/evitable bit –

She shoves him.

Marina   Get out!

Putin   Wow, you're touching me. This is assault.

Marina   Get out!

Putin   That was assault, you all saw it!

Marina   MURDERER!

Putin *reads the room. He leaves the stage, preferably through the auditorium, trying to maintain his dignity.*

Putin   (Mad woman, obsessed with me. It's quite sad actually.)

Our theatricality is gone.

Here, Now

The artifice of the play is revealed, and of the theatre. **Marina** *has the mic.*

Marina   Hello?

No answer.

Marina (*into mic*)   Hello?

This is very much to the audience. Being mostly British, they will not respond to her. **Marina** *approaches someone on the front row.*

Marina   Hello.

She puts the microphone out for them to respond.

Audience Member (*probably*)   Hello.

Marina   How do you do.

Audience Member (*on mic, probably*)   How do you do.

(*If not,* **Marina** *goes on to next audience member, asks the same until they do.*)

Marina   See? There we are.

She talks to us.

Marina   I have always believed in British justice. I think it is the best in the world. And I thought there would be an inquest which is a thing that happens to determine the cause of someone's death, what happened. But the government didn't want it. And then a new government and the Conservatives, that was even worse. The suspects had escaped back to Russia. And I think for everyone it was inconvenient. Wealthy Russians bought a lot of houses here, they send their children to private schools here, they go shopping here, they settle their legal disputes here. A lot of money. Newspapers. Political parties. Ties with the far right. Oh and the far left, for sure. The writer of this play tells me there were parties thrown for people all through entertainment at this time to 'build relationships'.

Friends of Putin and high-up politicians and celebrities. Theatre people. Lots of things exchanged. Influence, cocaine, the editorship of London newspapers. We call it soft power. I borrowed money for lawyers. But for six years, nothing. During this time I asked the Home Secretary, Theresa May, for a public inquiry. I went to see her with my son, with Anatoly, not as a stunt but because there was no one else to take care of him. I asked if her husband had been murdered in this horrible way, wouldn't she want the truth? She turned down my request. These are her actual words.

Theresa May   It is true that international relations have been a factor in the government's decision-making. We must also consider the cost to the public.

Marina   'The cost to the public.'

I am obviously not Marina Litvinenko. Alexander Litvinenko died at the University College Hospital three miles north-west of here. These are his actual words.

Marina *gives the actor playing* **Sasha** *her microphone.*

Sasha (*read, not memorized, uninflected, actor's true voice*)   I wouldn't like you to think that this is some kind of pompous political statement, but since all this happened I would like you to know. As you understand last month I was granted British citizenship and I very much love this country, and its people. Yes, they did try to kill me and possibly I may die, but I will die as a free person, and my son and wife are free people. I would like to thank my doctors, nurses and hospital staff who are doing all they can for me, the British police who are pursuing my case with rigour and professionalism and are watching over me and my family. This may be the time to say one or two things to the person responsible for my present condition. You have shown yourself to be unworthy of your office, to be unworthy of the trust of civilized men and women. You may succeed in silencing one man but the howl of protest from around the world will reverberate, Mr Putin, in your ears for the rest of your life. May God forgive you for what you have done, not only to me but to beloved Russia and its people.

Marina *is handing out cards to members of the audience. The law turns up in the form of* **Emmerson**.

Emmerson   Three High Court judges agreed that the Home Secretary's reasons for withholding a public inquiry were insufficient. By this time Putin had annexed Crimea and Russian soldiers shot down Malaysian Airlines plane MH17, and the UK government's relationship with Russia was sour enough for them to give up their fight against Mrs Litvinenko.

Thanks to her tenacity, we had a public inquiry.

Marina   Ten years after the death of Alexander Litvinenko, a report was finally published. This is judge Sir Robert Owen's conclusion and these are his actual words. (Would you help me?)

Marina *hands cards to various audience members to read.* **Marina** *gives them the microphone to contribute the verdict.*

Audience Member   'I am sure that Mr Luguvoi and Mr Kovtun placed the Polonium 210 in the teapot at the Millennium Hotel on 1st November 2006.'

Marina   Thank you.

Audience Member Two   'I am also sure that they did this with the intention of poisoning Mr Litvinenko.'

Marina   Thank you.

Audience Member Three   'It is probable they did so under the direction of the FSB.'

Marina   Thank you.

Audience Member Four   'The FSB operation to kill Mr Litvinenko was probably approved by President Putin.'

Marina (*to the audience*)   Thank you.

Emmerson   You have our ear now, Marina Litvinenko. London is listening. Is there anything else you wish to say?

Marina *shakes her head. There are no big words.*

Marina   I miss him.

We are outside. It is raining, **Emmerson** *holds an umbrella over himself and* **Marina**.

Marina   I was not expecting that! I thought they would say how, but not all the way back to Putin.

Emmerson   Very occasionally we get it right.

Marina   There will be justice now, yes?

Emmerson   I can't see Russia ever extraditing them.

Marina   I know, I know. And I cannot ever go home now? Yes?

Emmerson   . . . Look, as a lawyer, I can't advise you on that, I haven't the legal framing for it. But as a friend, I would ask that you, no, that you stay here.

Marina   My mother is very ill.

Emmerson   I understand.

Shall I walk you home? It's late.

Marina   No thank you.

He checks his phone for the time. He sees something.

Emmerson   Oh shit.

Marina   What is it?

Emmerson   . . . David Bowie died.

Marina   David Bowie?

Emmerson   Yeah. I didn't even know that he was . . . Sorry. He was . . . important to me growing up.

Marina   I'm so sorry.

Emmerson   No no. It's ridiculous. Um. It's fine.

Marina   Ben. I'm sorry.

Emmerson   No! It's –

But he's crying. She hugs him.

Emmerson   I'm going to go. Fool I am. Right. You keep this. I will see you again in not too long.

She nods. He leaves. **Marina** *comes forwards to us, under the umbrella.*

Marina (*to us*)   That is all that I have. So. Good night. Thank you. And. Please.

She reaches out from the umbrella to check if it's still raining. Of course, it isn't raining at all.

So she takes down the umbrella. She bows.

The cast join her.

End.